George East has enjoyed a spectacularly eclectic career path including stints as a pickled-onion manufacturer, gravedigger, radio producer, publican and professional bed tester. Now dedicated to writing full-time about his small adventures as an innocent abroad, George and his wife Donella spend their year travelling around the regions, restaurants and bars of France. 'It's a tough life,' says our hero, 'but someone has to do it . . .'

Home & Dry in
Normandy

*A Memoir of Eternal Optimism
in Rural France*

GEORGE EAST

An Orion paperback

First published in Great Britain in 2005
by Orion
This paperback edition published in 2006
by Orion Books Ltd,
Orion House, 5 Upper St Martin's Lane,
London WC2H 9EA

Based on the books originally published as
Home & Dry in France (1994) and *René & Me* (1997)

1 3 5 7 9 10 8 6 4 2

Copyright © George East 2005

Illustrations drawn by Delia Delderfield
Map drawn by Hemesh Alles

The right of George East to be identified as the author of
this work has been asserted by him in accordance with the
Copyright, Designs and Patents Act 1988.

A CIP catalogue record for this book is available
from the British Library.

ISBN-13 978-0-7528-7738-9
ISBN-10 0-7528-7738-0

Printed and bound in Great Britain by
Clays Ltd, St Ives plc

The Orion Publishing Group's policy is to use papers
that are natural, renewable and recyclable products and
made from wood grown in sustainable forests. The logging
and manufacturing processes are expected to conform to
the environmental regulations of the country of origin.

www.orionbooks.co.uk

My wife and I first met René Ribet when he moved on to our land and in to our lives at Le Moulin de la Puce. During an eventful year, he taught us much about the countryside and people of the Cotentin and, in the process, much about ourselves.

This book is also respectfully dedicated to Jean Chevalier, former mayor of Néhou.

Contents

Néhou

René's ditch

Le Moulin de la Puce

Longest Day Route -------

Roadside mirror

La Puce farmhouse

St-Sauveur-le-Vicomte →

Bike shed

Mr Janne's ditch

René's goldfish pond

Grey Lady tree

His 'n' hers vegetable patches

his

hers

Orchard

bridge

Stone bridge

cart track

Mushroom copse

Millstream

Slough of Despond

Le Lude

Preface

As a result of detailed research (mostly in pubs) I am convinced that at least 100 per cent of all English homeowners at some time consider buying a property in France.

This usually transient enthusiasm often results from:

a. Speaking with friends who have a friend who knows a chap who said he had just snapped up a seventeenth-century Breton farmhouse in thirty-seven acres with more than enough outbuildings to convert to a fair-sized holiday village... and all for the price of a second-hand Citroën.

b. Reading enthusiastic – but completely inaccurate – articles and PR puffs in magazines and newspapers about characterful cottages for conversion from as cheap a price as £15,000, and magnificent *manoirs* merely in need of a lick of paint and the odd roof tile for less than a three-bed semi in the UK.

The following pages are not an attempt to set the record straight about buying a property or living in France. This is merely the (hopefully entertaining) story of how one couple started a conversation in a pub with a friend who had a friend who had a friend who had just bought the cheapest property in northern France – and how they eventually ended up with an old mill... and a new life.

And how we wouldn't have had it any other way.

George and Donella East
Le Moulin de la Puce
Cotentin
Normandy

AUTHOR'S DISCLAIMER

Every effort has been made to ensure that any information with regard to French property (and other) laws, procedures, traditions and general goings-on is accurate. However, general inattention, lack of contemporary notes and the imbibing of strong drink at the time may well (and probably will) prove some details false.

Also, and to safeguard against any future actions which may threaten the author's financial and physical status, readers should note that all characters and events in this book are purely fictitious, and are intended to bear no reference to any person living or dead. Or absolutely anyone with the resources and enthusiasm for litigation.

ONE

The Little Jewel

'There is another place at around the price you're looking for,' said Mark, 'and it's in a much better condition than the others.' By this, we had by now learned, he meant that there would be at least four walls.

Mark Berridge was, by that stage, our fifth property agent in Normandy. His predecessors had understandably grown tired of chauffeuring us around the rural hinterlands to see and pick holes in a procession of abandoned cottages, pig sties and cattle byres with the slightest potential for human habitation. As usual in these situations, we didn't have the money to buy the property we wanted, and didn't like what we could afford.

But our new representative was made of sterner stuff. A charming and thoughtful – if sometimes vague – expatriate with a penchant for wearing odd socks and the expression of someone who has just remembered he has left a cake in the oven on the planet Zarg, Mark was determined to help us fulfil our quest.

Working on what we now realised to be an almost impossibly optimistic budget, our man in la Manche had come up with a handful of properties which were, in the broadest sense of the word, redeemable.

We had seen a totally gutted end-of-terrace cottage for £7000, which had a fair-sized garden and potential, but fell short of the remnants of our shortlist of priorities by having extensive views – of an acre or so of rotting corrugated-iron cowsheds.

Then, there was the detached cottage in nearly derelict condition, but with fine views across open fields. Unfortunately, it was detached by virtue of the wall with the adjoining ruin having collapsed. There was now, apparently, some degree of strife and impending legislation between the two owners as to just where one property ended and the other began... and therefore as to who was responsible for the very necessary structural repairs.

We had also seen a tiny terraced cottage on a hill with superb views across Cherbourg harbour, it was in surprisingly sound condition, and lacked only a kitchen and bathroom. This could be created, with a lot of imagination and reasonable cost, from the covered-in yard. More importantly, Mark reckoned it could be had for a shade under £9000, including taxes and fees. At last it seemed we were close to achieving our goal.

But, having mentally filed the cottage at Tourlaville away as a definite maybe if nothing better could be discovered, we firmly applied the 'Let's see just one more' rule of engagement, and went on our way in a much happier frame of mind.

As Mark explained during our journey south, the property we were to see was the sole remaining place on his books that approached our price range and requirements. Belonging to an elderly widow from Paris who had not visited it since her husband died on the premises ten years previously, the one-bedroomed stone cottage was at least two hundred years old. But in this rare case, it had been extensively and expensively renovated before her husband's demise. It was therefore in sound condition and was one of the handful of original properties which made up a hamlet outside the village of Yvetot-Bocage. The fields surrounding the village having been declared a general zone for building approval some twenty years before, Yvetot and the adjoining hamlet were now ringed by a welter of very posh houses for white-collar commuters to Valognes and Cherbourg – exactly the sort of built-up location which we hadn't wanted to even consider, but something about the way Mark described the place brought a frisson of anticipation, and straight away we liked what we saw.

On the corner of a lane leading to open fields, the sombre grey-stone building with tall gable-end and sharply pitched slate roof looked more like a Welsh Methodist chapel than our idea of a Normandy cottage. But it had bags of character.

Having given us a moment to take in the external aspects of the cottage and its surroundings, Mark (after a manful, if embarrassing, struggle) threw open the door and invited us across the threshold into the living room. We did, and immediately experienced that magical moment of silent communion and confirmation that comes only when finding exactly what you have been looking for... even though you hadn't realised it before.

The floor of the large square room was paved with irregularly sized flagstones, shiny with the wear of centuries. The ceiling was engagingly beamed and whitewashed, and taking up literally three quarters of the far wall was the biggest, most inappropriate and beautiful fireplace we had ever seen.

Filled with enthusiasm, we walked into the adjoining kitchen – and straight into a sudden manifestation of Dr Who's Tardis. The property, Mark explained, had no bathroom, so Madame had erected the huge plastic shower cubicle in the only available space, which happened to be the centre of the kitchen.

Undismayed, we eased our way past this monument to Madame's standards of personal hygiene, and climbed the open rustic staircase to where an ancient panelled door led, with a satisfying creak, from the wide landing to a beamed and airy bedroom. There was also a spacious loft ripe for conversion to a second bedroom, and altogether the whole place felt exactly and completely right.

The wallpaper throughout – circa 1974, depicting an incongruously British hunting scene – was peeling from the soaking (in some places sagging) plaster; the electrical circuitry was less than basic; the shutters, window frames and kitchen doors were rotten; and the chemical toilet looked as if it predated the house. But it was, we both knew without a word being exchanged, the place for us.

Yes, we told our man in la Manche, yes, yes, yes.

We had, of our own accord and with a little subtle help from Mark in the psychological plotting of our viewing route, settled for the type of property we hadn't even considered. But what a property. And with quite an *histoire*, it seemed.

Local legend had it, Mark explained, that the whole terrace had once been living quarters for the peasants working in the grounds of the local château. Come the revolution, the workers had invaded the home of their former master, and carried off everything that wasn't actually part of the building. Part of the haul had been the magnificent fireplace in the lounge, which had once graced the grand hall. This explained why it quite literally stood out to such a degree in the tiny building, and the tantalisingly defaced crest on the mantle. Local legend said that it, like the accursed aristos themselves, had been expunged at the height of the Terror to erase even the memory of their long and oppressive rule.

To be honest, the cement holding the faceless crest in place looked suspiciously modern, but who would spoil such a good story?

So, we had finally come to the ultimate compromise experienced by virtually all property seekers. The place we had so painstakingly detailed in our minds and even on paper being either non-existent or not yet found, we were perfectly happy to settle for something with equal if differing charms.

Providing, that is, we could settle a price with Madame; and providing, as we were shortly to discover, she could gain agreement to the sale from a list of blood relatives as long as our journey to the front door of *Le Petit Bijou*. For it now transpired that the current owner of The Little Jewel was, in fact, the second wife of the deceased original owner... and his first spouse was still alive.

But, said Mark with a casual optimism that gladdened our hearts, he was sure that all would be well if we kept cool, steadfast, and above all patient. The most important thing was that Madame wanted to sell, and we wanted to buy. The local *notaire* would be similarly enthusiastic, so all we had to do now was to return to the office in Cherbourg, and put in an offer.

This, it transpired, was not a simple matter of telephoning Madame with the figure we had in mind. The lady was not on the telephone, and even if she were, she was a lady in the proper French sense of the word; it would be very bad form to actually call her up and talk turkey. The proper way to do it was by letter, with the correspondence politely meandering through the local weather, news of the neighbours and mutual acquaintances, a pen profile of our backgrounds as suitable buyers... and finally, the little matter of the offer we were prepared to make.

The best way to approach the making of the right offer to Madame, advised Mark, was to adopt the Three Price Philosophy. This consisted of first equating how much we wanted the property with how much we could and would pay for it. In our case, this obviously equalled at worst the asking price plus the relevant taxes and fees.

Having agreed that we would be content to pay full whack and still feel that we had made a bargain, we now had to settle on not one, but two other figures. The middle offer would be the asking price less the calculated amount of fees and taxes. The third sum would be a cheeky bid, which would be low enough to make us feel we had stolen the place, yet not so derisory as to insult Madame's sensibilities and threaten the transfer.

Accordingly, back in Cherbourg we made out three written offers, signed a proxy to Mark so that he could make use of any or all of them in our absence, and made our way back to the ferry port and the next boat home.

Sitting in the bar in mid-Channel a few hours later, we both confessed to a strange and totally unjustified sense of anticlimax. Our great adventure had begun in earnest three months ago after more than a decade of dreaming and scheming, and had involved travelling around three thousand miles to see more than a hundred properties of all shapes, sizes and conditions.

We had fantasised about a small farmhouse with an acre or so and a wonderful view, and had settled on a tiny cottage in the middle of a modern estate, with not so much as a backyard.

But at least, and at last, we had found a perfect little jewel, and our French equivalent of a starter home. Now all we had to do was wait for Madame's acceptance of the top, middle or – dare we hope – bottom offer, and Le Petit Bijou was ours to lovingly restore and enjoy for a year or so.

At least, that was Plan A.

Waiting for news of progress on the purchase of Le Petit Bijou was like experiencing the extremes of emotions suffered by front-line troops dug in for a long battle. There were to be months of inactivity, days of action, and moments of sheer terror.

At first, we phoned Mark every hour, hoping to hear good news; then we called every day, hoping to hear any news. As he patiently explained after our twentieth summons to the telephone, property exchange in France was a shade more measured and complex than at home, and consequently took a little longer.

Madame now having been duly approached by mail, we just had to wait until she responded to our first, almost audaciously low offer. When she almost certainly turned that down, Mark would immediately fire off our middle bid, and we would see what we would see. The fact that Christmas was nearly upon us would doubtless complicate matters further. It would most likely be a matter of months rather than weeks before we would get our hands on the keys to Le Petit Bijou.

We were understandably a little more than pleased when Mark called on Christmas Eve to tell us that – to his complete surprise – Madame had said 'Yes'. Providing all went to plan, The Jewel would be ours in a couple of months... and at the first bid price.

After intense celebrations over the Yuletide, we now had to get to grips with the fact that we were actually going to own a home in France, and set up the necessary systems and procedures to do so.

To begin with, a bank account in France would be a more than convenient arrangement to take care of the ten per cent deposit, completion costs and further financial requirements like buying materials, furniture and furnishings and servicing regular bills.

This we duly did with no problems, visiting and setting up an account in the Crédit Agricole branch at Valognes, where the very fluent and obliging under-manager Philippe Boulet turned our bundles of English currency into what appeared to be a considerable fortune in francs. Losing almost a hundred pounds in the process by failing to study the current exchange rates and picking a better moment and method also provided a valuable lesson in basic European money-changing techniques. Ergo, remember that a point or two on or off the exchange rate can make a lot of difference when you are dealing in big money.

But with our folding stuff now transferred from a wallet

strapped to my chest to the security of the computer screen before us, Philippe issued us with the ultimate status symbols for the Briton with property across the Channel – a French cheque book and cashpoint card.

We now had a bank account with more than enough francs to pay the deposit on Le Petit Bijou, and had provided Maître LeFrançois the notaire with all the necessary details. But we still could not sign the *compromis de vente* (the first official stage of the contract) until Madame's relevant relatives gave the go-ahead. And this was proving more than usually difficult.

The problem with Madame being the second wife of the deceased owner was, apparently, no problem. The thoughtful chap had signed The Little Jewel over to his new spouse as a gift shortly after their marriage. This meant that his first wife no longer had any claims on the property, and those other former or existing relatives who did had no objection to the transfer.

Except in one case, where the relevant relation was unfortunately in no position to either make his wishes known, or even sign the necessary documentation if he were in total accord with the proposal. The only signature now required belonged to a young man in a mental institution somewhere in France. When he was located and approached, it was more than probable that he would, under French law, be judged as unable to make the necessary decision. This would mean a special sitting by a special court, with a specially appointed judge deciding on the matter, and then signing on the unfortunate young man's behalf if he thought it right to do so.

Shattered by this turn of events, we were foolish enough to return to the property we had rashly assumed would be ours in the nearish future. Under a gently protective layer of the first snowfall in Normandy for years, it looked even more like a perfect *pied-à-terre*...

TWO

Good Pub-licity

The next two months were to seem the longest (well, until later that same year) in our lives. It was not that we had not endured more important and dramatic times. The birth of our children, George and Katie, the finding and buying of our first home and a dozen other major milestones during our married life easily outweighed the significance of this particular event. A second home was, after all, a complete indulgence. But finding and buying The Little Jewel meant much more to us than acquiring a status symbol.

For more than twenty years, we had worked to find a combined lifestyle and occupation to which I could settle, and, more importantly, one which would give us some degree of financial and emotional security.

Before our marriage, I had tried my hand at being a welder, building-site labourer, gravedigger, private detective, author, brewer's drayman, nightclub disc jockey and bouncer (sometimes these last two at the same time). I had managed pubs, hotels and restaurants before managing to meet and entrap my wife. Since then, and after deciding on past evidence that I was basically unemployable, we had set up and run with various degrees of near-success a number

9

of home industries, including a sitting-room pickled-onion factory, a kerbside used-car concern, and a dual clothing-repair and creative-writing company.

This particular example consisted of mornings spent by my wife inserting zips in and generally repairing clothing for a local chain of dry cleaners. In the afternoons, Donella would disappear on her bicycle under a mountain of anoraks, dresses and trousers, to deliver the day's repairs. I would then move to the typewriter to take on Donella's name as author of (somewhat) predictable stories about the exploits of lovelorn young ladies for inclusion in such picture-story publications as *Honey*, *True-Love Tales* and *Bluejeans*.

Having received more than 500 rejections of my three novels and countless articles, I had finally found a niche for my talent in creating the storylines for a number of photo-magazines. As Donella East, I would churn out at least a dozen Girl Meets Boy, Loses Him And Loses Him Again episodes a week, which, together with our profits from the garment-repair business, would keep us in funds till my true literary talent would inevitably be discovered.

Unfortunately, it all came to an embarrassing end when the publishers – with whom I had only corresponded by post – arranged a convention of their totally female complement. Artfully turning up with my twenty-stone bearded maleness disguised only by my wife's name tag on my lapel proved not to be a successful ploy, and it was on to our next venture.

After a stint in local radio, I returned for one last try at the typewriter, and found the world still not ready for my emergence as a best-selling novelist.

Basing our game plan on the logic that I already spent more time in pubs than anywhere else, we then took the lunatic step of actually leasing one... and quickly discovered that I was the world's worst landlord. Ironically, I also briefly became the best-known publican in the world when our bed above the bar collapsed one night, and I related the story to a journalist regular over a leisurely half.

Being the archetypal hack with an ear for a good story and the credo of never letting the truth get in the way of one, he spoofed the bare details up into a steamy and torrid tale along the 'Twenty-Stone Bonking Bar Owner Breaks Bed During Night of Passion' lines. He then sent it off down the wire to a major news agency... and all hell broke loose. Within a day of the story being circulated, I was lying in the broken bed, being interviewed by the star reporter from the regional television magazine programme, while a horde of press photographers fought to get the best angle for their wide-angled lenses.

Never one to miss the opportunity to give customers what they wanted, I asked my wife to make me a voluminous Wee Willie Winkie nightshirt and cap. I had also been coached by my reporter chum now showbiz agent in a number of ancillary and totally untrue details. Such as how the legs of the divan had been driven through the bedroom floor by the sheer force of our nocturnal gambolling and, in the process, woken the dog, whose barking had alerted the neighbours, who had, fearing a break-in, called out the police...

To further validate the story, we had bought a set of disembodied bed legs from the second-hand shop over the road and screwed them into the ceiling of the lounge bar in the appropriate position, providing a great shot for the slavering cameramen. The legs also became a draw for hundreds of new customers who would come and buy a pint just to stare up at the evidence of my enthusiasm for marital gymnastics.

From then on, I appeared by the medium of the telephone and taped interviews on more than 300 American radio stations, made a splash in every popular national daily in Britain, and received copies of such disparate publications as the *Singapore Straits Weekly* and the *Sydney Herald*. The story also featured in a late-night 'adult' cable TV show in California... and the final accolade came with the news that I had been granted an honorary doctorate in Bedology by a correspondence-course college in Nebraska.

Shortly thereafter, I was approached by the largest manufacturer of beds in the world with an interesting offer. They had just invested a quarter of a million dollars in a robot, which spent a day a week replicating the movements of the human body in sleep to test their new bed designs. Would I, in return for a free king-sized double divan and a modest retainer, take on a contract with them as the world's first human bed tester?

Of course I would, and did.

For the next few months and while the story still had, as they say in the trade, legs, I toured the country's trade shows and exhibitions. In my nightshirt and cap I would leap every hour on the hour from the top of a stepladder onto one of the company's unbreakable beds. Far below, a shapely model in the briefest of nightwear would be lying spread-eagled on the coverlet to provide additional interest for the spectators, and an incentivising target for me.

Eventually, like all such silly stories, the exploits of the Bed Bustin' Publican lost their appeal for the great British public. It had, however, served its purpose by making me aware of just how easy it was to hit the headlines with a fairly plausible tall tale.

The pub was doing badly by now, thanks, I told myself, to the combination of my frequent absences on bed-testing duty and the drying up of the story. Truth to tell, the drop in takings was a true measure of my declining interest in spending countless hours listening to the same joke for the tenth time that session in return for the slender profits on a pint of Old 'n' Filthy.

I had created a 'character pub' which depended totally on its main attraction (me) being there to prosper, and I just didn't want to be there any more. It was obviously time for a change, and I had just received a lesson in the basic rules and requirements of the publicity game.

Impressed by this and other free examples of my prowess at picking up on the publicity value of what they at least thought was a true story, the brewery agreed to take me on as a freelance public relations specialist, and for the next five years, I came up with a regular diet of tallish stories concerning the company's premises, and began to dabble in putting people who wanted to buy pubs in touch with those who wished to sell them. It was a precarious existence, but that was nothing new, and above all, it was an interesting way of bringing home the bacon.

Then came the day when a casual conversation with the owner of a pub chain led to its disposal to a client in the mood to expand rapidly. I earned more in commission for a week's work than my usual yearly stipend, and suddenly, after ten years of talk, it seemed we just might be in the position to realise our long-held fantasy of buying a second home. We could keep our freelance publicity jobs working for breweries and still enjoy the good life in France.

Having almost resigned ourselves to an interesting but Micawberish life together, the prospect of actually owning a pied-à-terre in a foreign country took on tremendous significance. In the midst of middle age I was going to give my wife exactly what I had promised her. A place in the country in another land. Providing, that is, that circumstances, good fortune, fate and the unknown judge let us finally through the obstinate door at Le Petit Bijou.

THREE

Minding Your Language

After waiting in an agony of suspense for more than three months, the good news came suddenly. In the depths of unreasoning self-pity, I had become convinced that there was a conspiracy against me and my dreams, and our late-night orgies of planning the decor of Le Petit Bijou down to exactly where we would hang the wok (already bought) had deteriorated into listless recriminations about my lack of ability to see anything through to a successful conclusion.

Then, at 09.04 hours precisely on 1 April, the phone rang 'You've got it,' Mark said, 'it's yours – if you still want it.'

The judge, he went on to explain, had ruled that the transaction could go ahead, signed the necessary documents, sealed the necessary seals, made the necessary declarations on the steps of the Bastille, and posted the necessary proclamations on the highways and byways of Normandy. All that had to happen now was the drawing-up of the compromis de vente by the notaire, our payment of the ten per cent deposit... and the signatures of everybody from ourselves and Madame to anyone who happened to be passing the office at that moment.

★

Having had a fair dose of the ecstasy, we soon found that the agony was not yet over. All that had actually happened was the agreement that we were now free to make an agreement to buy Le Petit Bijou. Up until the exchange of initial contracts, Madame could still change her mind or take a better offer. Even after the signing of the compromis de vente, we now discovered, Madame was at liberty to withdraw. We would then benefit financially by receiving a compensatory ten per cent of the purchase price from her, but that was small cheer.

Even blacker thoughts came with the information that – due to the extent of property exchangers avoiding fees and taxes by passing large amounts of the actual purchase price under the table – Le Petit Bijou could still be snatched back from us months after we bought it.

French law, we were told, provided for an official investigation into and assessment of the true value of any property changing hands at what seemed to be an inordinately low price. If the authorities thought some underhand and private financial transactions had been taking place, they were at liberty to purchase the suspect property from its new owner at the price paid on paper, thereby leaving the miscreant short of what he had privately given the vendor.

It was a very rare occurrence, explained Mark, and we, of course, had not actually entered any tax and fee-saving conspiracy with Madame. The notaire was satisfied that the price we were to pay was a fair one, given the condition of Le Petit Bijou. But it was as well that we should know about all the little hiccups that could occur between signing for, and permanently acquiring, a property in France. We would, he said on a brighter note, be receiving our copy of the compromis within the next week or so, then we should read it very carefully before signing and returning it with the deposit.

After a week of playing who-can-get-to-the-front-door-first each morning, we took delivery of a bulky package from the perspiring postman, and ripped it open with trembling fingers so that we might now read, digest, analyse, check over and sign the contract it contained. Providing, we immediately discovered, we were fluent in ancient and legalese French...

We now had to find someone not only totally fluent in written French, but also in the complexities of phrases and codicils, paragraphs and points laid out in an archaic usage which made the average UK solicitor's communication look like a page from a Janet and John book.

~

Here is perhaps as good a place and time as any to tackle the complex and controversial question of just why the French insist on refusing to speak a perfectly acceptable language like English. And why they pretend not to understand their own tongue when used by us.

The question of the apparent inability of the French to comprehend their own language when spoken by a foreigner is a perplexing mystery I have spent thirty years trying to solve.

I first got to grips with the inconsistencies of the language at junior school, where I spent a whole year coming to terms with the idea that, in France, tables, chairs and other inanimate objects had a sex. Just as I was beginning to acquire the vital ability to tell any French persons in earshot that my aunt wrote with a feather, a sudden descent into the 'B' stream was enough to convince the curriculum organisers that my future lay in plumbing or carpentry rather than international diplomacy, and French was no longer on the menu.

For the next three decades, I visited France on hundreds of occasions, and picked up a handful of useful nouns and phrases each time. This left me with a fairly extensive vocabulary, if not the grammatical wherewithal to join them all together in the right order and context. This understandably made social intercourse on any subject a frustrating exercise for both parties, especially given the apparent French refusal to give a little when it comes to the fine-tuning of pronunciation.

A typical exchange preceding the frequent and (one might expect) simple purchase of any item from any shop or store is invariably played out in the following manner:

ME (entering Pierre's Pâtisserie or Edith's Épicerie): Bonjour, Monsieur/Madame/Mademoiselle.

HIM/HER (suspiciously): Bonjour, Monsieur.

ME (enquiringly): Vous avez gâteaux?

HIM/HER (face contorting into an expression of total bewilderment, angst and even acute pain): Pardon, Monsieur?

ME (even more slowly and clearly): Vous avez gâteaux?

HIM/HER (with shrug): Pardon, Monsieur?

ME (pointing directly at a selection of at least fifty-seven cakes on prominent display): VOUS AVEZ GÂTEAUX?!

HIM/HER (understanding spreading like dawn across their features): Ah... gâteaux!!!!

You have to believe me when I say that, throughout the engagement, I have pronounced the simple key word in the absolutely approved and precisely correct manner – i.e. 'gatt-oh'. What's more, the person with whom I am trying to do business will always, always arrive at totally over-the-top pantomime awareness by repeating the word in exactly the same way I have been saying it. Repeatedly – i.e. 'gatt-oh'.

Either I have been missing some incredibly subtle inflection or stress on the key word throughout these voyages to final understanding, or the persons to whom I have been speaking are, as we would say, playing silly buggers. Sometimes, however, one has to accept that a slight difference in inflexion or pronunciation can make for quite innocent yet dramatic misinterpretation by the French recipient.

Arriving cashless in the square of a strange town just after acquiring our French bank account, for instance, I went off in search of the local branch of Crédit Agricole. Unable to locate it, I chanced upon a rather striking young woman standing alone outside a bar.

Approaching her and falling back upon the old mime ploy, I proudly whipped out my new cheque book and waved it under her nose, at the same time making the universal finger-rubbing sign for money.

For a moment the lady stared at me uncomprehendingly. Then she smiled radiantly, nodded and said, 'Ah, you are looking for a bonk?' With that, she took my hand and set off at a fast pace down a side alley.

Needless to say, the bank was at the other end.

Faced now with translating the arcane wording in the initial contract on Le Petit Bijou, we eventually found invaluable assistance in the shape of a member of the UK Institute of Translators. After an hour or so going through the Gallic equivalents of The Party of The First Part and the Party Hereinafter to be Referred to as The Party of The Second Part, she pronounced herself satisfied that the terms and conditions were as we understood them. With the exception of the actual boundaries of the property.

Were we aware, she asked, that we were only buying the downstairs rooms of the cottage?

No, we replied in high-pitched unison, we were not.

A phone call direct to the notaire's office at Valognes was duly made. Maître LeFrançois, we were told, had conducted the previous transaction on the cottage some twenty years before, at which time there simply had been no first floor. The same information had been used to draw up the new compromis, and nobody had realised that there was now a bedroom and landing where once had been only an open space to the eaves.

It was, we were assured, a detail of little consequence as far as legal provenance and established ownership went. The necessary changes would be made when we returned the signed document, and there was no risk that we would at some time in the future find ourselves with distant relatives of Madame scaling the outer walls of our home and claiming squatters' rights to the upper floor.

Thus reassured, we signed each page in the appropriate place and sent it on its way with the deposit. We also in the process established and mentally filed another law regarding French property exchange: make sure you know exactly not only what any contract contains – but also what it means.

'I must demand to know,' said Maître LeFrançois through Mark, '...if there is anything under the table?'

Resisting the impulse to get on my hands and knees in front of the notaire's desk, I shook my head vehemently. The maître nodded in apparent satisfaction and continued with his checklist of formalities. The big day had finally arrived, and we were convened in his Valognes offices for the culmination of the transfer. And, like a young couple fighting a fit of the giggles at the altar, my wife and I were both on the border of nervous hysteria.

We were now less than an hour away from completing the final phase of the transaction (the *acte de vente*) but I was still waiting for the inevitable last-minute stymie. At any moment, I was convinced, he would leap to his feet and demand in ringing tones if anyone knew of any just cause or impediment why the union of George and Donella East and Le Petit Bijou should not take place. The door would then burst open, and a long-lost second cousin of Madame, previously believed to have been lost in a Foreign Legion action in the Sahara would appear with sand on his boots, and a claim to the cottage in his hand.

Or the phone would ring just as the maître reached for

the rubber stamp, and it would be Madame's physician to say that she had just expired in her Paris apartment, so the deal was off till the next of kin were consulted. Or the fire brigade would call – just after completion – to say that a spark from a nearby stubble fire had reduced Le Petit Bijou to cinders.

As it happened, none of these events occurred, and the proceedings went like clockwork.

We signed yet another ten pages of documentation, Donella made out a cheque with the largest number of digits she had ever written... and I was handed the keys.

Suddenly, it had happened. The maître shook our hands warmly and welcomed us to the community, and we walked out into the market place at Valognes as fully paid-up French homeowners. We didn't look any different, in fact we didn't, when comparing notes, feel dramatically different. All we felt was a burning urge to get to our cottage... and really make it our own.

Accordingly, we piled into our cars and sped the two miles to Yvetot-Bocage to prepare for the ceremony.

Mark having presented us with a bottle of champagne, a custom-made congratulations card and (very discreetly) the bill for his services so far, we were ready for the Grand Entrance. I picked my wife up, turned the ancient key in the lock, kicked the door open and stepped forward into our dream cottage. In doing so, I caught my right foot behind a raised section of genuine eighteenth-century flagstone, dropped the champagne and my wife onto the unyielding floor, and cut my hand badly on the broken bottle as I joined her.

Thus, we shed the first blood in the conversion of Le Petit Bijou.

The sweat and tears were to flow in copious quantities at a later date.

FOUR

Doing Your Homework

I had organised my work schedule to leave the next fortnight free by the simple but effective method of ripping the relevant pages from my desk diary. We had booked the first-floor *gîte* at Mark and his new wife Fiona's *château* for that period. I had also spent the previous weeks at auctions and bankrupt stock sales in the UK buying up job lots of rusty tools, tins of congealed paint and all manner of discontinued plumbing and electrical fixtures and fittings, most of which were to prove as useless as they had been cheap. But, in our present situation, far more important than these material considerations was to be the location and commission of that elusive and most treasured aid to the British property owner in France – the general (and generally competent) builder.

At home, most of us have tackled DIY tasks of varying complexity and scale. As a nation with a property and property-value improvement fetish, we have only to nip down the road to our local builder's merchant or mega DIY store to find everything we could possibly want for the job. Should the project be too ambitious, there are general and specialist craftsmen by the hundred, always courting our custom.

We can ask a friend or neighbour who has had a job

completed to his or her satisfaction, or refer to the Yellow Pages or local newspaper. We can then give the candidates a thorough grilling, ask to see references and examples of their past performances, provide a very specific specification, and finally haggle over the price and demand a very specific and non-negotiable estimate. We can also keep a very close eye on proceedings as the job progresses on our home base. And still we manage to come unstuck.

Now consider the problems implicit in taking on any major form of homework in another country, where you don't know the way the system works, let alone the correct phraseology for 'You will be sure to put the electricity points high enough to clear the worktop which will go against that kitchen wall, won't you?'

Quite apart from the language barrier, there's the scale and size of most operations required when you buy a home 'in need of some renovation' in France. You may have had your UK home rewired; you may even have had new windows or doors fitted. But have you had new foundations and walls built, damp-proofed, rendered and plastered to take those windows and doors? How many times have you felt the need to have a septic tank or cesspit installed to ease the waste disposal system situation in your UK semi?

Luckily for us, we had the good fortune to meet Hugh Jones, subsequently dubbed Hugo the Hod in deference to his Welsh ancestry. Hugo was a small builder in the truest sense of the term. He employed around a dozen tradesmen and general labourers in his home territory of west Hampshire, and stood about five feet six in his terminally disintegrating working boots.

He had come across the Channel to find, buy and restore his own farmhouse in south Normandy, but on his arrival with materials, tools and skills, Hugo was immediately set upon by a horde of desperate second-homeowners. He became so preoccupied with the septic tanks, subfloors and extended extensions for his new and unsolicited customers that his own property looked like having a completion date somewhere in the twenty-first century.

Apart from his rarity value, Hugo's worth also lay in his attitude to any commission. He was as honest a builder as any I have encountered, his rates were reasonable, and he took an eminently sensible approach to estimating costs. Experience had taught him that very few of his customers actually had the first idea of what they wanted or needed doing, beyond a vague conviction that the holes in the roof shouldn't be there, and it would be a good idea to have a bathroom somewhere on the premises. Therefore, Hugh had developed a system of pricing an initial job to its bones, knowing that more would come as his clients got to grips with further tasks.

There was, inevitably, to be a downside to our relationship. His value to the British house-restoring community meant that he was permanently in demand in all parts of the peninsula, and had a tendency to pop into Cherbourg for a length of timber and disappear for several days.

Eventually, we found that such underhand devices as hiding the keys to his van or even locking him in a room he was renovating were not just advantageous but absolutely essential.

In the process, we also formulated another discipline to be observed and even cherished by any property owner in France: first find your best builder... then keep firm hold of him till he finishes the job. Completely.

Hugo the Hod's tendencies to take French leave in the midst of a job were, however, only to emerge after work started on Le Petit Bijou, where we met immediately after we had taken possession (and my slashed wrist had been attended to). Walking around the cottage, we were relieved to hear no particularly loud intakes of breath as he casually tore lumps of wet plaster off walls and put his foot through rotten boards and door panels.

An hour later we had retired to a local bar, and got down to the business of agreeing upon what we would need to have done as against what we wanted to have done, and how much it was all going to cost.

We, for instance, lusted after a stable door and minstrel gallery. During innumerable late-night sessions with a sketch pad and every ideal-home magazine on the market, we would design our dream domicile around these two hallmarks of gracious country living, and they became the symbol of all our hopes and aspirations. Regardless of the basic condition or suitability of any property we were to look at, my first job was to work out exactly where the minstrel gallery could dominate the interior. And, of course, where the stable door could be hung.

Fortunately, Le Petit Bijou was already graced with what could, at the longest stretch of the imagination, be called a minstrel gallery.

Actually, it was just an open staircase and unusually wide landing, but our chums in the UK would never need to know that when we dropped the fabulous feature into the conversation. But The Little Jewel didn't have anything remotely resembling a stable door, or a proper place to put one. Therefore, regardless of all other necessary work to be done, our first instructions to Hugo the Hod were that at least one stable door was a must.

Dissuading us from ripping out the particularly sound and attractive nineteenth-century front door, he eventually conceded that the rotting chipboard sheet in an external entrance to the kitchen (which had originally been a stable so provided a politically correct and authentic setting, we argued) could be replaced by our twee townie's fantasy. The outcome of this example of style fetish over common sense was an expense factor equalling one tenth of what the whole cottage originally cost us. And a series of painful encounters for passers-by unused to the English tradition of sawing a perfectly good door in half and leaving the top bit open.

The other problem was that the wall in which our pride and joy was eventually fitted faced the worst of the Norman weather head on. Although Hugo had done his best to create the first totally watertight stable door, we were on permanent mopping-up duty whenever it rained and the wind blew from the southwest. Which was most of the time from September to March. The fact that for these seven months of the year we couldn't open it because of swelling and had to trail the rubbish bins through the parlour only served to underline the futility factor.

With this and subsequent costly, self-indulgent exercises, we were finally led kicking and screaming to the establishment of another French home homily: let the house tell you what it will and won't bear. As Hugo pointed out, the original builders of all those properties that had stood the test of time and elements for a few centuries obviously knew what they were doing. If a wall already had a window, it was a safe bet that it faced the direction from which the most available light was going to come. Bricking it in and putting another one elsewhere just to satisfy aesthetic desires was not only expensive, but a insult to the original builders who had proved across the centuries, among other things, that they knew which way the wind blew...

With the basic building projects decided upon and apportioned out between Hugo the Hod and ourselves, it was now time to start phase one of the conversion of Le Petit Bijou.

Hugo would take care of the unexciting but essential tasks like ripping out and replacing the plumbing and electrical services, rotten wood and plaster, and the Dr Who shower cabinet and immobile mobile loo. We would fetch and carry, pick up any materials from the local hardware stores and builder's yard, and generally get in the way until it was time for the finishing touches of painting and decorating.

A plumber by training, Hugo was more than a fair hand at electrical work, bricklaying and the other disciplines of property improvement – and a wizard at woodwork. He was never happier than when knee-deep in sawdust and shavings, with a length of virgin timber wedged in a makeshift vice set up in the road, the piercing scream of his trusty electric plane in his ears, and his ghetto-blaster, tuned to the regional pop station, turned up to full volume.

Meanwhile, Young Steve would be knocking down a (hopefully) unwanted wall with a sledgehammer slightly taller and heavier than himself, while listening (?) to another rock song on another radio channel – and singing his version of yet another heavy metal anthem. Young Steve completed the team of craft-persons engaged on the conversion of Le Petit Bijou. General assistant, pipe- and plank-holder and straight man in the double act of relentless banter with regard to his drinking, eating, sexual and other social activities, Steve came complete with earring, wispy moustache, and a constant yearning for his girlfriend and other familiar comforts back in the UK. He did not like the local food, drink, language, flora, fauna or air.

A good-hearted and enthusiastic worker, he was actually a shrewd choice of assistant artisan, as Hugo employed the common building sub-contractor's incentive of 'job jobbed and home'. This meant that at the start of their weekly stint in Normandy, Hugo would set a target of tasks to be done during their time away from home. If the work was completed to his and our satisfaction, it was hotfoot to Cherbourg ferry port and back to the bosom of his family for Hugo; and the open doors and arms of his local pub and young lady for Young Steve.

The result of this piecework arrangement was a very early start and late finish for the two weeks it took Hugo to polish off his part of the restoration programme. Both teams staying at Mark and Fiona's *Château de B&B*, we would compete to be first to leave in the mornings, and last to get back at night. Because of our quickly established tradition of stopping off at a Valognes bar for a swift *demi* or three and a debrief on the day's progress each evening, it was often close to midnight before we arrived at the château, a perfect time to gather around the massive fireplace in the owner's quarters for a nightcap.

Having relayed the latest news of What We Had Found Under The Floorboards or the Pumping Out Of The Portaloo, we would then settle down to listen to some extraordinary tales about other homebuyers who had used Mark's services. There was, for instance, the man who bought what Mark considered to be a perfectly habitable and attractive cottage at a bargain price on the peninsula, and had taken a month's leave of absence from his executive UK post to get to grips with the decorating. Dropping in to see how the straightforward task of putting up a few rolls of wallpaper and painting the window frames was going, Mark was bemused to find the picturesque cottage obscured from the road by a veritable mountain of rubble. Inside, he found the new owner frantically trying to stop a bedroom ceiling becoming the kitchen floor with the aid of an upended suit-case on the top of a pair of stepladders. His wife was on her hands and knees trying to reduce the rising level of water from a broken pipe in the ceiling space with a designer dust-pan and brush. Being totally fluent only in restaurant French, they had done their best to summon the fire brigade, police and every other emergency service, but had got no further than initial connection before a breakdown in communications.

After Mark had helped locate and call out a local builder who arrived with the necessary lintels, piping, adjustable support trusses and an anticipatory gleam in his eye upon seeing the extent of the damage, the white-faced executive had explained what had happened.

His wife had felt that the wall between the lounge and the kitchen of their holiday home was unnecessary as well as unsightly. Also, she reasoned, it would save the cost of dec-orating materials and the time to apply them if they just removed it. Neither was she too keen on the wall dividing the lounge into two small rooms. In fact, she didn't like or see the need for any of the downstairs walls. Accordingly, her husband had gone to the local hardware shop and purchased the only equipment he believed he would need – the aforesaid stepladder and a heavy sledgehammer. Going at it with a will, he had quickly removed the offending walls, and in the process removed all internal structural support to the first floor.

Two months later and with a new set of walls exactly where the old ones had stood happily for several hundred years, the couple were facing a bill for £5000 from the builder, plus a not inconsiderable charge for the removal of the rubble mountain.

FIVE

A Night by the Fire

Work on Le Petit Bijou was now progressing at a pace, and we could see exactly what we were getting from Hugo the Hod's whirlwind activity. The rest of the village could also see and hear what was happening from around seven in the morning till eight at night each weekday, and in some cases, over the weekend.

I had already made a tour of all the houses in sight and earshot, delivering bouquets of flowers and a letter of apology couched in Mark's suggestion of the most apt and multiple ways in French of saying sorry for the row. Strangely enough, our near neighbours seemed not at all worried about the upheaval, noise and regular blocking of the main street by Hugo, Young Steve and their competitive concerto of electric plane, sledgehammer and Greatest Hits of Grateful Dead meet Iron Maiden and Val Doonican. We were improving the appearance of Le Petit and therefore making the village a more attractive enclave for its residents... and potential buyers.

This benign reception of our clamorous activities was to make their attitude to the village's oldest and longest resident even more discreditable. We met the last surviving reminder of how our hamlet must have been in previous times just as I was picking myself, my wife and bits of the broken champagne bottle off the floor after our crossing-of-the-threshold ceremony. Straight from Central Casting as the ancient French *paysan*, Georges had apparently been living in the hamlet since before it had been built.

While all around him had changed beyond recognition, Georges had calmly carried on in his own way. In carpet slippers, brown overalls and the first beret we had seen in Normandy, he would shuffle along his daily beat, with string bag containing a bottle of red plonk (always half empty) and a broken baguette (always half eaten). When not working on either or both of these at the same time, his toothless gums were permanently welded to a monstrous hand-rolled cigarette apparently containing the sweepings of a particularly rank cattle byre.

Unlike the rest of the village, he lost no time in offering us a warm welcome and showing his honest curiosity about his new neighbours. Within moments of our arrival, he had appeared and invited us back to his nearby cottage to meet Madame, take a cup of tea or something stronger, and inspect his home – which was made entirely from wine bottles. At least, that's what Mark thought he said, as Georges spoke his own version of a regional patois that even the locals would have found difficult to crack.

Chez Georges, in which his parents and grandparents had been born, lived and died, was just around the corner from Le Petit, and stood out like a sore thumb among the smart new residences with their manicured lawns and imitation wells.

In the very basic kitchen (which basically consisted of an old sink, cooking range, mangle and a host of empty wine bottles), we were introduced to Madame Georges. Also from Central Casting, she was short, stout and clad entirely in black. With her shiny, kind face, calvados-apple red cheeks, tightly drawn-back hair and twinkling, humorous eyes, she looked every inch a model for a tourist poster of Normandy.

While Madame busied herself with the preparation of strong, black, sweet and handleless cups of tea, Georges took us on a tour of what remained of his domain. In the back garden, pigs rooted, chickens scratched, a goat was trying to eat the remnants of an ancient Citroën which had found a new purpose as a henhouse, and the evidence of Georges' personal recipe for longevity and good health entirely obscured the gable-end wall.

Stacked end-on and horizontally in a pyramidical tribute to Georges' daily consumption was every bottle that he had emptied over the years. Or, from later observation of his prodigious capacity, it might have just been the past month's tally. Exactly why he chose to make such an ostentatious display of his empties, we were never to discover. Mark surmised that it might be a canny way to add extra insulation to the cottage walls. My wife thought it was a traditional Norman hobby equivalent of making a model of the Tower of London from used matchsticks. I preferred to think that it was Georges' unsubtle way of showing the neighbours that he didn't give a fig for their nouveau-rural pretensions and censorious views on his lifestyle.

Back inside, we sat down to tea, and moved rapidly on to *vin rouge*, and from there to a totally lethal, local distillation of apple juice which tasted like molten lead... Not wishing to be outdone in this display of hellfire hospitality, I made my way back to the car in search of a donation to the proceedings. Having found and unlocked it some time later, I returned unsteadily with a bottle of malt whisky, which we had brought over as a medium of barter worth virtually unlimited local use of the telephone at Mark's château.

The afternoon turned to evening, the evening wore on, and with it I made an astonishing discovery.

After years of struggling to pick up, assimilate and

remember the odd French phrase, and testing and finding wanting a string of expensive tutors, I could now speak the language fluently. Moreover, I could converse in the local patois with ease just hours after meeting Old Georges. I exchanged witty anecdotes about examples of our respective cultures with our hosts without recourse to Mark's services. I even told perfectly a long and involved joke about a vicar, a virgin and a verger, which had previously given me much difficulty in my local pub after no more than three pints of ale. And all due to the magical qualities of Georges' homebrewed calvados.

Eventually, at least another foot of the glass mountain having been emptied for later erection, we bade our new neighbours and now close friends '*tonto*' and walked meanderingly back to Le Petit Bijou below a stunning canopy of real and imaginary stars.

Although we had originally intended retiring to the château that evening, Georges' hospitality had proved a greater attraction than the prospect of a bed to sleep in, and we had determined to spend our first night as French homeowners at Le Petit Bijou. Accordingly, we stripped the car of all available cushions, blankets and newspapers, and settled down for a momentous, if chilly and uncomfortable, night on our very own French floorboards.

A deep and dreamless slumber was interrupted some hours later, when I woke to see a blue light flashing at regular intervals on the newly whitewashed wall of the bedroom. Still under the influence of Georges' hospitality, I was not particularly interested in the phenomenon, but considered it my duty to rouse my wife and suggest she investigate.

Eventually finding the window, she studied the scene outside for a full ten seconds, then made her trancelike way back to our makeshift bed.

'What's afoot?' I muttered.

'There's a policeman fighting with a fireman outside and all the villagers are watching in their pyjamas,' she reported, and promptly went back to sleep.

'Oh,' I said, and in the best British tradition of minding one's own business in matters of domestic disturbance, joined her.

~

Next morning we awoke to find the road outside our cottage several inches deep in water, and one of the buildings opposite no longer there.

Hastily dressing, I went downstairs, checked the car for damage, and met with one of our neighbours, who did her best to explain the circumstances in a combination of French, English and sign language.

Exactly opposite our cottage was an equally ancient stone property owned by a retired couple that let an outbuilding to a student at Valognes university who enjoyed the odd late-night candlelit *soirée*. During the previous night there had apparently been another such convocation, which had ended with the occupants falling into as deep an alcohol- (or other substance-) induced slumber as ours, and a candle catching fire to the sacking curtains. The resultant conflagration had attracted the attention of the local *gendarmerie* and fire brigade, as well as the entire hamlet. Except, to Madame's mystification, us.

She went on to explain that, our car taking up much of the narrow lane leading from the main street to the scene of the disaster, there had been some difficulty in getting the fire engine close to the blaze. All efforts to raise any response from within our cottage proving unsuccessful, it had been assumed that we were sleeping elsewhere. There had then been a healthy and most entertaining altercation between the two senior police and fire officers present as to the legality and logistics of moving our car out of the way.

Actually, as I learned later, the real cause and outcome of the dispute was very French. Each of the combatants insisted that the duty (and drama) of shifting our ancient and

very *solide* Volvo should be theirs alone. There being no outright winner in the verbal punch-up, and the local mayor
and notaire not being on hand to arbitrate, they had left it
where it was.

As it transpired, Madame assured us, there had been little problem in reeling out the hoses to within quenching
distance of the fire, and all had obviously turned out most
happily. Another eyesore had been removed from the village,
and the miraculously unscathed student debating society
would now have to move on to more distant quarters.

A further bonus to the community was, as we were to
learn from Old Georges at a later date, that we had unwit-
tingly provided a valuable after-dinner anecdote by our
seeming indifference to the drama, which had unfolded so
close to our front door. How typically English, it was being
said, that Madame and Monsieur chose to ignore the dan-
gers and attractions of such an occasion, and sleep serenely
through the most dramatic event locally since the D-Day
bombardments. We did not, of course, enlighten them with
the explanation that our behaviour owed more to Georges'
firewater than British phlegm.

~

The ambivalent attitudes of our neighbours at Yvetot-
Bocage were highlighted again during the removal and
replacement of Le Petit Bijou's unique toilet facility.
Virtually all of the double-income executive class, their attitudes mirrored many of those of a typical Home Counties
dormitory village in England. They seemed to keep themselves very much to themselves, and spent most of their
spare time either mowing lawns that already looked as if
they had been painted rather than grown, or holding discreet dinner parties. The local *épicerie* and bar was going out
of business because the residents preferred to buy their
weekly groceries at the *hypermarché* at Valognes, and to
drink and dine in the far swisher café-bars at Cherbourg.

There was little feel of a real community, and once they were safely inside their modern detached chalet-style executive homes, the residents of Yvetot-Bocage seemed to avoid any contact with the outside world. Except during such ideal opportunities for mutual concern as provided by the recent Great Fire, and then the Case of the Lethal Loo.

Although most fastidious in other matters of personal hygiene – as evidenced by the Tardis-like shower cabinet – Madame had obviously been quite content with the services of an extremely strange and temperamental toilet during her residence at the cottage. Located in a recess off the kitchen, the huge throne-like apparatus was a weird mixture of portable and permanent loo. Having used it, the intrepid operator would then, we were told by Mark, pour liberal doses of a sinister-smelling chemical into the bowl. The final step was to frantically pump away at a handle that (theoretically) built up the pressure to squirt the hastily treated sewage along a narrow pipe and out through the nearest wall. Tracing the pipe's progress, Hugo discovered that it actually ran no further than under a large stone sitting across a ditch, which had originally been dug to dispose of surface rainwater from the road. This being a somewhat unsatisfactory state of affairs as far as we were concerned, it was decided to replace the former arrangements with a state-of-the-art electric toilet. But before this item could be installed, its predecessor would have to be removed and shipped back to join the ever-growing selection of period domestic apparatus now housed in one of Mark's outbuildings.

Having planned the operation in detail and taken an early lunch, Hugo and Young Steve moved into action, myself and wife standing nervously by with buckets and mops as they wrenched the exotic edifice from its moorings.

To our surprise and relief, the old loo came cleanly away from its billet, and was safely carried from the kitchen to the waiting van. It was during this journey that Hugo observed just how heavy it seemed, how something was slopping around inside the bowels of the device – and just how revolting the odour of that something was.

Understandably reluctant to spend the next twenty minutes in the back of the van with the source of the stench, Young Steve hit upon the idea of giving the handle an experimental series of pumps. The result was swift and spectacular. A solid jet of old (yet still extremely odiferous) sewage vacated the insides of the toilet and, compressed by the narrow outlet, shot like an Exocet missile clear across the road to splatter all over the whitewashed garden wall opposite. Once started, the stream continued unabated, with Hugo and Young Steve receiving liberal coatings of tangential spray, while my wife made futile thrusts with a mop at the spreading lake of effluent now threatening to make the D49 impassable.

Having spotted the doors of every house within scent opening, I took the coward's way and disappeared inside Le Petit Bijou to inspect the inner recesses of the cupboard under the stairs. It was at least ten minutes before I emerged casually into the sunlight and found as many spectators surrounding the still-lethal loo as had been in attendance on the night of the Great Fire.

Astonishingly, rather than being outraged at this deadly assault on her garden wall, Madame opposite was demonstrating her intimacy with the finest traditions of French sanitary plumbing by pumping vigorously away at the handle to show how it should be done while the other neighbours urged her on with a flood of advice and encouragement almost equalling the tempo of the effluent jet stream.

An hour later, the reservoir having been finally emptied, Hugo and Steve disappeared to the château for a bath and change of clothes, while my wife attacked the road with a couple of gallons of disinfectant and countless buckets of water. The villagers returned reluctantly to their homes, obviously satisfied justice had now been done in demonstrating that, while the English might be cool in a conflagration situation, it took true French *brio* and initiative to cope with a real crisis.

The two weeks we had set as a target to complete the restoration of Le Petit Bijou passed all too swiftly, but their passing had transformed our uncut gemstone into a jewel. The old plumbing, wiring, rotten woodwork and other defunct features of the cottage were now mere memory, and the property looked more enchanting than even our most optimistic predictions.

Inside, the peeling paper and dank and crumbling areas of plaster had been replaced with virgin wall surfaces as smooth as the icing on a wedding cake; the ancient beams and stone surfaces once covered with layers of green gloss paint were now revealed in all their former glory, and, most importantly, the Tardis had miraculously transformed into a modern shower cabinet and re-materialised in an alcove on the landing, and the lethal loo had been usurped by a sleek electric toilet of savage efficiency.

Outside, the windows were embellished with snow-white wooden shutters, each held against the walls by the traditional male and female figurine catches which also served as good luck talispersons. Other indulgent additions included an ornate carriage lamp and wrought-iron nameplate beside the front door, and serried ranks of hanging flower baskets that obviously fascinated as well as endangered (like the half-open stable door) passing locals. We had also proudly screwed a brass plaque to the wall, giving full details of our ownership and UK address, and even affixed a totally incongruous alpine cowbell and chain alongside the long lusted-after stable door.

A pile of logs, which had been a literally intended house-warming present from Old Georges, was artistically arranged against one wall, and the apparently dead climbing rose bush which I had almost torn down upon taking possession of the house had burst into glorious life across the gable-end. As a finishing touch, a platoon of Home Counties garden gnomes frolicked territorially upon the narrow strip of newly laid gravel defining the boundaries between our property and the rest of France. It was all a little over the top, perhaps, but it was all ours.

For us, Le Petit Bijou now lived fully up to its name, and was as pretty as any picture postcard. It was ours to cherish and enjoy for many years to come. Or so we thought at the time...

SIX

The Hazards of Smoking

With Phase One of our restoration programme completed, it was time for our private housewarming party. In spite of the season, Donella was going to let me get to grips with our giant fireplace and build a blaze to rival the recent conflagration over the road. And this despite the gloomy predictions of Hugo the Hod.

While standing in the grate and peering morosely up the chimney, he had on more than one occasion opined that our prize possession might look the business, but was simply too big to do the job in its new location. At the château, the giant winged construction would have had access to an equally commodious chimney breast, and then to a lofty open stack that would provide sufficient draught to maintain a roaring blaze and take the smoke away. But this, said Hugo, would more than probably not be the case if we insisted on an open fire at Le Petit Bijou. Although our chimney breast was roomy enough to consider turning into a second bedroom, the large stack had been topped with a slab of stone and a single, small pot to keep the perennial Norman rain at bay.

In another prime example of not letting the house (or expert builder) tell us what was best for it, we had airily rejected Hugo's suggestion of fitting a smoke-free stove and flue in the giant fireplace. Apart from the stable door and minstrel gallery, the fantasy in which we had most indulged during the search for our dream cottage had been that of spending the long winter evenings sitting around a real fire and we were not going to be thwarted by the pessimistic prophesies of Hugo the Hod.

Following his departure, we gleefully purchased a suitably capacious wrought-iron fire basket from the local hardware store, together with what looked like a square squash racket. This, we had learned, was traditionally used in the region for cooking anything from a hamburger to a whole joint over an open fire.

Having assembled all the accessories needed for our first real fire- and home-cooked meal, it was time to begin the ceremony. After laying an artfully constructed huge pyramid of Georges' logs on top of several screwed up copies of *La Presse de la Manche*, I applied a match and stood back. Meanwhile, my admiring wife stood by with the metal squash racket, now bearing two prime cuts of fillet steak.

Straightaway, Hugo's dire predictions of a lack of draught were proved totally wrong. The pine-branch cuttings caught immediately. Ablaze with joy, we literally danced with delight as the leaping flames cast our shadows against the whitewashed walls, and the room was suffused with the inimitable fragrance and glowing warmth only achieved by a log fire.

For a full five minutes we revelled in the sight and smell of the blazing logs and sizzling steaks, before noticing that it was becoming difficult to see each other across the hearth. As Hugo had calculated, the chimney breast was easily large enough to take the several hundred cubic metres of smoke now resulting from our mammoth blaze. The problem was that the single chimney pot simply couldn't cope with releasing more than a fraction of it into the night air.

The cycle having been set up, the dense smoke had

nowhere to go but out from under the mantelpiece, and into the room. Within ten minutes, we found it more acceptable to sit on the floor rather than the chairs. In half an hour, we were crawling on all fours towards the door, fire and the steaks abandoned, our only thoughts of finding a way out and breathing again.

Outside and having regained the blessing of sight, we observed that approximately the same numbers of interested parties as had gathered for our neighbour's fire had now assembled for ours. Luckily, none of them had so far called upon the services of either the local *pompiers* or gendarmerie, and we were able to make some sort of explanation, bid them a hugely embarrassed goodnight, and sit in the car till it was feasible to return indoors.

Then, all we had to do was rescue the charred steaks from the fire, and attempt to remove the smoke stains from the carpets, walls, woodwork and furniture, while discussing the likely price of a bland but efficient and smoke-free central heating system for Le Petit Bijou.

~

Following our re-redecoration, all was at last *complet*. All that faced us as we sat in our incomparable holiday home was the prospect of a long and happy enjoyment of its charms. Then came the knock at our freshly painted front door, which was to announce the arrival of our man in la Manche, his two newest clients, and a quite dramatic change to our future plans.

Jeanne Jackson and Val Pennington were the latest of Mark's clients to have made the pilgrimage across the Channel in search of a holiday home in Normandy. Teachers at the same Leeds school, they were looking for a small home to share for holidays and future retirement on the Norman peninsula. So far they had seen nothing that appealed to either of their aesthetic sensibilities. Or anything in remotely good enough condition to be restored without more time, trouble and expense than they would wish to afford.

Their dream, they reminded Mark, had been of finding a small but characterful cottage of distinguished age and appearance and fairly good condition. They were not fussy about where it was on the peninsula, and couldn't care less about the size or existence of a garden, as they had acres enough to look after at their house outside Leeds. Surely, he must know of somewhere that would suit their wishes and budget?

Well, said Mark (in all innocence, he later assured us), he did know of just such a place. Not only was it almost exactly as they described, but it had also been totally restored and renovated in the most imaginative and sympathetic blending of the old with the new. What's more, it had British electrical wall sockets. Unfortunately, it was very definitely not for sale, as the owners had just put the last lick of paint on the walls, and were looking forward to enjoying the fruits of their labours for many a year to come.

But, he suggested, why not drop by and ask Mr and Mrs East if they objected to a quick guided tour? Then his clients could see exactly what could be done with a tight budget, and a lot of imagination and enthusiasm.

And so they arrived, and fell as completely and hopelessly in love with Le Petit Bijou as we had a scant few months earlier. Half an hour after arriving, they held a whispered conversation with our man in la Manche, and there and then made us an offer for The Little Jewel which we were to find difficult, and eventually impossible, to refuse.

What our first British visitors had offered for Le Petit Bijou represented, on paper at least, a whacking profit on our total investment of something like £5,000.

That, of course, did not make any allowance for the time and money we had spent in looking for our little jewel, the weeks of labour we had put into renovating it, or the months of worry while waiting to clinch the deal.

It would be easy, as Mark said, to say no for the time being, and promise the girls that they would have first refusal when and if we decided to sell. But, as he also shrewdly observed, it was a very good price, and the average selling period in Normandy was around two years from a property going on the market to a buyer being found. We had, he reminded us, originally wanted something with some land. Le Petit Bijou, beautiful as it was, had not so much as a back or front yard. He was pretty sure that he could find us another property with as much promise as The Little Jewel, and at worst a big garden.

Opportunity seldom knocked twice, he reminded us, and this could be Fate's way of telling us not to cast aside the chance to finally find the property we had originally set out in search of. Everything Mark said made good sense. Especially, as my wife pointed out rather tartly, from his point of view. A quick resale of Le Petit Bijou represented a second agent's fee on the same property, and within a couple of months of collecting the first. He would say exactly what he had said, wouldn't he?

If we did agree to sell after investing so much time and emotion in searching for and finally finding, buying and restoring our perfect pied-à-terre, how did we know we would find anything remotely as appealing? We could sell in haste and repent for a long, long time. Besides, she said, what would we do about storing the furniture if the girls didn't want to buy it with the cottage?

Now it was my turn to speak on behalf of the motion to move before we had spent even a single day of leisure enjoying our holiday home. It was true, I agreed, that our agent was in the business of selling property in Normandy. But Mark obviously cared about the people and the properties he brought together. And he had observed me pacing around the confines of Le Petit Bijou when the renovation was nearing completion, as if looking for a secret room we had overlooked and would offer a further challenge. He had been with us as we looked wistfully from the car at *À Vendre* signs outside derelict and rambling farmhouses which could be given new life with effort and imagination. He was absolutely right, in my case anyway, that now we had a taste for it we would be prepared to start all over again... and on a much more ambitious scale. And finally, he had offered to let us store the furniture in his barn till we found another uncut but even more promising jewel.

As ever in our long and eventful union, a sort of rickety compromise won the day. We left the keys to the cottage with Mark, and a promise to the girls that we would sell at the agreed price – providing that we could find a replacement property within the next few weeks of hard looking.

For the next month we were such frequent passengers on the Portsmouth to Cherbourg crossing and back that even the captain was greeting us by name. The customs officers at our homeport were also beginning to make ostentatious notes on their clipboards as we drove smartly through the Nothing To Declare channel yet again.

SEVEN

Starting Over

From the start, we set down rigid guidelines for our second property purchase in France. The building would have to be detached, away from the road, and surrounded by at least half an acre of land. Preferably it would have a few trees dotted about, and a good view from an elevated position. Ideally, there might even be a small pond or stream on or near our land. Even more ideally, the house would look exactly like Le Petit Bijou. The condition of the premises would be immaterial. With my newfound confidence in taking on major structural work based on our painting and decorating successes at Yvetot-Bocage, I reckoned it was even better for the new place to be a complete wreck. That way we could get everything just as we wanted it from the start.

But after viewing more than fifty properties within 150 miles of the Cherbourg ferry port which offered *any* potential, our task seemed hopeless. Nothing looked anything like what we had in mind, and everything seemed much, much dearer than we had hoped. It seemed that the canny country property owners of northern Normandy were getting wise to the growing demand from UK second-home seekers.

We saw a near-derelict detached cottage with an acre of flat scrubland for £30,000, and a scruffy terraced village property, even smaller than Le Petit Bijou, priced at much more than we were going to get for our completely renovated French home. On one occasion, we went on a round trip of more than a hundred miles to see what the farmer owner claimed to be a semi-detached cottage in its own grounds. On arrival, we found him driving his trio of cows into a grisly barn, the end section of which had been hastily partitioned off to form a snip for the right sort of British mug. All this, we were told, could be ours for just £25,000, not including fees and taxes, of course.

After ten trips across the Channel in as many weeks, we were very close to the point of giving up. I even wrote Jeanne and Val a mournful and rambling letter, apologising in advance of what we both now believed would be the inevitable conclusion to our search. We would have to shelve our plans for moving on, and in the process stop them from achieving their dream of owning Le Petit Bijou.

It was now the last day of what we had decided would be our last chance in the foreseeable future of finding another home in Normandy. Unless a small miracle happened, we would be departing on the next day's early morning boat having admitted defeat.

That morning, we decided to really put the pressure on and literally stop at every single À Vendre sign we came across in an unplanned drive around any part of the peninsula to which the nearest road would take us. After collecting Mark and telling him of our random attack plan, we arrived at a crossroads on the Valognes to Bricquebec route, and I took out a ten-franc piece and spun it to determine which way we should turn. Realising afterwards that we hadn't decided which side was heads, I chose left and headed for the nearby market town of Bricquebec.

For the next two hours, we pulled up at every sign we saw.

It didn't matter whether the place was on the main road, or how ugly or hopeless it looked from the car. We would walk beyond the house, hoping each time that we would come upon a magical property tucked away in a leafy copse, undiscovered by passers-by and estate agents alike.

Inevitably, what lay behind every grim façade was even more unattractive and tacky. Disheartened and dejected, we pressed on, passing through Bricquebec and taking at random the D900 to St Sauveur-le-Vicomte. By mid-afternoon, we had climbed in and out of the car on another dozen occasions, and clambered in and out of lofts, cellars and windows at least twice that number of times. We had not exchanged a word in twenty minutes, and then, just as I was about to say that Mark would have to call the girls and tell them the deal was off, I saw the ubiquitous bright yellow card on a broken gate to our left.

Automatically, I stepped on the brakes, and drew up out-side the gable-end of a particularly unattractive and dilapi-dated farmhouse. Standing right on the edge of the D900 and approximately halfway between St Sauveur-le-Vicomte and Bricquebec, it was not the most prepossessing of sites or sights.

'Surely,' said Mark, 'you don't want to look at this place? I had it on my books, but scrubbed it because it was so tatty, and so near to the road.'

'Don't care,' I snapped petulantly. 'I'm still going to look at it.'

And so we forced our way past the rotting gate, which had obviously not been opened for years. Close to, the house was even more unappetising. Basically, it consisted of a small flint cottage in average disrepair for a place which had obviously not been lived in for a decade or so. A rotting stable and barn of baked mud walls supporting a broken-backed roof were tacked on to the back. Opposite was a low building which looked rather like my old school bikeshed, and by the end of the barn stood the remains of an old water pump. Alongside the bikeshed we found the entrance to an orchard, now knee-deep in grass and decomposed apples from three particularly tired-looking trees.

'At least,' I said, 'this one's got a bit of land.' My wife smiled bravely, and looked as if she would rather be somewhere else.

Then came a shout from Mark. We found him standing at the pump, pointing across a shallow gully to a clump of trees some seventy yards distant. 'There's the corner of a roof just showing,' he said, 'and I can't see a single bit of barbed wire anywhere between here and there. I think that could go with the property.'

Somewhat less than excited by his discovery, we chose to stay by the farmhouse while he fought his way down the overgrown bank and disappeared out of sight behind the nearest line of trees. Twenty minutes later, his face alight with enthusiasm, and with just a hint of a tremble in his voice, he told us that down in a clearing and hidden by a ring of trees was a ruined water mill. Moreover, not one but *two* sparkling streams gurgled contentedly past the mill, and a huge water meadow stretched forever behind it. *And* there was a riverside walk leading to a magnificent water cascade and pond. And a line of majestic beech trees guarding the journey from the enchanted grotto to a series of undulating fields with views across open land to a distant forest. *And* he still had not come across a single fence, length of barbed wire or other obstacle to his progress.

This, as we now knew, was a most significant discovery. As we had learned over the past months of exploring, the Norman attitude to property and land ownership meant that every and any possible passage from one person's terrain to another's was always protected by some form of impenetrable barrier.

'It looks,' said Mark almost casually, 'as if there could be more than three acres going with the mill... and the mill could go with the farmhouse. And, if I remember correctly, the asking price is only £14,000. That's why I didn't bother to look any further than the roadside. I still can't believe that it's all part of the same deal. But if it is, would you be interested?'

EIGHT

The Flea Lands

A phone call from Normandy the next day confirmed that *Le Moulin de la Puce* was still for sale; and also that Mark had been way out in his estimation of how much terrain went with the cottage, outbuildings and ruined mill. Rather than the three uninterrupted acres he had paced out, the property extended to almost ten. We had stumbled upon a rare treasure indeed.

The ancient water mill ripe for conversion was almost an estate agent's myth. One for sale which sat among so much unworked wood and pastureland was as rare as a Frenchman with a good word for English cooking.

The night before, we had caught the ferry home to attend to pressing business in the UK. Mark, under equally pressing instruction from us, had been waiting for the local notaire's office in St Sauveur to open. From there, he had learned that the property had been for sale for the best part of a decade. Built around the time of the Revolution, it had served as the area's only mill for more than 150 years. Unworked and largely unvisited save by illicit hunters, fishers and berry, nut and mushroom gatherers for a half century or more, the terrain had evolved into a natural habitat for virtually every tree, grass, bush, plant and flower known to the region.

With a long and mostly unrecorded history, even the name of the property had become the source for debate. Some residents claimed that the tiny mill was known as 'The Flea' through natural affection and tradition. At least three local dogs rejoiced in the name of *petite puce* after all. Providing precious flour for the community for so long, they argued, it was only natural that the little *moulin* would earn a name usually reserved for pets and wives of good nature and small stature.

Others, however, believed the name came from the ancient custom of using the millstream as a rustic laundromat. The Lude, having its source less than a mile away and running swiftly past the mill towards its rendezvous with the Douve at St Sauveur, had proved ideal as a communal laundry site. Given the general standards of domestic hygiene in those far-off days, it was only natural that a weekly washday for the whole village in one spot would result in a thriving community of pre-Revolutionary predators. Ergo, The Mill of the Flea.

Whatever the origins of the name, the local farmers and their wives had long been wooed away from *La Puce*. A posh new hydroelectric mill nearby and the introduction of running water to local homes at the turn of the twentieth century had caused the thriving little estate to fall into disrepair.

The mill, the farmhouse and barns by the road and the triangular sliver of just over four hectares of unfarmable land adjoining them had been bought by a local man some fifty years before, Mark had discovered.

Monsieur Ole the Elder had unfortunately passed on to his reward before being able to enjoy the earthly delights of La Puce as a retirement home, and his Paris-based son had not been interested in maintaining the fabric or even exercising ownership of the property.

It was assumed by Maître Gancel the notaire, said Mark,

breaking the news as gently as possible, that the four younger brothers of the vendor were still equally in favour of disposing of the property. If, after sleeping on the matter, we still wanted to proceed, it was now time to put in an offer.

Having sat trancelike for the total ferry crossing, then spent the intervening hours babbling about the incredible good fortune of stumbling upon precisely the property we had dared imagine owning only in our dreams, we said yes please (or words to that effect), we would like to proceed.

In that case, said Mark, all we had to do now was put in the right offer to secure agreement by the clan Ole to the purchase of La Puce, then check out the Rights of Way, Tenure Agreements, Restrictions, Covenants and likely views and actions of SAFER.

Taking it from the top we said that, as far as we were concerned, there was no question of risking the loss of exactly what we had been seeking physically during the past nine months and mentally for the past decade by putting in an unsuccessful offer. We would pay the full asking price without demur; in fact, we would pay more than the asking price if that would speed the process up and ensure that we won the favour of every Ole relative in Normandy. But, much more importantly, what was this long list of potential problems starting with Rights of Way and ending with SAFER, whoever he, it or they may be?

To begin with, Mark patiently explained, as with our previous transaction on Le Petit Bijou, we must not rush in with the full price. Not only could that be seen as unseemly behaviour, but it could also give the appearance to the vendor that (a) we were desperate to buy, and (b) that the asking price was too cheap because we knew something that he didn't.

Having accepted an offer, any vendor was bound to honour the originally agreed price. But there was, we must remember, nothing to stop him withdrawing from the deal between initial contract and completion stage. He would pay the ten per cent fine almost cheerfully if the buyer's original eagerness caused him to look for and find someone prepared to pay much more.

As to the list of other potential obstacles, the Rights of Way complication was much more of a problem than it had been at any of the much more urban properties we had seen. It wasn't so much that there was a likelihood of someone maintaining the right to walk through our front room en route to the house next door, as there wasn't one. But it was almost certain that a fair number of farmers with adjoining fields would have long-established rights of passage through the land. The point to establish was where those paths led to and from... and what was in between. The prospect of a neighbour trundling over your patio or carefully cultivated rose garden was bad enough. But what if he was sitting on a tractor at the time...

There was also the strong possibility that there would be some Tenure Agreements between the current owner or his predecessor(s) and any number of the local farming community. It might be a simple situation of grazing rights to the fields next to the road, with a local farmer paying a minimal rent for regular access for his sheep and cows, but bearing in mind one of the established uses of the stream alongside the mill, it might also involve the entire female complement of the two communes of St Jacques-de-Néhou and nearby Néhou having the inalienable right, should they so wish, to launder their smalls there on the first day of every month in return for the annual payment of one goose egg.

Regarding the possible restrictions and covenants, it might simply be a question of any new owners not being able to work the mill or farm the water meadow in perpetuity. Unlikely though it was, the owners of the posh mill up the road might also have wangled some informally made but nonetheless binding arrangement with the local mayor that nobody would ever be allowed to live on the premises, let alone work in them.

Finally, SAFER was the French equivalent of our National Farmers' Union, only with much more clout. This organisation, given the fiercely protective French cultural attitude towards archaic and inefficient agricultural procedures, held more actual power than the American Gun Lobby. If the members felt like it, they could block the sale of potentially useful farming land to any non-farmer or union member. If the potential buyer was a foreign devil from the land of cut-price lamb, their vetoing ability was virtually limitless.

Also, SAFER had the power to use their veto at any time before, during or after the initial contract exchange and right up to mere weeks before completion. It would be operated by the simple expedient of the local branch requisitioning all or any of our precious hectares at a set price of less than 8000 francs an acre.

Looking as ever on the bright side, Mark pointed out that this was (quite) unlikely to happen. Even if it did, we would be better off by several thousand pounds, and would therefore have bought the ruined mill and farmhouse for even more of a snip. But looking at the downside, if the worst happened, we would end up with two wrecks to convert... and owning hardly a blade of grass surrounding them.

We sat by the converted bathtub fishpond in the twelve-yard-square garden of our Portsmouth home, and discussed and considered our options exhaustively, then phoned Mark.

Please go ahead with the offer, we said.

~

It was now that our man in la Manche really came into his own.

Realising our depth of feelings and desire for La Puce, he threw caution and French protocol to the wind, and persuaded the notaire to abandon virtually all the time-consuming and traditional procedural activities. We had given Mark the go-ahead at just before noon, French time, and in less than an hour after the inevitable lunch break for the whole of France, he was back on the line.

'The Flea,' he said almost casually, 'has landed...'

In less than sixty minutes Maître Gancel had managed to contact and present Monsieur Ole and all his brothers with our offer. Astonishingly, he had managed to achieve this miracle of communications despite the fact that three of the younger brothers were living and working in separate corners of France, and the fourth was presently residing somewhere in the barren northern wastes of the UK. Even more astonishingly, they had all agreed to the offer (which was substantially below the asking price) on the spot.

The notaire would now go ahead with drawing up the necessary papers of exchange. Given this evidence of the efficiency and ability of Maître Gancel, we could, all things considered, look forward to a speedy and relatively trouble-free completion to Operation Flea.

Once again, however, we were to find that arriving home and dry in a French property is not always the most straightforward of operations.

~

The next three months were to prove quite interesting.

As with the first and last voyage of the *Titanic*, it was all optimism, celebration and plain sailing at the start.

Val and Jeanne, steadfast, honest and unflappable as ever, had applied for a suitably small mortgage to cover the cost of buying and furnishing Le Petit Bijou, and were more than ready to sign the compromis de vente. The completion date, as was quite usual in this situation, would be filled in and duly signed when the anticipated good news came from their French lenders.

We would be in the enviable situation of buying La Puce outright with the funds released by the sale of Le Petit Bijou, which would happen, care of Maître LeFrançois, about a week after the completion date on The Little Jewel. Knowing for how long all commerce in the UK is abandoned before and after Christmas each year and arbitrarily doubling it in the case of France, we were determined to have the dual transfer smoothly transacted before the first office parties of Yuletide were even planned. Accordingly, we instructed Mark to make all haste in his dealings with Maîtres Gancel and LeFrançois in the matter of drawing up the necessary contracts. Totally against his advice, we set a provisional date for completion on La Puce of the last day in November.

We were confident – even if Mark was not – that everything could and would be tied up in a whole three months. Obviously, thanks to our crisp and concise instructions, the compromis de vente documents for both Le Petit Bijou and Le Moulin de la Puce arrived on our front-door mat almost simultaneously. It was a mere matter of hours to go through them (one with and one without a translator) in fine detail, sign and countersign each page, and put the contract relevant to Le Petit Bijou in the post for similar attention from Jeanne and Val.

In the case of La Puce, it would be more convenient for Donella to pop over to the peninsula with the papers, as by now yet another deal was in the offing. During our initial and heady tour of the land, which we hoped might go with the mill and farmhouse, we had walked through a delightful copse of beech and oak trees. It was alongside the orchard and fell within the natural boundaries of the whole parcel, but was not owned by the Ole *famille* and the one string of barbed wire we had encountered during our further explorations of the estate ran straight across the riverside walk beneath a stately avenue of beech trees.

Mark's call to the notaire following our departure for the UK had revealed that although every other square inch within the boundaries was part of the deal, neither the half-acre copse nor the hundred metres of river path were included. Also, each belonged to different people, but given our savings on the purchase price of La Puce, we would now be able to make an offer for those two small additional plots. This would then make the boundaries of the property more constant, and what lay within them even more perfect.

Madame, who owned the copse, would be agreeable to a deal – provided that the price reflected the value of the land, the trees upon it, and the wealth and diversity of mushrooms that grew there. Also that she would be allowed to choose and remove a single oak tree, promised to her nephew as a suitable and very supportive donation towards his soon-to-be-built *maison de mariage*. We were charmed by the prospect of future dawn raids on our very own fungi factory; and even more so by the idea of one of our trees forming an integral feature in one of the otherwise bland new houses sprouting around St Sauveur and every other old town in the region. We therefore instantly agreed to pay what the notaire judged to be a fairly fair price for what would henceforth be known as the Mushroom Wood.

In the case of the riverside walk, Madame number two was not sure if she could afford to let such a valuable strip of terrain go. It had been in the family for centuries, was a priceless and peerless example of unspoilt (because it was unworkable) Norman terrain, and so on. However, if the price were right, who could say? It might just be that she could see her way to bearing the loss. While she and we thought about just how much the narrow strip was worth to each party in emotional and financial terms, we gave the go-ahead to Maître Gancel to draw up the first stage contract for the Mushroom Wood, which Donella could sign at the same time as delivering the compromis on La Puce.

On her return, she bore even more good news. Maître Gancel seemed a very nice as well as unusually efficient notaire. Also, the owner of the riverside walk (evocatively described in the deeds as Hunters' Walk) had by now decided that she could face the loss of the most precious part of her cherished terrain in return for a suitably large remuneration.

The initial contract for this final part in the glorious jigsaw that would hopefully soon be all ours would be signed during the completion on La Puce and the Mushroom Wood.

Then came the first bulletin of bad news. Val and Jeanne had proved exemplary candidates for a loan on Le Petit Bijou from the French finance house. But there was no way that all the documentation prior to the releasing of funds would be ready before our completion date on La Puce. It would, Mark recommended, be best to apologise to Maître Gancel and to ask him to kindly rearrange completion on La Puce to a date which would definitely fall after the exchange on Le Petit Bijou. Which, as he had said in the first place but was far too polite to remind us of, would make the end of January a fairly near and definitely safe target time.

It was at this stage that I totally lost any sense of reason. Okay, I said reluctantly, I would write a nice and suitably contrite letter to Maître Gancel asking to move the completion date on La Puce onward. But I would not allow it to be moved a moment further forward than the second half of December.

I would thus allow another three weeks for the girls to get the okay on their mortgage. And for us to complete on La Puce before the Christmas celebrations threw a spanner in the various administration processes on both sides of the Channel.

My letter to Maître Gancel was posted, received and acted upon within the week.

On the same day Mark phoned to say, without a trace of 'told you so' in his voice, that his latest enquiries of the French finance house revealed that there was now no way that Jeanne and Val would be in a position to complete on Le Petit Bijou that year, let alone a week before 19 December. But it was still not too late to send another even more contrite letter to Maître Gancel cancelling the amended completion date and replacing it with another in January.

I refused to see sense. No, I said, English honour required that we stuck to the December agreement. If the money wouldn't be available from the sale of Le Petit Bijou by then, I would simply borrow sufficient to pay for La Puce on a short-term loan.

Although our overdraft arrangement at the bank was perilously near to its limit and we had not a bean in the form of cash reserves, it would surely be no great problem to extend the mortgage on our UK home, using the deeds of Le Petit Bijou as security. This, as Mark gently predicted and our mortgage company brusquely confirmed, was not to be a viable option. Without actually laughing at our proposal, which was made with the visual aids of alluring photographs of Le Petit Bijou and my wife wearing her shortest and tightest skirt, the branch manager briskly pointed out:

1. It was rigid company policy not to advance mortgage extensions on foreign property, no matter how attractively the rose bush fanned across the gable-end of Le Petit Bijou.
2. It was also current company policy not to extend mortgages on property in the UK, even if we chose to change our story about the reasons for wanting the money and claim it would be used for our third loft conversion in seven years.
3. Regardless of (1) and (2), the recent collapse of the UK housing market and subsequent devaluation of all properties meant that the difference between what we owed on our Portsmouth home and what it was now worth was not really enough to cover an advance for the ferry fare to Normandy, let alone a collection of ruined buildings and land (however picturesque) in that foreign place.

Walking or, in my wife's case, hobbling, away from this unexpected setback, I had an even better and, when you thought about it, more obvious idea. If we were going to have so much difficulty borrowing the necessary cash in the

UK because, among other reasons, La Puce was in France, why not borrow the money over there? We were, after all, in good stead at our Valognes branch of Crédit Agricole. That banking company had recently started a major advertising campaign for their *Le Mortgage* facilities. Moreover, French interest rates were much lower than ours.

Arriving home, I immediately phoned Mark, secured the name of a reputable UK-based company specialising in such matters, and phoned their senior director. As, at this stage, the unfortunate Don Clark had no inkling of the unreasonable pressure we would be putting him under during the coming weeks, he was extremely pleased to hear from us. Apprising himself informally of the circumstances *vis-à-vis* our yearly turnover and current outgoings, he was also pretty sure that we would have no problems with regard to raising the necessary monies from Crédit Agricole.

Hearing about my weight and smoking and drinking inclinations, he was even surer that I would be required to take a medical for insurance reasons. This would pretty certainly be followed by a weighting of the premium, dependent on the exact odds of my surviving for the duration of the loan period.

Learning of the need for us to have the loan agreed and in place at least a week before 19 December, he was a little more circumspect. Without actually hearing a sharp intake of breath on the other end of the line, I should have gathered from his cautious optimism on this point that three months, though a lifetime in French politics, could be but the blinking of an eye, administration-wise.

The moral of this necessarily convoluted tale therefore is, or should be, painfully clear: allow plenty of time for completing on French property.

If you are selling as well as buying, allow much, much more…

19 NOVEMBER

The completion date on La Puce was now just a month away, and it seemed that my self-imposed deadline had been a tad optimistic. By now, Crédit Agricole had received all the information they required, and the insurance company had (amazingly) agreed to give me health cover on any loan forthcoming.

Shortly, a panel would be sitting to approve the proposed mortgage. Their decision being favourable, we would be sent an offer, and following a set cooling-off period of eleven days as required by French law, we would be free to accept it. The funds would then be transferred to our account at Valognes, and the notaire notified that we were solvent enough to complete the deal on La Puce.

Given a fair wind, the best intentions and attentions of all concerned and not a single administrative hitch, everything should be in place on the day before the completion date. It would have to be, because Maître Gancel had already said that he would not proceed with the exchange unless that were so.

It was going to be the closest of calls...

2 DECEMBER

The phone rings. It is the normally imperturbable Don Clark, calling in (for him) a near frenzy.

He has just heard from Crédit Agricole in St Lô that the mortgage has been agreed, and an offer is on its way to us as we speak. When the agreement forms reach us, we should fill them in and take the package directly to the main UK branch of the company in London on the morning of the eleventh day after receiving the offer. This will give us the best chance of speeding up the business of Crédit Agricole in London forwarding the documents to their Manche HQ at St Lô. By special arrangement, the funds will now go directly to the notaire instead of to our bank at Valognes. It is just possible that the funds will be in place by the day before the completion deadline on La Puce.

5 DECEMBER, 7AM

The documents arrive, and with shaking hands we fill them in. We will be required to add our final signatures to the forms in the presence of a Crédit Agricole representative at the bank, and not a minute before the cooling-off period is officially over. We put the forms on the mantelpiece and look at them for the next ten days.

16 DECEMBER, 5AM

Turning off the two alarm clocks and answering the early morning call from BT, I make my way downstairs to get ready for arrival at Portsmouth Town station in good time for the 7.20 to Waterloo. I turn on the radio, and just catch the end of a bulletin reporting that a bomb has exploded at or near Clapham Junction, and all trains into London have been cancelled till further notice.

Determined not to let even the IRA thwart our chances, I get the car out of the garage and my wife out of bed, and we set off together with a few million other commuters to the log-jammed capital.

11.27AM

We arrive at Crédit Agricole in London.

Because of the station closures, a journey of ninety minutes has taken a shade under six hours, but we are here. With a total lack of parking space within a three-mile radius of Fleet Street, my wife drops me off at the ornate entranceway and circles the block for the next hour.

I meanwhile meet the extremely helpful young lady in charge of our case, and sign both my and Donella's signatures as she looks out of the window to see if it is raining. She also promises to lose not a minute in speeding the news of our acceptance of the offer to St Lô. We cover the distance back to Portsmouth in the relatively speedy time of four hours, and wait.

17 DECEMBER, 10AM

Don Clark phones to say he has just spoken to a top executive at Crédit Agricole in Paris, who says he has just spoken to the notaire at St Sauveur.

The Maître has now agreed unconditionally to take CA's word for it that the funds are on their way, and complete the transfer as planned on the nineteenth. Whether the money has reached him or not. We sit down and cry with relief for a bit, then load the car ready for the overnight ferry trip to Normandy, and the completion of our purchase of Le Moulin de la Puce.

18 DECEMBER

After a tranquil crossing, we made straight to La Puce to see if it was actually there and the preceding three months had not been merely a dream.

It was just as perfect as when we had last seen it ablaze with the golden shades of early autumn. Excepting that the largest and most visible tree from the farmhouse was missing, and in the near distance, we could hear the sound of a chainsaw ripping through the early morning air. Evidence of the murder was all around. Amputated branches were strewn across a wide area, and a deep track showed where a tractor had dragged the corpse away across the water meadow and up to the road.

The unearthed stump of the giant beech, which had guarded and shaded the riverside walk for the best part of fifty years (we counted the rings), was pointing accusingly towards the sound of yet more wanton destruction further along the bank.

There, beyond the barbed-wire fence once dividing our (as from tomorrow) terrain from our neighbour's land, two large men in sawdust-stained overalls were struggling to fit a set of chains from their lorry to a giant tree trunk which we had earmarked as a rustic bench. Selecting a suitably heavy branch from the carnage around me, I went to reason with them.

My knowledge of French was obviously too limited for any detailed conversation, but my body language was equally obviously expressing our concern with more than adequate fluency.

Our adversaries were, they hastened to assure us, not the perpetrators of the crime on 'our' land, but were merely following the instructions of our neighbour to remove the long-dead oak tree trunk before we took over on the morrow. In impotent fury, we watched as they shackled it to the lorry and dragged it unceremoniously along the riverbank, across the ford and past the mill up to the road. In the process, they left a quagmire, which had once been our beautiful riverside walk.

We had previously liked to think of ourselves as fairly liberal, easygoing people, and had often been extremely miffed to be told we were on private property when walking our dog in the Hampshire countryside. Why, we had asked, should anyone object to someone else enjoying their land when they had so much of it?

Now, before we became even the most modest of landowners, we were already suffused with the same antisocial tendencies. Before phoning Mark to rage about the stolen tree, we looked into the hardware shop at St Sauveur to price the rolls of their thickest, sharpest and most savagely intimidating rolls of barbed wire.

As if discussing a recent death in the family, Mark explained that he had learned of the theft of the giant beech the day before. He had spoken to Maître Gancel, who had explained that the culprit had already been identified and made aware that it was known that he had transgressed the local countryside code.

To the alleged letter of the law, the buyer agreed in the compromis de vente to take his purchase over as it was on the day of completion. Theoretically in the case of a house, the vendor could probably take the roof with him if he thought the effort worthwhile. When land changed hands, the same situation occurred, and the vendor was at very technical liberty to cut down every tree on his domain up to the moment of completion. In practice this didn't happen, as a totally abandoned feeding frenzy on the remaining trees in the region would ultimately be bad for the land, and therefore virtually everyone who made their living from it.

In our case, the anonymous intruder who had seen the opportunity to help himself before we took over at La Puce had won himself about £200-worth of firewood. But he had also earned the condemnation of most of the community, so Maître Gancel was fairly confident that it would not happen again. Nonetheless, we decided to spend the rest of the daylight hours before we signed for La Puce on Operation Treewatch.

19 DECEMBER

At last, the appointed hour had come, and with it our arrival at the St Sauveur offices of Maître Gancel. A business-like but affable chap, the Maître confirmed through Mark that SAFER had decided not to sequester a single metre of our land. He named the three local farmers who had the right to cross our terrain, and assured us that the ladies of the local commune would not wish to avail themselves of the laundry facilities at La Puce.

After dealing with every other clause, codicil and condition of the sale, Maître Gancel then introduced Monsieur Ole to the proceedings for the final signings. This was relatively swiftly followed by the completion of the contract on the Mushroom Wood, and the appearance of the owner of the additional strip of riverside walk we were to buy.

The initial contract on that final piece of the jigsaw

having been signed with a hopefully not too tree-less completion date in the New Year, everybody shook everybody else's hand at least twice, and we walked from the office as fully paid-up owners of Le Moulin de la Puce and all its environs.

Now, the only major challenge remaining was to spend the next however many years restoring the farmhouse and mill.

For the moment, we would have to go through the painful but very necessary process of saying goodbye to Le Petit Bijou. But before that we promised ourselves the most relaxing Christmas of our lives together. For once we would spend a little time in the Cotentin without looking at a single For Sale sign. Or allowing Mark to bring a single frustrated client to inspect the as yet unexploited promise of La Puce.

NINE

Innocence Abroad

Midnight, and the Néhou Christmas party is in full swing. I am outside counting stars from the vantage point of the village *pissoir*. My wife is dancing to 'The Birdie Song' with Christian the Goat, and Mr Maurice is telling an audience of schoolchildren about the night the Yanks invaded his wardrobe. René has not begun his whirling dervish routine, but the night is still young.

All is as it should be at this trial run for the seasonal celebrations, but I am worried about the bar bill. Since we arrived tonight, our Jolly Boys' Club has been drinking its way around France, and I have not bought a single bottle. So far on our journey of exploration, detailed analysis and criticism, we have visited the Loire, Bordeaux, Burgundy and Gascony. Along the way, we've paid tribute to food of the relevant region, with JayPay (Jean-Pierre) unveiling and presenting each complementary course like a magician pulling a ready-cooked rabbit from the ether. Every time our table reaches the bottom of a bottle, another takes its place courtesy of Big Freddo, official vintner for the evening.

As he leaves to visit the open-air facilities, I follow to tackle him about the likely size of the bill and, most importantly, who will be settling it. Now, standing shoulder to shoulder beside the épicerie window, we solemnly observe local custom by aiming at the epicentre of the enamelled Gauloises poster. As usual, Freddo is spot on. Across the road, the church clock chimes the witching hour and a nearby stallion snorts with derision at my feeble efforts to match my companion's head of pressure, trajectory and pinpoint accuracy.

Eventually, as relief comes, I ask how we are to sort out the finances. I appreciate his generosity, but surely it must be my turn to buy a round? Sighing with contentment, Big Freddo turns towards me and I see that his nickname is not entirely attributable to the size of his moustache. Casting a sympathetic glance downwards in my direction, he explains that as it is Christmas, we will be playing the sausage game. Pressed for further details of this ancient Cotentinese ritual, he summarises the basic rules. At the end of the evening, all the men at our table will line up at this very spot. As one, we will unzip, display and compare our assets. The member of the cartel with the furthest to reach to the cigarette poster will be (like the poor chap's wife) the loser, and must stump up for all bottles consumed that evening.

'If you like,' says Freddo politely as we zip up and make our way back to the celebrations, '…we can ask your wife to be the judge?'

'No need to bother,' I reply limply, '…will you take a cheque?'

At our table, Freddo explains in an unnecessarily loud voice that I have offered to pay for all the drinks this evening, and suggests another round. He then orders a giant two-litre bottle of farmhouse cider.

In final and complete capitulation, I call for a miniature of scotch.

~

Some hours later, and we are nearing the end of our vigil by the big pond. At this time of year, we do not expect any sightings of the local wildlife, but are determined to savour every minute of this, our first night as proper residents at La Puce.

For the past three years we have made a monthly pilgrimage from Portsmouth, knowing we must desert our Normandy home in a few days time. Each visit has been a frenzy of activity, battling to restore the ruined farmhouse and make some impression on the even more ruined mill cottage at La Puce before time and funds ran out. We had slept with the cement mixer, learned the patois for 'actually we wanted the toilet bowl in the bathroom, not the kitchen', and experienced the full horror of employing French and British craftsmen at the same time and in the same place. Like a Gallic *Brigadoon*, La Puce would vanish into the legendary Cotentin mists as we left, existing only in our imagination till the moment we drove again down the old cart track to walk the fields, touch the trees and pretend to live there for another heartbeat of its long history.

Back in England my thoughts kept drifting away to the water meadow and leaking septic tank while discussing the practicalities of a topless darts match with a Nottinghamshire licensee, I would find myself driving on the right-hand side of any road without a white line down its middle.

Each night in Normandy we would sit beside the grotto at La Puce, listing a dozen good reasons why we should take the final step across the Channel. The following week in the UK we would invent thirteen excuses why we could or should not.

Then, as if an impatient deity had grown weary of our excuses, three of our best brewery customers called in the same week to give us the sack. Re-organisation, re-shuffling and reducing costs meant that they would not be renewing our retainer fees in the autumn. They would, of course, still be interested in any ideas for public-house publications, PR and publicity packages I might wish to offer, but could not guarantee us an income.

Something had to be done, and as usual when big problems surfaced, we went down to the pub. In our Portsmouth local, we took stock of our situation and our options. On the debit side, we had a badly failing business, minus equity in our English home, an overdraft and no pension or source of regular income. On the plus side, we had La Puce, in hock to Crédit Agricole for a relatively small sum, and the farmhouse was virtually ready for habitation.

Starting her fifth *pastis*, my wife observed that we could just cover our UK and foreign mortgages by renting both properties out. When I pointed out that this would leave us with nowhere to live on either side of the Channel, she responded swiftly that I had forgotten the mill cottage at La Puce. It had been good enough for cows to live in for the last half-century: with a little imagination and a lot more work, it could make a comfortable, if basic, home while we sorted ourselves out. We could simply reverse our situation and base ourselves in Normandy, the move we had endlessly discussed and rejected. Then, we could return each month like latter-day Vikings to raid and pillage any pub publicity business in England, and virtually live off the land at La Puce in between times. And just think of the book I could write about our time in Normandy with René Ribet and all our other friends at Néhou.

It would be an adventure, and if, after a year, we had not waxed fat on the fruits of the land and my fertile imagination, we would be on the spot and in a much better position to sell La Puce and return to reclaim our home in England. To surrender now and meekly await certain financial disaster would be unworthy of us. It would also be an insult to all our ancestors, who had set forth from Portsmouth harbour to make a new home in far remoter corners of the earth than the Cherbourg peninsula with hardly a sovereign in their breeches. Were we going to talk about it for another thirty years, or were we going to make the break and follow our hearts' desire?

As a young couple at a nearby table broke into spontaneous applause at my wife's moving address, I considered the arguments for the defence. I could – and probably should – have pointed out that her experience of living off the land was limited to a yearly harvest of grow-bag tomatoes in the backyard of 87 Laburnum Grove. That the closest she had come to animal husbandry was taking the dog for a walk. That we had seen dozens of other people's schemes for survival in France go tragically wrong. And that most of our immediate ancestors had limited their adventuring to the odd trip on the Isle of Wight ferry. Finally, thanks to Peter Mayle, there were now more British people trying to write and sell books about their adventures in France than actually live there. But the way things were, it seemed to me that someone somewhere was trying to tell us something. It was time to put up or shut up. I ordered another pint of Dutch courage and agreed that it would be so. We would have our year with René, and take each day as it came.

René Ribet and his mobile home arrived in the big field last year, shortly after he told us that he was being evicted from his tiny cottage on the outskirts of Néhou and needed somewhere else to stay till times became better. The arrangement, he said, would be to our great benefit, as his presence would deter poachers, burglars and other miscreants who would otherwise take advantage of our absence. Under his stewardship, our estate would be in safe hands, and he would not only manage the land, but also carry out all restoration work on the buildings at La Puce at half the price of any other specialist tradesman in the area. As anyone would tell us, there was little he did not know about nature, farming and building work.

In fact, most people in the area seem keen to tell us that

René is known locally as Ribet the Fox and is not to be trusted, but, for all his failings, he has a big heart and has become my friend.

~

Above us, the big Normandy sky goes on forever, and the night is as still as death. I start to tell my wife that she was right, and that I love her for it. A terrible fear for the future still grips my heart, but I would rather be here with her at this moment than anywhere else in the world. I reach towards her but she stays my hand and silently bids me listen.

Somewhere, from out in the velvet blackness, a visitor has arrived. A crackle of breaking undergrowth is followed by a regular series of low, breathless grunts. Donella turns to me, her face alight with joy.

'There,' she says, voice trembling with emotion, 'I told you we had a badger. Now will you believe me?'

I smile and nod and take her hand.

I have heard that sound before, and know it is René trying to re-start his moped after falling into the roadside hedge. Unlike him, sound travels best at night, and the Christmas party at Néhou must finally have ended. I shiver and suggest we return to the mill, lest we scare the badgers away and spoil a perfect day.

23 DECEMBER

Having driven straight back from visiting friends in the Dordogne, we arrive home to find a new member for our ditch-of-the-month club.

It rains frequently in Cotentin, and the sensibly deep channels on each side of every road and lane lie in wait for unwary drivers like still and patient lions at a waterhole. Curiously, it is invariably the locals who play the part of doomed gazelles. Visitors soon learn to keep clear of the treacherously soft verges, while the Cotentinese seem almost

proud of the way their clinging embrace claims so many victims. There is still talk in the village of an encounter with *les
accotements non stabilisés* by a rather proper English lady
some years ago. A new member of the Bricquebec-twinning
committee, she arrived very late for a reception and meal
and apologised during her after-dinner speech, in her best
Franglais. She had, she haltingly explained, pulled off the
road to get her bearings on the way to the venue, and
become bogged down.

'Everything about your countryside is so charming,'
she gushed, '...but you do have such soft... *verges*.'
Understandably, she had not known the French term for the
dangerous grassy bits on the side of the road. She had also
obviously not known that *verge* is the French word for penis,
and that she had consequently offered the male members
present the most deadly insult imaginable. After convening
a hasty meeting, the bemused leader of the all-male hosting
committee had responded by welcoming her to the region
but passionately rebutting her claim that it was famed for its
impotence. Necessary steps should surely be taken to dis-
prove this regrettable misunderstanding, and the entire
committee was happy to volunteer with a demonstration at
the time and place of her choosing. Local legend does not,
sadly, record whether the offer was taken up.

La Puce sits alongside the main route from St Sauveur to
Bricquebec, so we have seen much evidence of the
Cotentinese affinity for ditches and their magnetic properties, but any offer of help will inevitably be met with a frosty
look and curt rejection as if acceptance would be an admis-
sion that the position of their vehicle is anything other than
deliberate. Of all the many examples of cultural idiosyn-
crasy, the French approach to driving seems the most
bizarre and potentially lethal.

I have never seen a copy of a French Highway Code for
British visitors, but have begun a manual, which will be

based upon some basic lore and laws. Sub-headings will include:

1. CLOSE ENCOUNTERS

The favoured position for any driver (male or female) is about six inches behind your rear bumper. So much do they like this position that they only leave it regretfully, and then preferably on a particularly dangerous and sharp blind corner, or just before a humpback bridge. In particularly bad weather and visibility, the distance between bumpers will decrease pro rata.

On one occasion my wife actually thought she was towing a car in a thunderstorm, so closely was it following her every move. Looking into the rear-view mirror after navigating a particularly tight bend, she saw that it had disappeared, and stopped to investigate. Rounding the bend on foot, she found the ancient Citroën lying wounded in a waterlogged ditch, with two elderly ladies sitting calmly inside. Both refused all offers of help and may, for all we know, be there still. On another occasion, I grew tired of counting the liver spots on the face of an aged pursuer through miles of winding country lanes, and after taking a dozen random turns to try to shake him off, finally careered into a convenient driveway to escape. As he arrived alongside and skidded to a halt in a shower of gravel, I got out to apologise for parking outside his house. He looked at me as if I were mad, and snapped that he was merely following me to see where I lived...

2. AFTER YOU

The right of way on any roundabout may belong to the driver already on it or arriving on it, depending on local tradition and established usage. All drivers with foreign – i.e. not local – number plates have no legal right to be there, and are therefore fair game. Local drivers may and probably will gang up to box in, intimidate or even force intruders off the road.

3. TAKING SIDES

Depending on the area, season of the year or time of month and day, traffic entering a main route from a side road or lane may or may not have priority. Tractors towing long and badly loaded trailers obviously win extra points for stalling halfway out on to the highway.

4. JUMP OR DIE

Pedestrian crossings are not there to guarantee safe passage, but to channel potential targets for bored or irritable motorists, and will always be located in a particularly ill-lit or obscure location. Some villages have as many as five crossings in a row, giving local pedestrians a whole range of choices as to where they would most prefer to be run down.

On an early visit to Bricquebec, I drew up at a pedestrian crossing as an elderly lady hobbled off the kerb without looking in my or any direction. Not only did the queue of drivers behind sound their horns in a frenzy of outrage at being cheated of their quarry, but the old woman glared ferociously and shook her fist at me before continuing on her painful way. There were two possible reasons for her anger. Either my actions implied she was now too elderly and infirm to play the traditional dicing-with-death crossing game, or she felt I had cheated her of the opportunity to ensure future security for her family, courtesy of a foreign (and therefore soft) insurance company.

NB *All or any of the above rules, regulations and conventions will not apply between the hours of 2 and 5 PM, when drivers are returning from their luncheon venue. During this time, any vehicle from a tractor to a seventeen-tonne juggernaut is likely to come and go to and from wherever fancy dictates, and on either side of the road.*

Investigation of the van occupying the ditch outside La Puce reveals that our new club member is Mr Janne. A local farmer, he follows the Cotentinese tradition of being close to the earth, and is somewhat wider than he is tall. On a good day he looks like his favourite breakfast dish is live rats. He is, however, a gentle and considerate man who raises thoroughbred horses at his farm a mile away. He presently lies slumped motionless behind the wheel of his Renault, and we fear he is injured. Closer examination of the empty lemonade bottle in his lap reveals, however, that he is merely paralytic.

We ease his giant bulk from behind the wheel and help him into the kitchen. Here, his story unfolds over several mugs of coffee, brewed to local taste. As they say, the perfect composition is as black as night, as sweet as a young nun, and as thick as a bull's most important appendage. The present condition and position of Mr Janne's van is, he explains with a shrug of his massive shoulders, entirely the responsibility of the ridiculous laws appertaining to the transport of the region's favourite beverage. It is simply because he is such a law-abiding citizen that things have come to this pretty pass.

At this point, it is perhaps useful to attempt an explanation of the complex relationship between Norman country folk, the apple, what they do with it and the importance it plays in their everyday lives. As with Somerset, the soil and climatic conditions found in the northwestern region of France particularly favour the growth of small, sweet and often exceptionally ugly apples. I have never seen a Norman actually eat one fresh from a tree, but they know more ways to preserve, cook or distil its essence for consumption than there are days in a leap year.

By tradition, every country dweller will have at least one apple tree in his garden, or access to someone else's. The harvest will be taken in October, either during the day or night depending upon whom it officially belongs to, and the apples left in a pile in the open air to mature, or as we might say, rot.

Over the long winter months, the ancient rituals then begin in almost obsessive secrecy and security. The basic ingredients for cider are apples and more apples, but most households will make some small addition at a vital stage to ensure unique flavour and taste. Pieces of dead animal are much favoured for the creation of further zest and body, and one elderly brewer of our acquaintance is alleged to add a pinch of gunpowder to every litre to increase its purgative qualities. As with English prize vegetable growers, competition is fierce to produce the best in class each year. Unlike vegetable growers, however, Cotentinese cider buffs will rarely allow anyone else to taste their produce without money changing hands, so most judging and subsequent status relies on the claims of the maker and the forensic evidence of the odd tasting or burglary. This leads to much debate and argument in the local bars as to who produces the superior vintage each year, but that's how they like it. Occasionally, a villager will bring a bottle of his best cider into the bar and leave it casually on a table for observation and comment, and a purely visual process of judging will begin. Points will be awarded for degree of murkiness and the number of small pieces of apple and other grisly remains suspended in the liquid, and even the age, design and general grubbiness of the bottle may win grudging approval.

Unquestionably the acme of the regional homebrewer's art is calvados, invented (according to our village) by the Cotentinese and subsequently hijacked by the people of the département of Calvados in Upper Normandy. (Cotentin is the top part of the département of Manche, which constitutes Lower Normandy. Manche is the peninsula with Cherbourg at the top and the border with Brittany at the bottom.) This fierce distillation of cider is loosely described by those who have never tried it as a sort of apple brandy. All patriotic Normans, however, place calva somewhere higher up the league table of great French beverages, and local conviction claims it to be the prototype for the mythical elixir of life which foreign alchemists have been trying to create since the dawn of time. As every Norman knows, a tot of classic calva will cure a host of maladies, preserve life when all other practices of modern medical science have failed, and start the most reluctant of tractors on a frosty morning.

Also known colloquially as *trou Normand* because of its traditional use to fill the hole between courses at table, locals may refer to farm- or homemade calvados simply as *goutte*, elsewhere meaning any small amount of strong drink. Though they will take a glass at any time and with the slightest excuse, most Cotentinese are also firm believers in its employment to cleanse the palate during meals. The smallest glass will briefly paralyse all nerve endings in the upper body while perversely liberating the vocal chords, stimulating the libido and burning out all sensation of taste. Having attended a number of Norman dinner parties, I believe this may provide a strong clue to the real reason it was first conceived and created. According to local tradition, regular consumption also negates the need for dental hygiene, and the purchase of toothpaste and brushes in Cotentin is, it is proudly claimed, the lowest in France.

Because of the special and enduring relationship between the Cotentinese and their calva, a whole set of rules and regulations governing its production have been in place for centuries. In our region, for example, it is still an offence for the orchard owner to allow foreign growths to infest his trees. Mistletoe flourishes on apple wood, and the gendarmerie has the power to call at an appropriate time to solemnly check that the parasite is not strangling its host and threatening the next harvest. In practice, every leaf and berry of *gui* will have been carefully collected for seasonal export by the bemused farmer, amazed at his good fortune that the English will actually pay to display the weed in their homes as an excuse (as if one were needed) to kiss a pretty girl.

An attempt to control the production and circulation of farm calva and placate the region's licensed vendors is enshrined in a law permitting each amateur grower to employ the services of a travelling still once a year. Then, the golden essence of the season's harvest will be created and reverently transferred to oak barrels, where it will hibernate contentedly for up to a decade. A considerable amount will never reach the barrel stage, however, as samples must be bottled for immediate assessment, possible trading, and to start the tractor when all else fails.

Officially, the amount produced by each orchard owner is regulated by the number of trees and their yield, and must be strictly for home consumption. Given the going rate for illicit calva, it is hardly surprising that there is a permanent shortage of empty bottles in our neck of the woods, and that manufacture takes place on a considerable scale in the most unlikely places. Many properties in our area have security systems worth more than the outhouses they protect, and we know of a local man who somehow produces 3000 litre bottles of goutte a year while living in a bedsitter.

To stem the annual torrent of bootlegging activity, there is also a thoroughly French law. A sealed and full bottle of calva in a car could be in transit for illegal sale, reasoned the authorities, so a suitable statute would have to be framed and enforced to prohibit the practice. With supreme Gallic logic, the legislators decreed that only the transport of unsealed and part-filled bottles of homemade calva should be permissible. Consequently, anyone found driving a car with an unopened bottle in the boot risks investigation and prosecution. If the bottle is loosely corked, half empty and rolling about on the front seat, the driver is obviously complying with state requirements and using it for personal consumption only, so is in the clear.

~

After a reviving goutte from our emergency supply, Mr Janne recovers enough to tell us his story. Hearing from René of our imminent arrival from the ungodly south, he had selected a bottle of his best calva to welcome us back in traditional fashion. Before departure, he had broken the seal and poured a little of the golden liquid safely into a jug to conform to the law. Obviously, it would have been unthinkable to have done so without ensuring that all had gone well since the contents of the bottle had last breathed the evening air. In all modesty, he assured us, it was close to perfection. To be doubly sure, he had tried another glass before setting out, and even stopped off at a convenient point on the mile-long journey to check that his precious cargo was travelling well. Somehow, and most probably due to a fault in the steering, he had eventually found himself in the ditch outside La Puce, and kept his spirits up while awaiting our arrival with the remains of the gift bottle. Now we must help him out of the ditch, but much more importantly, out of trouble with Madame Janne.

Would it be possible, he pleads, for us to go to his farm and find Henri the labourer, explain the situation and return with the necessary equipment to rescue the car? If he were to return on foot, Madame would ask all sorts of awkward questions, and the implications with regard to both his capacity for strong drink and driving skills would surely diminish his standing throughout the region...

A little later, and Henri, the tractor and a towrope have been summoned, and the road is completely blocked with motorists anxious to observe and advise, if not actually help. They are mostly dispersed by a passing policeman, who arrives on his *mobylette* to sympathise with Mr Janne's predicament, make copious notes about the incident and officially take over arm-waving, traffic-directing and shouting responsibilities.

At last the van is parked in our yard while Mr Janne, Henri, the bobby and two complete strangers settle down in the kitchen to celebrate a successful conclusion to the evening's drama. Donella visits the medicine cabinet for another bottle of emergency calva and suggests she run Mr

Janne home to ensure that he arrives safely. All the men look at her as if she has just suggested they have soft verges. A better idea, proposes Mr Janne, would be for him to drive us all to the Bar Ghislaine, where he may properly thank us all for our assistance and relate the story of our adventures to the Jolly Boys' Club. In spite of much nodding and general agreement, we politely refuse his invitation.

There are at least two miles of ditches en route, and besides, we know of Ghislaine's general opinion of men, men drinking, and especially men drinking off the premises.

25 DECEMBER

Christmas Day. We rise late and exchange presents. Opening mine, I solve a month-long mystery regarding the contents of the large and strangely shaped parcel beside the gaily-decorated fir tree in our orchard. Donella has bought me a new wheelbarrow, complete with a list of pressing out-door tasks attached by a pretty bow to the handle. She seems equally pleased with the second-hand chainsaw, which I bought from René after his assurances that it is as good as when his father bought it twenty years before, and far superior to modern rubbish with all those unnecessary safety devices.

Like children impatient to play with our new toys, we decide to spend the day outside. Loading my new wheelbarrow with a picnic, bottle of wine and the chainsaw, we make our way down to the water meadow so that my wife may give her presents to the livestock.

Unable to keep our own animals in the past as mostly absentee landlords, we have sublet the land to a variety of tenants in an attempt to keep the land in trim, and Donella has adopted them all. Two goats belonging to our distant neighbour Christian do good work on the scrub in the one-acre garden behind the farmhouse, and my wife has bought them a gift-wrapped packet of extra-strength Capstan cigar-ettes, their favourite brand.

We learned of this enthusiasm for tobacco from an eccentric Englishman in a neighbouring village who shares his house with an alpine goat. While most amiable, the creature also likes pot plants and is not house trained, so even my wife has not invited the happy couple to dinner as yet.

Apart from the occasional arrival of friends' sheep or pigs in need of rough grazing, the two sloping and well-drained roadside fields at La Puce are reserved for the beef cattle owned by Jean Chevalier, the mayor of Néhou. Typical of the farmers in the region, John and his wife Solange have their own fields around their farmhouse in a nearby hamlet, but rent extra grazing land at a very nominal fee. Apart from their keeping the land, hedges and gates in impeccable condition, having such a close relationship with the local mayor has been of great practical assistance during the restoration of La Puce. Every commune in France has its own elected mayor, and each wields considerable power, particularly in matters of planning consent for building works and improvements.

~

Down at the big pond, we find the crayfish gang have extended their territory and reign of terror.

Reggie and Ronnie Cray and their heavy mob appeared in the east end of the pond shortly after we had it dug, and immediately set about ruling their new manor with inhuman ferocity. We first noted their territorial ambitions when they put the frighteners on the artistic and sensitive Triple Salco and his troupe of aquabatic frogs, and even the largest trout would turn tail when the Cray Brothers and their firm swaggered aggressively through the shallows. Burrow holes had regularly appeared around the bank as new generations of the gang set up home, and now it seems they hold total sway. They are, according to our enquiries, a particularly large and succulent species of native freshwater crayfish, which have reappeared since we began clearing out the stream and generally attempting to restore life to the polluted waters of La Puce.

Hearing of our new tenants during a visit to the Café de Paris, Freddo the patron had told us of his happy childhood days at our grotto fishing for crayfish and trout, and advised that we keep their return secret. The first action we should take would be the removal of the No Fishing signs Donella has put up. Their very presence would let everyone in the area know there were now fish to be caught at La Puce, and the temptation would be too strong for the most law-abiding Norman angler. Even more importantly, we must make sure that René does not find out there is anything remotely edible or saleable in our waters.

We know this to be sound advice, having become aware of our friend's appetite for unusual delicacies when we dug a tiny pond in the garden at La Puce and filled it with goldfish cunningly smuggled across the Channel in a couple of large thermos flasks. The day after they had taken up residence, Donella had found him looking thoughtfully at the innocent creatures, and asked if goldfish are as popular in France as they are in England. He had nodded enthusiastically, and told her his special recipe for *poissons rouges* in batter.

Given the rapid expansion of the Cray gang as evidenced by their territorial gains, René has hopefully not yet noted their presence, in spite of their tendency to wreak havoc when in drink. We had first become aware of the Crays' own liking for alcohol when preparing a special dinner for a visiting Burgundian friend. Wishing to impress him with our mastery of his regional classic dish, we had visited JayPay with a bottle of scotch and a request for a crash course in *boeuf bourguignon*.

Following the lengthy verbal and written instructions to the letter, we marinated the beef for the requisite time, and then fished out the carrots, which had been sitting in a bottle's worth of best Burgundy for a day and a night. This, JayPay had stressed, was a vital step, as they would become discoloured in the process and totally ruin the overall visual effect if left in place. Having read that crayfish are not averse to vegetables, we had taken the thoroughly soused carrots down to the big pond and dropped them by Reggie and Ronnie's front door. In moments, the duo had emerged and snapped up the unexpected treat. Inevitably, the alcohol had taken effect and trouble broke out. With nobody else to pick on, they started drunken brawling with each other and we were unable to separate them. Eventually, a lost claw declared Big Reg the winner, and all was still again as they retired to sleep it off. So knowing their susceptibility to strong liquor, Donella has prepared them some pork crackling in low-alcohol lager, and respectfully leaving their special Christmas lunch at the entrance to their manor, we continue our rounds.

~

At his caravan, all is quiet, which means René has either found an open bar, is visiting the Widow of Negreville, or is sleeping off the effects of the night before. We leave his present of real-ale-flavoured Christmas puddings and a bottle of malt whisky, and an invitation to join us for dinner.

The roast is almost ready when René arrives. As Donella prepares the drinks, he explains he has been out on the traditional Christmas Day hunt, in full hue and cry for what must be one of the few surviving mammals bigger than a water vole in Cotentin. Before we sit down at the table, René passes me a carrier bag containing our Christmas present, and I see that it is a dead squirrel. I thank him and slip the still-warm corpse into the rubbish bin while Donella hands him a glass of mulled wine spiced with nutmeg and ginger. Our guest takes a sip and grimaces. It is the first time in our acquaintance that he has not finished a drink.

After dinner, René accepts a tumbler of whisky and asks if our burglars had taken anything. Pressed for details, he describes a dramatic incident at La Puce during our visit to the south. Just after dusk, the mayor had arrived at René's caravan in a state of high excitement. Knowing of our absence, he had stopped off at the farmhouse to check all was well. As he had walked around the building, however, an outside light had turned on and off, indicating that intruders must be inside. Armed with René's ancient shotgun and a billhook, they had surrounded the farmhouse, when once again a light had signalled the presence of careless trespassers. As the official key holder, René had then led an assault through the front door, only to find the building empty.

They had concluded that the would-be thieves had made good their escape during the search upstairs, that the flashing lights had been operated by a power surge, or even more likely and satisfactory, that it was the manifestation of some supernatural force. I express our thanks for their brave action in protecting our property, and think it best not to point out that, before leaving to visit our friends, I had installed a set of newfangled British security floodlights with special sensors which react to any movement in the yard.

And so, the legend of the *fantôme* of La Puce is born.

30 DECEMBER

We are invited to dinner with the mayor, a signal honour. It should be an interesting evening. The guests will include my mother, who has joined us to see the New Year in, and Helen Patton, granddaughter of the famous American general. Patton was based at an orchard just down the road from La Puce during the D-Day operations, and Helen is restoring a grand house in Néhou in his memory. A considerable celebrity in the area, Helen Patton is much respected in the village, and has just asked John Chevalier to take on the responsibility and honour of aiding progress with restoration work on the orchard and house.

Over a simple but excellent dinner of pressed bull's

tongue followed by roast chicken in a special sauce made from its entrails, John tells us how his farm was a billet for German troops during the occupation. He was just fourteen at the time, but some of the soldiers were even younger. Others were too old to do much more than wear a uniform, and none were brutal or even unfriendly. In stark contrast to our long memories and dislike of those who have as much as threatened our shores, we have found that none of the residents seem to bear any malice towards their former occupiers. Donella believes this to be another example of Norman pragmatism, as German visitors contribute greatly to the economy of the area by revisiting the scene of their crimes.

As the evening progresses, we learn that La Puce saw some honourable action during the D-Day landings. According to John, a German machine-gun nest was set up in the roadside attic, frustrating the efforts of a platoon of American infantrymen to advance on St Sauveur-le-Vicomte. After a lively exchange of fire, the platoon leader called on the services of a passing fighter plane, which strafed the farmhouse until the inhabitants surrendered. According to elderly locals, they were then marched away to our copse by resistance fighters and never seen again. The holes in the kitchen ceiling and great chunks missing from the attic rafters are evidence of the aerial attack, as I will have noticed. It would be fitting, the mayor ventures, to leave the wounds intact during our restoration as a permanent reminder of the incident and the ultimate pointlessness of war. I agree, wishing I hadn't spent so much on getting the rafters repaired and timbers treated by René, who had assured me the culprit was a particularly savage termite, which would eat the whole building if not exorcised.

After dinner, we are introduced to yet another variety on the calva theme. The regional economy version of Grand Marnier, *quarante-quatre*, is made by every rural housewife to serve at special occasions and the method of marinating an orange and some coffee beans in calva for the required forty-four days could not be simpler (see recipe on p.88). The resulting sweet and fragrant liqueur is just as lethal as calva but has an innocence of taste, which invites overindulgence, as my wife and Mother proceed to confirm.

It is now time for us to present our party pieces, and Helen breaks the ice by performing a tuneful American folk song. Rather thoughtlessly, I respond with my speciality of standing on a chair and declaiming some of the loud and very francophobe extracts from the St Crispin's Day address in *Henry V*. Happily, the text appears to lose much in the translation, and Solange calms us all with a patois lullaby, serenely delivered in her pure, sweet voice.

Emboldened by the quarante-quatre, my wife stops the show with 'Land of My Fathers' in the original Welsh, and Mother gives a stirring rendition of 'Hearts of Oak'. To even the score a little, I suggest we all sing 'la Marseillaise' before going our separate ways.

Fuelled with another glass of the calva liqueur, Mother is now beginning to make tart comments about the overall performance of the French and the late entry of the Americans into the war, and unfortunately Helen is translating. I thank our hosts and escort Mother to the car as she recalls how her great-great-great-grandfather played a leading part in the Battle of Trafalgar, and how he would oft recall that the Lords of the Admiralty quite rightly considered one English tar to be worth at least eight French matelots when planning engagement tactics.

Around midnight, I have a strange dream, in which I am visited by a grey lady in eighteenth-century clothing. She summons me, and I follow her down the stairs and out to the orchard. There, she points at the base of an old apple tree. I wake Donella and tell her of my experience. It is well known, I point out, that all millers were renowned for fiddling their customers and burying a spare pot of gold somewhere on the premises. Perhaps this is a supernatural visitation to tell me where a fortune in *louis d'or* is buried. She yawns and reminds me that I ate nearly a whole round of goat's cheese after dinner. Knowing the Norman reputation for closeness to a shilling, any treasure would have been discovered long ago. Perhaps, she grudgingly concedes, I might find our German storm troopers there.

I return to bed, nevertheless determined to buy a metal detector on our next visit to the UK...

Recipe for Quarante-Quatre

1. Take one orange
2. Pierce with forty-four coffee beans
3. Place in a jar and cover with rough farm calva
4. Leave for forty-four days
5. Taste in sitting position and on a day off
6. Drink some more
7. Go and lie down...

11 JANUARY

An uneventful crossing home – yes, *home* – on the overnight from Portsmouth.

Now that Christmas and the worst excesses of the booze cruises are over, it is at least possible to use the toilet and avoid certain confrontation with a pool of vomit or its previous owner.

The last time we ventured into a Cherbourg supermarket in the run-up to Christmas, a British youth wearing a monstrously inflated condom on his head was being sick over a table in the cafeteria as his mates made encouraging comments on style, volume and content. Thankfully, the table was not occupied at the time. As we hurried away trying to look like locals, I commented admiringly on the reaction of the French diners. Rather than looking angry or disgusted, they were watching the display with the bemused air of foreign spectators at a village cricket match.

I put their attitude down to classic Gallic tolerance and respect for individual liberties. My wife thought it was probably because they are so used to being invaded, the odd barbarian at a neighbouring table is no big deal.

We have been over the water to raid the dwindling supplies in our Portsmouth bank account. We could have had the money transferred direct, but our manager doesn't yet know we have moved, so it seemed a good idea to show our faces in the Southsea branch and forestall any awkward questions about why we prefer banking in a foreign country.

At Bricquebec, we stop off at Crédit Agricole to inject some life into the separate restoration and survival funds, which are both dangerously close to extinction. When we bought La Puce, we thought it best to take out a mortgage with our French bank, and it has proved to be a serious mistake. At that time, the exchange rate was more than ten francs to the pound, and the interest level comparatively low. Now the rate is little more than seven francs, and we appear to owe more on La Puce than this time last year.

In a black moment last month, Donella calculated that if things go on as they are, we would end up with a bigger debt than the place cost to start with. This bizarre equation is reflected by our experience in the bank, where the longer we wait, the further we get from the counter. If there is a French word for queue, the Cotentinese have obviously yet to learn it.

Eventually, there is only one customer in front of us, a very small monk with a very large sack of cash to deposit. We have seen him before, and know him to be the bagman for the Trappist monastery overlooking the square, where it is said the finest *charcuterie* in all France is made. The impressive gothic building is next door to a grocery store where it is said the finest cheeses in all France are to be found. Naturally, stocks are limited to the twenty-seven varieties made in Normandy. As the monk is fortunately from a silent order, the usual ten-minute dialogue on intimate health details and exchanges of x-ray plates from recent operations does not take place, and we are soon at the counter. After all this excitement, it is time for a coffee break at the Café de Paris.

Of the half dozen bars in Bricquebec, the Café de Paris is our favourite, a popular haunt for most of the town's serious drinkers and socialites. As the owner of the most monumental moustache in Bricquebec, Freddo is naturally an important figure in the community, and we come to him for advice on all matters of local etiquette and best practices. But as it is a Tuesday, our host will be at his day job as a master at the local secondary school. Donella is sure he teaches English, but as a smattering of German appears to be his only foreign language, I think this is unlikely, even in Cotentin.

Madame Collette and her mother are at their usual posts, and we are each awarded the four kisses normally reserved for close friends. There is a special bond between us, as the kind and gentle Collette was born in Néhou. In the reverse of the usual situation in an English village, we have been almost instantly accepted as members of the community, unlike the foreigners at nearby St Jacques-de-Néhou. We have yet to discover the reason for the fierce rivalry between the two villages which stand in permanent antipathy on either side of the D900, but believe there was a serious falling out a hundred years or so ago and the two neighbouring communes keep strictly to their own territory, shops, bars and affairs. Scandals concerning each other's residents are, of course, very much in the public domain.

As ever, it is difficult to see more than a metre inside the Café de Paris due to the comfortable fog of tobacco smoke.

Last year, we were traumatised to learn that a universal ban on smoking in public places, including all bars, had been decreed from Paris in our absence, and was shortly to come into force.

From the dawning of what for some unfathomable reason was dubbed Blue Elephant day, every bar in France would be strictly smoke-free, with just one table in a clearly defined separate area set aside for hopeless addicts. An orgy of posters, leaflets and advertisements bearing the blue elephant logo having prepared us for the day, we visited the Café de Paris determined to show our intransigent British dissent by sitting outside and sullenly fuming in the rain. As it transpired, Freddo and every other bar owner in the region had taken a very French approach to the new legislation. There were now two overflowing ashtrays on each table instead of the usual one, and the few non-smoking regulars had lit up to express their contempt for this unacceptable threat to fraternity and liberty. Bets were also being placed on whose glass the ever-growing column of ash on Freddo's *disque bleu* would contaminate as he puffed with his usual determination over the pumps. The law being the law, however, Freddo had taken all due precautions. A single table marked *non-fumeur* had been placed in the dingy passageway at the rear of the bar, wedged in between the fridge-freezer and toilet door.

Nobody, he told us, had chosen to use it so far, but you never knew when a spy from the relevant ministry might drop in to check that the new law was being scrupulously observed and administered.

~

After catching the *Huit-à-Huit* just before the standard two-hour lunchtime closure – which allegedly also applies to some restaurants in our area – we depart for La Puce. Making our way straight down the ancient cart track to where the remains of the tiny mill stand beside the Lude, we are greeted by a host of snowdrops and a newly delivered mountain of sand.

Now that René has finished restoration work on the farm-house and has promised to find us an impeccable tenant, *tout de suite*, he is obviously preparing to turn his attentions to the mill. As all interior and exterior stone walls are to be left unplastered and the heap of sand is almost as big as the building itself, it appears he has over-ordered. Probably, I reassure my wife, René has gained considerable savings on our behalf by buying in bulk, and sand always comes in handy. She sniffs and reminds me that her researches and our latest bill from Mr Ribet prove it would be cheaper to have a lorry load delivered by the local builders' merchant than a wheelbarrow's worth via the Fox of Cotentin. I promise to do something about the situation, and pointedly suggest she might like to spend the afternoon re-stocking her feeding stations with the expensive selection of quality victuals she has brought all the way from the Portsmouth branch of Pets R Us.

22 JANUARY

René arrives after lunch to find me tooled up with my new metal detector, carefully Hoovering the spot next to the apple tree where the Grey Lady indicated the location of the miller's gold. Thinking quickly, I say that I am ensuring there are no water pipes below the earth, as I have decided to plant a new cherry tree. He sucks his teeth, looks at me for a long moment, and then explains patiently that it would be stupid even for an Englishman from a city to dig so close to an ancient apple tree. The ground will not bear two trees so close together, and besides, cherries are a waste of time. The birds will eat all the fruit before it ripens. René has a keen interest in the welfare of the orchard trees, because, as he explained when we made our original arrangements, honourable tradition and long-standing custom dictate that the estate manager has the rights to the entire harvest. In exchange, we are awarded one bottle of calva per tree. As, thanks to his year-round ministrations, our trees produce the finest goutte in Cotentin, I would be most ill advised to risk the health of this one. I nod in agreement, and determine to start digging at night when he is safely tucked up in bed.

25 JANUARY

René has called a caravan conference to begin discussions on the creation of another *étang* in the water meadow. Now that the crayfish gang have taken over at the big pond, Donella is anxious to create a safe haven for the victims of their protection racket. René says he and his tractor-owning pond specialist can start next week, so I calculate that the first sod will be turned over around June.

This is one of the reasons why my relationship with René is so important. In my dealings with our estate manager, I am daily learning how to adapt to the ways and wiles of the Cotentinese, said quite unjustly in other regions to be as crafty as two barrels of particularly cunning monkeys.

Over the past year we have learned that, in the local work vocabulary, 'tomorrow' means at least a month or so, and 'next year' more than likely never. The Cotentinese are recognised as past masters at avoiding future start dates, and have their own version of *mañana*. When asked if he will be sure to arrive at the agreed time and place, the local craftsman will invariably shrug, look at the sky for a while, remove his hat and cigarette, scratch his jaw, fiddle with his moustache, then grunt *'p'tet bankwee… p'tet bankno'*. Technically, this means 'perhaps yes… perhaps no'. In practice, the acceptance of the negative option is usually a very safe bet.

From the beginning, my understanding of the Fox of Cotentin has been developing through a series of encounters, with each of us striving to establish and maintain the advantage. He has knowledge of the land, the people and the ways of the region. I like to believe I have the worldly-wise sophistication of the modern city dweller, and am experienced in striking a shrewd business deal in the urban jungle. Since we arrived and the game began, my wife has been keeping score and says there is no contest. René has been playing with me like a farm cat with a particularly stupid mouse. What she does not know is that I have been biding my time, learning the local rules of engagement, and while appearing to appease him at any cost, am actually conducting a complex strategy which will result in a sound working relationship for the future.

Now, the sand mountain outside the mill has become a symbol of our struggle, with the advantage to him growing with its size, and to me as it diminishes. I am resolved not to become obsessive about the sand pile, but have my plans.

Our original deal to start a suitable working arrangement was struck over a bottle of my best malt whisky at his former home, and concluded with the general agreement that all restoration and development projects should be carried out by him or his representatives, and in exactly the way he proposed. This, he argued, would work completely to my benefit, as he could secure the sort of labour charges and material costs that I, a foreigner, could not hope to achieve. In return, he would merely ask for the odd specialist commission for himself, and that our refrigerator be kept stocked with an adequate supply of beer. After a year of being a mostly absentee landlord, I had not been able to ensure that the first part of our bargain was working to my advantage, but had achieved considerable success with the beer rationing.

In mid-summer and when an acre or so of garden grass needs cutting, René will operate his scythe to optimum efficiency and safety standards on one bottle of Kronenbourg 1664 every twenty minutes. Any less and he begins to dehydrate and sulk, and his lunch break lengthens to three hours;

any more, and he will work faster, but endanger his own limbs and those of any creature within range of the flashing blade.

Initially, not knowing that René was the River Authority for the region, we had asked for an estimate from a professional pond maker. He had arrived with all sorts of machinery and complex equipment, surveyed the water meadow for an hour or two and finally declared the terrain suitable to hold a lake. This came as no surprise to us, as the meadow floods to gumboot level every winter, is marked on old plans of La Puce as *le réservoir*, and was used as a storage lake by the miller for around two centuries.

What did come as a surprise was the price quoted for a fairly large pond, complete with feed and drainage pipes from and to the river just fifty feet away. A suitably large lake would cost us only slightly less than we had paid for the ten acres, farmhouse and cottage. It was time to consult with René.

Having changed the location, size and shape of the pond and dismissing the professional pond builder as a rank amateur in a few minutes, it took him three hours and eight beers to come up with a price. Finally, the calculations were completed, scribbled on the back of a beermat and slid conspiratorially across the wet table top beneath his horny hand.

Getting into the spirit of things, I picked the piece of card up like a particularly secretive poker player, looked suspiciously round the empty bar, then tried to decipher his computations beneath the table. The special price for our pond would appear to be *trois* millions. At ten francs to the pound, this would be approximately £300,000, which would appear to be a little optimistic of our presumed wealth and gullibility, even for René. I sighed, expressed my disappointment with an English expletive and rose to go to the pissoir.

René frowned, caught my arm and waved me back to my seat. I must understand, he hastily explained, that the price was, according to the countryside tradition, couched in ancient francs. In modern terms, it would, *naturellement*, be 3000 francs. And the grand lake would be built before our next visit. I clasped his hand and sealed the deal.

A year later, and our pond was ready, at the wrong end of the water meadow and much smaller than we had hoped, and, without any piping to or from the river, the water level drops alarmingly in summer. It's also difficult to reach as René and his *spécialiste* disposed of the excavated earth by simply dumping it around the edge and creating a massive rampart, which is almost impossible to scale in the rainy season. However, at £300 the price was exactly right.

This was my first experience in negotiating with and getting the better of the Fox. My wife still feels that had we been as incredibly wealthy and stupid as René had hoped, he would have taken the £300,000 without a blink, and disappeared to a pleasant retirement in the south. She also believes it was the last time I got the better of him, and that Ribet the Fox has been making up for it ever since. But at least, as I constantly remind her, we have the cheapest artificial lake in Cotentin.

I 2 FEBRUARY

Spring must be on the way. A straggle of jaundiced daffodils has appeared in the farmhouse garden. I call to my wife to share the good news, but she is obviously out on her morning feeding patrol. I note that at least half the specially imported catering pack of bacon is missing, together with the six eggs and couple of cold sausages I had earmarked for a fry-up. Obviously, the Cray gang are going to have a better start to the day than me.

My wife returns in a state of high excitement. Not only has she spotted a red squirrel among the giant beech trees lining Hunters' Walk, but also something big enough to move in on Reg and Ronnie's territory has taken up residence in the pond. From what I can gather, Donella was feeding Trevor the lone trout when a large, furry creature appeared on the opposite bank, slipped into the water, submerged and swam under the surface leaving a wake like a submarine. I turn to our *Illustrated Book of European Mammals*. After much discussion and interrogation with regard to the size, shape and colouring of the beast, my wife regretfully rejects the possibility of an aquatic badger. Against all the evidence, however, she will not accept that it is merely a common or water meadow vole or rat.

We are lunching with Jacko and Mauricette Laiznay tomorrow, so will ask them about the mystery creature. That way we can determine whether it is considered edible locally, and therefore should be kept a secret from the Fox.

I3 FEBRUARY

Setting out early to the supermarket to buy flowers for Momo and a bottle of good wine for Jacko, I check the mailbox and see that we have had yet another letter about the roadside mirror from the St Sauveur planning department.

Soon after moving into the roadside farmhouse, we found that the locals had devised a special game to enliven their travels between St Sauveur and Bricquebec. The frontage to our terrain is just short of 500 metres, and runs downhill from the crossroads to St Jacques and Néhou. This enables drivers to reach at least seventy miles an hour before hitting the hairpin bend after our copse, and it is local sport to see who can clock the highest speed in the measured distance without leaving the road, finding a ditch or killing a stray cow. I have heard them discussing it in the bars. Normally, we don't mind as their speed is such that the one vehicle every five minutes has raced by almost before we hear it. However, as our exit from the courtyard is halfway down the piste, it makes it rather risky to leave La Puce without one of us standing in the road with a red flag during the day, and a flashing light after dark. Because of the situation, one of my first installations at La Puce was a large convex mirror located just outside our courtyard wall, pointing in the direction of the oncoming traffic. Apart from attracting a few sniggers from locals at our killjoy and wimpish attitude to their little game, the mirror also attracted an official letter from the *mairie* at St Sauveur. In brief it said we had erected the *gros miroir* without planning consent, and it must go. Appealing against the decision, I explained that I had made the unapproved erection only so that local lives and cows might be saved.

My artifice fell on stony ground, with my anonymous correspondent pointing out that the mirror was a grave impediment to anyone walking along the public highway (i.e. the bit of verge just outside our yard). Resorting to British irony, I responded by explaining that a full survey of the locals had revealed that no pedestrians had been seen on the relevant stretch of verge since the American infantry in 1944, and that my only neighbour within half a mile was Mr Pigeon, now eighty-five and not likely to jog past on his way to town three miles away.

But it was all to no avail. Back came a stern letter, warning me that the mirror must go immediately, lest further proceedings be taken. Taking this as a veiled reference to checking out our lack of other planning permission for all sorts of recent additions like the television aerial and the mailbox itself, I compromised by taking the mirror off the post between visits. This worked well till we found the stout piece of oak uprooted from the verge and left pointedly by our front door. Taking its presence as the throwing of a symbolic gauntlet, I then dug a huge hole alongside a suitable power pole on the opposite verge, and set the mirror post in a two-foot-square block of reinforced concrete. Upon our next arrival, we found the mirror, post and block by the door, and the power pole leaning dangerously over the road. Realising that the situation was getting out of hand, I appealed to our mayor for advice. After listening attentively, John explained with grim relish that we would never, ever win a battle with the bureaucrats at St Sauveur. Everyone in the region knew that they were almost as unreasoning and unreasonable as the mayor of St Jacques. Far better to consider the possibilities and come to an accommodation which would satisfy all concerned. I should leave it with him.

A week later, he called to say that a solution was in sight. Where, he explained carefully, the verge was the property of France and therefore in the sole keeping of the relevant authority at the St Sauveur mairie, the ground beneath the hedgerow of the field opposite our courtyard was the property and responsibility of the owner of the orchard beyond. John would approach the proprietor and negotiate on our behalf for permission to erect my mirror in his hedge.

On our next visit, our friend called with good news. He had talked with Mr Margot (the owner of the hedgerow), who would be arriving that evening to begin negotiations.

A small, tidy and most correct personage, Mr Margot accepted a tumbler of scotch after the mayor had effected the necessary introductions, and explained that he worked in St Sauveur but tended the orchard to keep his hands dirty with good Norman soil and provide a yearly stock of calva. Then, with a flourish, Mr Margot produced a two-page document, giving us, our children and our children's children the sole rights and privileges to the twelve square centimetres of land in which our mirror post would rest for all eternity. The paper having been duly stamped, witnessed by the mayor and signed by both parties to the accord, we finished the bottle of scotch. It was not till much later that we were to discover that Mr Margot not only worked in the planning department of the mairie at St Sauveur, but was allegedly also the informer who had originally laid a complaint against the illegal siting of the mirror.

~

We arrive at the local supermarket and I go in to search for flowers and wine for our luncheon hosts. Donella remains in the car in case there is another *grand tableau* on the meat counter. Last time it was Veal Week, and the display was centred around the skinned yet otherwise complete head of a calf. My wife said she accepted that other cultures must be respected by those who chose to live within them, but it was the way they had left the eyes in place, and how they seemed to follow her accusingly around the store.

Returning with an expensive bouquet and a bottle of wine that seemed neither too pretentious nor too niggardly, I see my wife talking to Mauricette, who is casually wringing the neck of an inoffensive-looking old hen. Nearby a throng of eager housewives besiege a lorry, which is obviously full of lively if elderly fowls.

Mo-mo explains that the now deceased hen under her arm is the main ingredient of our lunch. I ask her politely if it would not be cheaper and less labour-intensive to buy one of the freshly dressed and plucked young chickens lining the shelves of the supermarket outside which we are standing. Patiently, she explains that *poule-au-pot* must be made with an elderly hen, and besides, only by killing it herself can she be sure that it is really fresh.

Three hours later and we are seated around the huge table in the Laiznay kitchen as the flesh of the late hen is boiled into submission.

Mauricette is a local girl, and Jacko a former fireman from Paris who took early retirement some years ago. Our friends live in a tastefully and obviously expensively restored house in a hamlet on the outskirts of St Jacques. I have heard in the bar at Néhou that Jacko left the fire service at the same time as his best friend left the Paris police force. While Jacko bought and restored the house, his friend set up in a bar and restaurant at Bricquebec. When this point in the story is reached, the teller usually winks, rubs finger and thumb together and makes some comment about the unseen benefits of working for the emergency services in the capital. I have no idea what is being alleged, but assume petty jealousy to be the cause. Whatever the case, I shall not ask Jacko. He is a small man, but has a badly broken nose, large facial scar and is said by the residents of St Jacques to be the finest shot in all the region, if not all France.

As Mauricette busies herself at the oven, Jacko shows me his gunroom, which would put Woolwich arsenal to shame. The only weapon not in his collection, I jokingly remark, is a heavy machine gun. He looks thoughtful for a moment, then explains that it would not be an efficient way of killing game as the number of bullets used in a single burst would be extremely expensive, apart from making a mess of the carcass.

Back in the kitchen, I hand over the flowers and wine with a flourish. Mauricette is obviously impressed with her bouquet, while Jacko thanks me politely but consigns my careful choice of table wine to the back of a kitchen cabinet.

As she serves the assorted parts of the bird we met so recently, Mo-mo explains the origins of poule-au-pot. It was the favourite dish of Henri IV, who issued an edict that it should be on the menu at any time and anywhere on his royal progress around France. Naturally, he was on record as saying that Normandy in general and Cotentin in particular was where they made the finest example of the dish in all France. It is very good, but I would have preferred the vegetables to have been added to the casserole at some time after the three hours the pot has been in the oven. Once again I reflect on the common misconceptions that afflict both our countries. The English believe that the French dislike and mistreat, if not actually eat, dogs, while we are claimed by them to overcook all vegetables. In our experience, both beliefs are completely untrue. They seem generally as sentimental about dogs as we are, and any vegetable we are given here seems to be cooked within an inch of its life.

The luncheon goes well until I top up my glass of wine

with water, as I have seen done in bars all across Normandy.

After almost choking on a piece of chicken and casting a glance in the direction of his gunroom, Jacko takes my glass and empties it pointedly down the sink. I am to learn later from a horrified Freddo that, by defiling the most expensive wine laid on in our honour, I have proffered an almost deadlier insult to our host than claiming he can't shoot straight. Silently, Jacko reaches into the kitchen cupboard, unscrews the top of my gift bottle and pours a generous measure into a large tumbler before pointing pointedly at the tap. It is at this moment that my wife looks across at a nearby worktop, finds herself in eye-to-eye contact with the head of the hen we have just eaten, and thoughtfully relieves the situation by swooning clear away.

Poule-au-Pot

1. Take an elderly hen and wring neck till dead
2. Dress and joint, reserving the head for garnish
3. Place the pieces in a heavy pot with suitable vegetables
4. Cook in oven for at least three hours, or until
the vegetables surrender.

25 FEBRUARY
It is our wedding anniversary. We decide to celebrate in the evening by going on a pub crawl in St Sauveur-le-Vicomte. This will not take long, but will give us the chance to get to know the local socialites better. Donella declares I must earn my wild night out and presents me with my anniversary present, a pair of thigh-length waders.

Since she first saw La Puce, Donella has been fascinated by the possibilities of our streams, ponds and waterlogged pastures as additional wildlife sanctuaries. Over the past year, she has spent a great deal of time and money undoing the massive works of past centuries aimed at channelling water past Le Moulin de la Puce as quickly and effectively as possible. Now we are here full time, she is daily coming up with schemes to turn the ten acres into one gigantic lake. What she does not fully appreciate is that running water has a mind of its own, and can turn quite nasty when interfered with.

Built to service the needs of the surrounding estate, the mill was positioned to take advantage of the tiny Lude, which sources at the manor house of the same name just a mile away. When grinding time approached, the miller would simply lower a stone slab across the stream, diverting the Lude into the two-acre field directly behind the moulin. When le réservoir field was flooded and the grain hopper full, a slab by the business end of the mill would be cranked up, allowing the reservoir lake to empty over the top of the wheel. The millions of gallons of water would then rush away down an otherwise dry river bed, under the stone bridge which led the carts to the mill, and finally alongside the copse to join up again with the Lude on its way off the property and on to the sea.

Over the years, the working end of the mill has been harvested by local builders and householders. The original wheel is said to be a feature at a nightclub a few miles away and rumour has it that even the local police station benefited from the plunder. One day, we will restore it to its former glory, but, now, rebuilding our lives and business at La Puce is a far more pressing concern. One of our ideas is a trout-fishing lake for use by visitors and local farmers.

The plan for the day, Donella explains, is to create a barrier at the stone bridge. By the careful placing of a few sandbags under the arch, rainwater and the constant dribble from the water meadow would be collected in the dry river bed between the bridge and the sadly depleted millpond, creating a natural and comfortable habitat for another hundred or so Hampshire goldfish which she will smuggle in via her collection of Victorian chamber pots still in England. An added advantage of the additional en-suite fish facility will be the protection afforded by the sweet chestnut trees lining the bank at this point. They will deter the heron which has been studying our goldfish pond almost as enthusiastically as René, and the new stretch of stagnant water will attract more frogs to join Triple Salco and his troupe. I forbear to mention that our estate manager has already brought me the good news that our frog colony is of the edible variety, with particularly long and plump legs.

Discussing the fine-tuning of the damming project, I ask my wife how she intends creating a sandbag barrier with no sandbags. With a snort of impatience at my lack of initiative, she points out that we have an adequate supply of plastic rubbish bags to hand, and a mountain of sand outside the mill which is threatening to attract its own cloud formation. I have my doubts about the suitability of the bin liners, but anything which reduces the sand pile will be to my advantage in the struggle for supremacy with René. We have had yet another tractor load from a crony of our estate manager, who I have now discovered is a close friend of the foreman of a nearby corporation yard. I have driven by and the mountain range of sand within seems of a very similar consistency and colour to our own.

In our experience, most Contentinese are as honest as a summer day is long when it comes to respect for personal possessions. However, certain natural objects like sand, gravel, trees and wild animals on one's land can be regarded as fair game or even a gift from heaven.

On a visit last year, we arrived to find a pile of huge and obviously valuable marble slabs dumped by the stream at Hunters' Walk. After agreeing to a knockdown price when my wife pointed out the difficulty of his shifting them again, René explained that they were almost a gift from yet another friend, and would make an unusual and sophisticated *terrasse* outside the caravan by the big pond. Apart from one slab, which was used as a makeshift but stout bridge across the grotto, they still lie beside the stream, comfortably hidden in summer by the long grass, and I feel reluctant to move or use them. There are no names or epitaphs inscribed on the shiny sides that I can see, but their texture and design looks highly familiar, and the funeral parlour yard at St Sauveur has a large hole in its fence…

~~~

René appears like a ghost in the early morning mist as I struggle to position unwieldy bags of sand beneath the ancient bridge, and helpfully points out that the rubbish tip is only a mile down the road. I explain that I am constructing, under my wife's direction, a barrage to fill the old millpond and a short stretch of the dry stream.

My friend looks at the untroubled sky, wags a grimy forefinger in my general direction and announces the arrival of a thunderstorm *extraordinaire* by midnight. The bags, he says confidently, will be no match for the deluge. For once, defending my wife's convictions I disagree publicly, and he stomps off to sulk in his caravan. I add another dozen bags of sand before climbing out of the miniature ravine for a coffee break.

As I walk to the mill it begins to rain.

~~~

We start our bender at Jackie's bar and grocery store in the shadow of the castle at St Sauveur-le-Vicomte. Once a thriving market town, St Sauveur has suffered more than most as a result of European unity and a common agricultural policy, and money is very tight. It is not a pretty town, and tourism has not been of great benefit. Mostly, the people seem to get by with seasonal farm work and help from the government when the winter sets in. Most English people we know seem to believe that rural poverty in France is found only in the Deep South, and is somehow picturesque, with the peasants contentedly living off the land while wearing striped jerseys and amusing berets. This is not true, and real life in the Cotentin can mean getting by in conditions which the average British reader of romanticised twaddle about the joys of living in rural France could not begin or wish to imagine.

Jackie is as usual dividing his time between serving at the Donjon bar and adjoining store and adjusting his wig. Just as the general mood and height of libido of the proprietor of the Café de Paris in Bricquebec can be determined from the condition and styling of his moustache, the location of Jackie's wig is a precise indicator of his current consumption rate of pastis. Dogs and drink are Jackie's consuming passions, and after taking our order and being persuaded to join us in a glass of Ricard, Jackie introduces a new member of the household, the tiny fox terrier nestling in his cardigan.

Donella immediately falls in love and curses the ridiculous laws that prevent free travel for pets between our two countries. She will not buy and keep a dog at La Puce because of the agony of separation when we must visit the UK together in future, and she has strong feelings on the subject of quarantine. In the past ten years, as she will point out to anyone who will listen, hundreds of thousands of dogs and cats have been incarcerated in British pounds, and not one has proved rabid. Many, though, have died through accident, disease as a result of their imprisonment, or simply from broken hearts.

A good and sensitive soul, Jackie consoles her and himself with another round of pastis, and offers her the unconditional use of the fox terrier between our monthly trips across the Channel. Thus, what we believe may be the first time-share dog scheme in France is established at le Bar du Donjon.

～

While Jackie slips next door to buy a bar of chocolate from himself for Albert the Alsatian and the as-yet-unnamed fox terrier to celebrate the arrangement, I visit the toilet facility, which is a minor classic in my list of Cotentin urinals.

Sited most conveniently at the bottom of the yard and alongside a stack of vegetable supplies for the shop, the urinal is a perfection of simplicity and ingenuity. The system consists mainly of a large, ancient and furry cider funnel clamped to the wall at the optimum height. From this device runs a length of garden hose which disappears down a drain in the middle of the yard. I have no knowledge as to where, if anywhere, the drain joins the local sewage system, and on a busy night there can be some backfill problems, as the route of the hose from the funnel runs slightly uphill. But it works after a fashion, and the open-air toilet offers some of the best views of the sky at night in the area. There is also a keen spectator interest from those in the houses overlooking the yard. One day I will write a definitive guide to the lavatories of Cotentin, which I find much more interesting than many of the more conventional tourist attractions.

Hearing a noise, I look down and see Albert has joined me for a bit of male bonding. He cocks a leg and pees with unerring accuracy over a sack of carrots. I look up at a sea of stars and contemplate the true scale of the universe and the relative unimportance of my petty concerns. As I return to the bar, the rain increases in intensity, and a grumble of approaching thunder rolls across the moonshiny rooftops before echoing round the yard.

As it is a special occasion, the bars of St Sauveur stay open late and all have record takes for a midweek night. It is almost ten o'clock before we arrive at La Puce and Donella puts me to bed.

I awake to find that the ghost of the Allied warplane is re-strafing the cottage roof, but my wife says it is merely a cloudburst. I look at the clock. It is almost midnight, so René may yet be proved wrong. An hour later, the storm is certainly extraordinaire. I get up to close the shutters, and hear a roaring noise from the direction of the mill cottage a hundred yards away. Full of foreboding, we dress in wet-weather gear and slither down to the wooden bridge. It is still in place, and we stand above the normally arid river bed and watch in awe as a raging torrent cascades down from the reservoir field into the old millpond, filling it to over-flowing for probably the first time in a hundred years. The flood boils and roars as it is forced along the ravine below us, to be channelled under the stone bridge and away into the night, howling in frustrated fury at its containment.

Looking over the parapet, we see that eight hours' work and the twenty plastic sandbags have been casually washed away by the deluge. Even now, they are probably heading out towards Jersey. As we battle our way back up the slope and in spite of the deafening roar of the deluge, I am sure I hear a grunt of triumph from René's caravan.

TEN

Gone Fishing

15 MARCH

It is not yet dawn, but we are already hard at work over coffee and calva in the Café de Paris. The deserted square calmly awaits the arrival of the livestock, hardware, clothing and food stalls, while a pair of rooks take their ease on the church tower, hoarsely discussing the possibilities of rich pickings when the day's trading is done. It is a very civilised way to start the day.

My wife and I are engrossed in our regular early-morning language lesson, with Freddo *le professeur* teaching us to talk like true Cotentinese.

Every region of the country has, quite naturally, its own way of pronouncing the standard words of the language. Each will also have its own special words and expressions. As with the other regions of France, Normandy has its own patois. It also has a customised version for the different départements and areas. According to some, every commune on the peninsula has its own verbal conventions for mystifying and excluding foreigners from down the road. In extreme cases, individuals in our area may have adapted the local dialect and sub-language, or even invented their own.

Quite apart from my own difficulty in communicating with him, there are some Néhou residents I know who find René Ribet mostly unintelligible, even when sober. This is why my wife and I have enlisted Freddo's help to learn to talk, if not on equal terms, then at least on the same subject with the locals. There are some very interesting insults relating to bodily parts, sizes and functions in which Freddo has painstakingly coached me during my wife's absence. They often come in handy when winding down the window to discuss relative driving skills with other motorists.

We have almost reached the end of today's crash course in complimenting a neighbour on the virility and volume of his cockerel when our latest houseguests arrive. I introduce Freddo to our friends, Rinaldo and Janet, who have come over to take advantage of the fortnight version of our special 'Real France' package. The standard terms are that we pay for their ferry and food, while our visitors contribute skilled labour to the terrain or restoration work on the mill cottage. Rinaldo has been running pubs in Hampshire for the past twenty years, but comes originally from a remote area of Italy almost as rural as Cotentin, so should know the lie of the land and how to best deal with it. He will therefore be in charge of ground works during their stay. Provided, as I have already warned, he gets on with our estate manager.

As they recover from the effects of an overnight crossing with a restorative goutte, the conversation turns to current events at La Puce, and I ask Freddo for his views on the latest inhabitant of the big pond. Listening to my wife's description of the mystery beast, our host's moustache begins to quiver like the tail of an overexcited pointer hound. It sounds, he says, as if we have a muskrat on our hands. This is very, very bad for the land, and he will come to La Puce tomorrow after school and shoot it.

Seeing my wife's expression, I quickly point out that, in my opinion, the beast is actually nothing more or less than a large water rat, or even an overgrown vole. Freddo shrugs, and says it does not matter what it is, he is still happy to come along and shoot it.

Other locals now enter the debate and make their judgements as to the identity of our new tenant. Whatever they suggest, Freddo declares it to be very bad for the land, and that it will be his pleasure to shoot it for us. By now, offers to visit La Puce and rid us of our dangerous intruder are coming thick and fast.

With my wife about to forget her normally impeccable manners and explain that she personally is thrilled to discover a wild creature larger than a butterfly still at large in Cotentin, I turn the subject to other matters. Rinaldo, I announce, is a keen fisherman, and I wonder if the assembly can suggest the best sport in the area. Freddo's best friend Pierrot is then universally acknowledged as the finest fisherman in the region, if not all France, and kindly agrees to show our Italian friend how to catch trout.

I now see another side of Rinaldo, whose own outsize moustache had not appeared as significant when on duty behind the bar of his pub in the Isle of Wight. Speaking in the overly polite tones of a character from *The Godfather* who has had his ability to effortlessly remove a horse's head questioned, he explains that he learned to fish in the limpid mountain pools of the Abruzzo before he could walk. Moreover, the teacher was his blessed grandfather, who was recognised nationwide as the finest fisherman in the region, if not all Italy.

Seeing the inevitable outcome of the debate, I ask brightly if anyone has visited the latest Millet exhibition at the Cherbourg *musée*, but it is too late. Over another round of calva, an international challenge is laid down. This weekend Italy, Great Britain and Cotentin will clash at the local fish-it-yourself pond. The one with the smallest catch will pay for the total haul. I remember the sausage game at Christmas, and mutter something about the need to plant a row of onion sets at La Puce, but Rinaldo's Latin blood is obviously up. We will convene in the Café de Paris this weekend, and the matter will be resolved.

～

All appears well when we arrive at La Puce and our estate manager is not in evidence, so I take Rinaldo to see the big pond and our trout colony. After an hour of casting our sliced English bread on the waters, we get a glimpse of Trevor, and I confess my belief that he is the sole fish in residence, though my wife is under the impression that the original four dozen are still there, and merely shy.

On the advice of René, after the big pond had bedded in, we visited the nearest commercial trout lake and bought a dustbinful of healthy yearlings. My idea at the time was to make a start on our own trout-rearing business. A spin-off would be the creation of a personal fishing pond, with inhabitants enticed out of the water and in to the pan in moments whenever the fancy took me. Obviously, I did not share the details of this part of the plan with my wife.

In the event, the water in the bin proved a little short of oxygen over the three-mile journey, and several of the fish lay gasping limply in the shallows when we released them into our new pond. Without a thought for personal safety, Donella jumped in and administered artificial respiration, after which they happily swam off to join their fellows. Her bonding with them in this dramatic and intimate manner was of course fatal for my ambitions, the pond immediately declared off limits, and my rod briskly parcelled up and taken back to Portsmouth.

It was particularly galling that, while I was banned from fishing in my own pond, the local angling fraternity felt free to enjoy the facilities in our absence. Each visit, it seemed fewer trout came up for their daily feed. It was even alleged by some of our friends that René Ribet had placed advertisements for the new *étang à truites* in bars that he knew we did not visit, and had been selling daily tickets, bait, cold beer and chips from his caravan while we were away.

Even if the story is true, now that Trevor is the lone tenant of the pond, the idea of fishing for more than five minutes without a guaranteed catch would have deterred the most earnest Norman fisherman, and he seems safe. Reluctant to restock the pond for the benefit of the locals or tell my wife of our losses, I now spend much of my time throwing feed pellets at the bemused crayfish gang, and claiming to have spotted at least a dozen healthy trout leaping after my solo visits to the pond. Donella says the colony must have developed a special relationship with me, as she has never seen more than one at a time, and they all look remarkably like Trevor.

The day of the international fishing competition dawns bright, cold and early, and Rinaldo and I report to the Café de Paris. Pierrot and Freddo await, and are dressed to kill in commando camouflage, balaclava helmets, freshly waxed moustaches and huge knives dangling from ammunition belts stuffed with heavy-duty shotgun cartridges. They are obviously taking the match seriously, and may intend shooting the fish if unable to hook them. As we walk to the car, I notice that each seems to be carrying at least three rods, and ask if others are joining us for the contest. Freddo explains carelessly that it is normal procedure for each competitor to have more than one hook in the water at the same time.

In the car, the rules of the *grand tournoi* are laid down. The pond and our individual places around it will be decided by the committee, which is to be made up as host nation of Freddo and Pierrot. We will fish for three hours precisely, and the country with the biggest catch will obviously be declared champion. The loser, says Freddo looking directly at me, will pay the fishing fee and drinks afterwards. I consider lodging an official objection on the grounds that the French *équipe* will muster twice as many men and six times as many rods as the GB team, but remember my mother's claims about the odds at the Battle of Trafalgar, and keep my own counsel.

As we speed through the winding lanes, I fall to musing about the particularly French attitude to freshwater angling. Having exhausted the countryside of most of its natural wildlife, our locals have turned to the new pursuit of trout-pond fishing with much enthusiasm. Every landowner here with a suitably wet piece of land seems to have turned it into a commercial trout lake. Having scooped out a large-ish hole and filled it to the brim with water and fish, he will park a caravan selling cold beer and hot chips alongside, and advertise the new facility by placing enticing posters featuring drawings of trout the size of sharks in every bar and available window in the area. Being Norman, his patrons will naturally demand the very best value for money, which means they must be able to enjoy a day's sport and go away with a satisfying haul of fish at less than they would have paid for the same weight at the fishmongers.

When the trout-fishing fever took hold in our area, one local entrepreneur tried charging by the hour regardless of catch, but soon saw sense when his unhappy patrons started using trawl nets to ensure value for money. Whenever I go to a local trout lake, however, the words 'shooting', 'fish' and 'barrel' spring unbidden to mind.

After ten minutes of careering along a bumpy track, we arrive on the shore of a magnificent lake at least half a mile across, and I prepare to eat my thoughts.

Sadly, Freddo ignores the parking facilities and drives on to a small clearing in a heavily wooded and secluded area. Here we find a square pond a little larger than a family-size jacuzzi. Unloading the gear and provisions, Pierrot leads us to our positions. I am given the side under a huge beech tree, the branches of which brush my head as I stand and survey my pitch. Obviously, our hosts are being considerate by allowing me the only place of shelter should it rain. Rinaldo is invited to take up his position nearby, while Freddo and Pierrot share the rest of the bank. Although they have two sides to our one, I notice that they have placed their rod holders very close together. We break out our kit, and I see that, as well as two rods each, Freddo and Pierrot have fitted swivel traces, each with two sets of double hooks. The rods supplied for Rinaldo and I are almost of the basic Huckleberry Finn patent. The maggots are doled out, and Freddo kindly sets our floats so that the hooks will hang no more than six inches beneath the water. This, he explains, is to avoid snagging on the roots of 'my' tree, which apparently riddle the bed of the pond. I note that he and his colleague set their hooks at least a yard from the floats.

After consultation, Rinaldo and I steal a march on our rivals and get our lines into the water without delay, while they are held up by the large amount of tackle and the baiting-up of at least two dozen maggots each.

The competition proper starts and the French floats disappear almost immediately. In five minutes, Freddo and Pierrot have taken a trio of fat trout between them. Rinaldo has struck once, and I decide it is time to employ my English initiative in bending the rules a little. Although I am forbidden from moving my pitch, I may surely cast anywhere in the pond, and as a former B-league Portsmouth darts champion, I should be able to drop my sinker within a whisker of the French happy hunting ground. A quick and dextrous flick of the wrist, and my hook finds a branch of the giant beech. Freddo and Pierrot sympathise and break out the beer while issuing instructions on the best way to disentangle my line. Unfortunately, they add, they have no extra tackle with them.

An hour passes, and the French contingent seem to have more fish in their bin liner than could stand comfortably shoulder to shoulder in the tiny pond. Rinaldo has notched up a handful, and I am halfway up the tree with my Swiss penknife.

A little later and a man appears carrying a dustbin on his shoulder. He shakes hands with Freddo and Pierrot, nods sympathetically to me, and discharges at least a gross of trout into the pond at the feet of his countrymen. The water boils as the fish compete to be the first on Norman hooks. The bin man disappears to fetch another load, while a queue of trout seems to be forming in a very un-French manner at the spot where Freddo and Pierrot are having difficulty in keeping up with demand.

At the end of the allotted time, the tournament is declared over, and the count begins.

The French haul is seventy-two, Rinaldo has managed a round half dozen, and my total tally is two undernourished juveniles and one of Freddo's discarded beer bottles.

Back at the Café de Paris, our host enlists the help of all the customers to carry his haul inside, where the giant glittering, twisting mound is displayed on the bar top as he makes a lengthy address to the assembly. After a blow-by-blow account of the action, he announces the official figures for the competition, and commiserates with the losers. Obviously, he says, it was harder for me as I was in foreign waters. It is also well known that the British have lost the art of fishing, as demonstrated by their morbid fear of French trawlers appearing in 'their' waters. I respond graciously, toasting the success of the craftiest coarse anglers in the region. I also agree with Freddo about the decline of our fishing fleet, and suggest that this is because we, as a nation, have been concentrating on efficient farming, which is why our exports of lamb seem to be doing so well in this part of France.

All this badinage is taken in good spirit, especially, I suspect, as the drinks are now on me.

The celebrations commence and Freddo takes up a proprietary position at the door. For the rest of the morning, he distributes largesse, trout and the story of the international fishing tournament in equal measures to passing pensioners. As we leave, he takes me to one side and hands me a bag containing a dozen of his catch with fondest compliments to Donella, and to ensure that we have enough to eat for lunch.

~

Late lunchtime, and we have set up our makeshift oildrum barbecue and oven under the balcony at La Puce. Rinaldo has barely got the fire beneath it going when René arrives to take charge. He has already heard about our defeat. We should, he says, have enrolled his help, then there really would have been some fish caught. In moments he has gutted, cleaned and lightly oiled the trout before dousing them in goutte and wrapping each one tightly in newspaper ready for baking.

It is the first time we have eaten *truite au calva*, and even Rinaldo has to admit that it works.

All agree that it is a meal to remember, and I do not spoil the moment by pointing out that, pound per pound, the trout have cost me more than lobster served at Maxim's of Paris.

21 MARCH

Rinaldo and I have started on the treasure hunt. I have let my friend into the secret of the Grey Lady and the miller's gold, and he agrees it sounds very promising. René is away on business with the Widow of Negreville, so the coast is clear. We set to with a will at the base of the apple tree, and have hit some obstinate roots when our distant neighbour, Mr Bellamy, arrives on his ancient khaki mobylette.

Renowned in the neighbourhood as the only person who speaks a word of English, he gained his singular skills in 1944 after acquiring a booklet issued to all American GIs to help keep them on friendly terms with the natives. This makes for interesting conversation when he practises on me, and as his everyday patois is even more colloquial than

René's and makes normal conversation impossible, we have agreed on the happy medium of sign language, wartime Americanese and conventional French.

Apparently believing we wish to move the old apple tree for some good English reason to a point a metre from where it has stood happily since before the Americans arrived, he joins us in the hole and shows us how to dig properly.

An hour passes pleasantly, and the pile of earth beside the hole is approaching the size of the sand heap by the mill. It is probably my imagination, but the tree now seems to be leaning towards us. So far, we have turned up some interesting old bottles and the remains of a giant horseshoe, but there is no sign of the miller's gold. By now our good friend Marcel Bernard has also joined the party. The first person to arrive to welcome us to the area, Marcel lives in the same nearby hamlet as our mayor, and is the proud owner of an ancient lorry, which he allegedly acquired from an enterprising supply sergeant when the American task force moved on in 1946. For as long as anyone can remember, he has hired out himself and the lorry for the odd haulage job and in between contracts, it makes a handy overnight coop for his free-range chickens.

Driving past the farmhouse years ago, Marcel had pulled over and watched in silent bewilderment as we started restoration work by removing at least a ton of elderly straw bales from the loft. As he explained later, they were the local equivalent of fibreglass lagging, and someone had taken a great deal of trouble to put them there in the first place to guarantee a comfortable winter.

Seeing his empty lorry we had asked how much he would charge to dispose of the bales, but he, good man that he is, had refused the commission. Instead, he demonstrated the simple and much more effective countryside way of getting rid of rubbish. Gauging the wind direction, he built a huge pile of straw, rotted sacking and feed bags and applied a match.

Our next guest at the digging party is Coco, returning from his weekly fungi raid on our woods. This crop and the other natural harvests at La Puce have long been regarded as fair game for anyone who will take the trouble to gather them, and we have long since given up trying to manage or deter the constant flow of locals arriving with stepladders, carrier bags and even the occasional horse and cart. When we first arrived, we had unwisely put up a series of signs at the boundaries of the property warning off all hunters and gatherers. On our next visit, the No Entry sign on the track down to the mill had vanished, and the *Chasse Interdite* placards were riddled with buckshot. We responded with bigger, more aggressive signs and rolls of barbed wire, but then they, too, went missing between visits. Finally, a truce was mediated by the mayor, who explained reassuringly that the vandalism was not aimed at us as foreigners, but a manifestation of the locals' objection to our changing the rules of common usage which had existed at La Puce for many years.

From now on, John promised, the hunters would respect our peculiar wish to protect the wildlife on our terrain, while all Néhou residents would continue to have access to the nuts, berries, wild flowers and herbs which we did not earmark for our own consumption. We would be welcome to shoot at any trespassers from St Jacques, naturally, and thought even more highly of if we managed to wing a couple.

Not a keen nut or berry gatherer, our estate manager had made no objection to the deal as long as the apple harvest was left strictly alone, and we had struck a private treaty with Coco for exclusive foraging rights to the copse. Apart from being the owner of a leading bar and restaurant at St Sauveur and a fervid anglophile, Coco is quite deservedly acknowledged as the finest fungi expert in the region (if not all France), and a true eccentric, even by local standards. He resembles a gothic engraving of an Old Testament prophet, who drives madly around the peninsula in a very battered

Land Rover with Mission Impossible crudely daubed on each side. Apart from allowing his wife to run the family business, he keeps busy with his constant quest for ever more exotic fungal growths and by staging musical extravaganzas in the church square next to the restaurant. Some malicious souls in the town allege that his wild eyes and erratic manner can be attributed to the regular consumption of a particular sort of mushroom, but I think it is merely his nature. Our arrangement, struck in his bar late one summer evening, was that he would have the full gathering rights to the copse, while in exchange we would be treated to an annual slap-up meal. Each course, of course, would contain suitable examples of La Puce fungi.

Last year, we arrived for our treat to find the town had apparently been invaded by the National Front. As the locals looked on with awe, huge youths with shaven heads, Union Jack T-shirts and lace-up boots gyrated happily in front of the church while a band advertised as the British Bulldogs performed on a platform beside Coco's Bar. Nervously, we ate our free lunch in the restaurant, before leaving, asking him if he was sure that he had picked the right band for the sleepy town. He smiled dreamily, and assured us that his customers were very fond of traditional English folk music. Surprisingly, the town remained unscathed, and all went so well that the band are booked for a return visit this summer. Coco also tells us that he is negotiating for an exchange visit of the St Sauveur Abbey choir to a forthcoming London folk concert featuring the Bulldogs and fellow artists Die for England and We Hate Fucking Foreigners.

By now, Coco has laid down his overflowing trug, and is instructing us on the care and handling of any rare fungi species we may uncover. Marcel Bernard, Mr Bellamy, Rinaldo and I are competing for spade room in the hole, and it is inevitable that René should suddenly appear like a pantomime demon king from behind the bikeshed.

Surveying the scene for a moment, he pronounces that

Donella has gone too far this time. The pond we are digging will be well above water level, and will kill his beloved apple trees stone dead. I have rarely seen him so angry. I make a weak excuse about testing his theory about there being no room for the cherry tree, and we sheepishly fill the hole in under his watchful eye. I invite the digging party indoors for drinks, and think I hear the Fox making an aside about fool's gold as we enter the farmhouse. The exercise has not been wasted, however, as I have now formed a cunning plan to reduce the sand mountain.

~~~~~

A long and diverting evening is over. Rinaldo and Janet have retired to the guest room, while our other friends have moved on to René's caravan for a nightcap to fortify themselves against the snow they all agree will soon be with us, despite the time of year and official forecasts of rain as usual until mid July. Our impromptu soirée passed pleasantly with a tasting of the selection of Italian wines Rinaldo brought with him, and a contribution of his finest farmhouse cider from Marcel. I weighed in with a pack of Somerset cider cans, and Marcel, René and Mr Bellamy were mildly shocked to learn that it can be produced in Britain, and even more surprised that it is drinkable, even good. They also expressed surprise that drinkable wine is made in Italy, and Rinaldo risked a row by pointing out that more bottles of allegedly French wine are produced each year than the amount of grapes grown in France could possible provide. It is well known in the industry, he claimed, that many tons of lesser-grade Italian grapes are bought in each year to enable the communes to overproduce their so-called *appellation contrôlée* wines.

Donella avoided potential unpleasantness by suggesting a game of ludo, which René as usual won. My wife says that he cheats but this is hard to prove as he insists on playing by what he claims are the local rules, even though we had thought the game exclusive to Britain. His version entails throwing the dice under one hand, then telling us what the number is.

Now we are alone, and walk out to stand on the balcony overlooking our land and say goodnight to La Puce. It is a bitter and breathlessly silent night, and yet again I am bewitched by the clarity and number of stars in the big Cotentin sky. An owl hoots on Hunters' Walk, and is answered by a tetchy whinny from a horse in a neighbouring field. Beyond the mill, the stream continues its endless cascade into the magical grotto, and the unseen creatures of the dark are surely going contentedly about their business on such a perfect night. In this region they call mills 'listen when it rains' but for once, there is not a cloud in the sky.

Baked Trout à la René Ribet

1. First catch your fish, or preferably someone else's
2. Gut, then rub skin briskly with olive oil
and a generous measure of calva
3. Season lightly
4. Wrap fish individually in outer pages of
Normandy West News *and place in hot oildrum oven*
5. Read racing results in remaining sports section
(Sunday edition)
6. Remove trout from oven, unwrap and
serve with deep-fried chicory and roasted
sweet peppers in a farm cider coulis.

I APRIL

Our guests have regretfully returned to their pub in the Isle of Wight, and we decide to mark the date by playing a joke on René. We present him with a bottle of Rinaldo's Italian wine after pasting the label from a French *vin de table* on it. When we meet later that evening, I ask if he enjoyed the wine. He says we were cheated. It was obviously Italian, and probably from the Abruzzo region, unless he is mistaken. Lost in admiration, we confess our little prank, and attempt to explain the April Fool's Day tradition. He is not particularly amused, and bids us goodnight after forecasting heavy snow for the morrow. I smile knowingly and explain that April Fool's Day jokes can technically only be played before noon. He shrugs and begins filling up the cracks in his caravan windows with the newspaper left over from the trout barbecue.

2 APRIL

The joke is again on us, as we awake to find La Puce has become a winter wonderland. Last year it snowed in late February, but the area has not seen *la neige* at this time of year in living memory, which is a long time. The locals are bound to blame the Common Agricultural Policy. We wrap up and set out to explore the terrain.

In the baby pond, the goldfish are happily swanning around underneath a thin layer of ice. Donella sets about it lest they drown, in spite of my suggestion that Triple Salco and his aquatic frog troupe might enjoy learning to skate.

We work our way steadily through the mill garden and grotto, stocking up the dozens of provision points. Although there were at least a million beechnut husks littering the ground after the remarkable summer last year, Donella still insists on providing a regular KP Family Selection Bag for our single squirrel. The nuts are always gone when we return, which, she says, proves they are popular. I think they may be particularly popular with the regular foraging and fishing parties who visit La Puce in our absence, and trout and almonds is a favourite in the area.

Three loaves, two tins of corned beef, a salami, a whole round of brie and two packets of bacon later and we have reached the caravan overlooking the big pond. Originally, I put it there as a guest annexe for visitors, but it has become a combination of wildlife observation point and feeding substation, crammed with sacks of trout pellets and bird-seed. I see that the patio of slabs I painstakingly laid last summer has provided further sport for the local mole colony.

Together with the moles, a variety of other small creatures have taken up residence beneath the caravan, and since a family of water voles has squatted under my upturned dinghy, Donella has forbidden me from launching it except in dire emergencies, such as the rescue of a drowning frog. She has even asked me to bung up the sculling hole in the transom in case it lets in a draught.

Thankfully, the big pond has not frozen over, so I will not be sent out on a dangerous ice-breaking mission, and the voles will remain undisturbed. We walk round the pond, and I see that the huge construction of underwater weed in one corner is getting smaller. According to the book, if our mystery lodger is, as Freddo claims, a muskrat, it will have built a lodge of weed to live in and off during the winter, then eaten its way out to go on an orgy of bank tunnelling at about the time Donella spotted it. Perhaps I will invite the patron of the Café de Paris and his shotgun to tea when my wife is not at home.

The Cray gang are not in evidence, but I see they have installed several new front doors below the water line on the west side of the bank, and the odd abandoned claw indicates violent territorial struggle. After throwing at least a pound of trout feed into the pond, followed by stones while Donella's back is turned so that I can pretend to have seen at least a dozen fish leaping, we catch a fleeting glance of Trevor, so she is content. Now our mercy mission has been completed, tradition demands it is time for cups of coffee and a ciga-rette at the grotto.

Sitting on the old railway-platform bench overlooking the cascade, I open the flask and we look contentedly down at the churning water, each alone with thoughts of how our adventure is progressing. Suddenly, Donella grasps my arm and points. I stare, and finally become aware of a flotilla of small fish, hanging almost motionless beneath the turbulent surface in front of the miniature waterfall. They are baby trout, taking on oxygen from the aerated water before making their journey downstream to be reunited with their mother. The months of backbreaking labour clearing the river have been worthwhile. We smile at each other like proud parents and I hug my wife in pure delight. After forty years, the river trout have returned to La Puce.

5 APRIL

I am worried that my wife's sense of relative values is catching. Early this morning, Donella arrived in a state of wild agitation as I was chopping firewood behind the mill and reported a confrontation with a young man on the track to the grotto; she said he was a stranger, and acting extremely suspiciously because he refused to return her greeting. He was also carrying a fully extended fishing rod.

I hastened to the grotto, forgetting to lay down my double-edged felling axe. The intruder was happily squatting on the other side of the basin, his line in the water at the exact point where we had recently seen the flotilla of troutlings. As I appeared, he looked first at me, then my axe, and hastily reeled in. On his hook was a large fish. Outraged, I forgot all the suitable Norman patois curses so carefully learned from Freddo and fell back on a stream of Anglo-Saxon while charging across the tombstone bridge to discuss the matter further. Obviously unwilling to argue his point, he made off, avoiding Donella's rugby-style tackle as he fled up the track and escaped, with mother fish still writhing on the end of his line.

I spend the rest of the day making a number of new No Fishing signs, crudely hewn from the copse with my felling axe, and executed in dripping and blood-red gloss paint.

9 APRIL

René brings bad news from the orchard. The old apple tree where we searched for the miller's gold has fallen over. We go to look at the damage, and our estate manager seems strangely pleased to see that his dire warning about digging near the roots has borne fruit. He tells us with grim satisfaction that the ancients believed apple trees to be sacred, and that for whatever reason the catastrophe had taken place, it is a certain harbinger of approaching doom. Someone connected with the land of La Puce is sure to die before long. It is certainly grim tidings for us, as René says he has already ordered not one but three replacement trees from his friend who owns the *pépinière* along the road, and they will be very expensive. He had no choice, he says as according to our agreement, the harvest is his, and the extra trees will barely make up for what he loses in fruit while they grow to maturity. He also claims salvage rights on the old tree for firewood to heat his caravan with the stove I know it doesn't contain. I learn of the cost of the new trees, and realise why we call French apples Golden Delicious. While bidding farewell to the dead tree, Donella points out what looks suspiciously like chain marks around the trunk, but René says that they were obviously made by a passing deer, desperate for food after the late snows.

14 APRIL

A choppy crossing on our return from a raiding mission. A pub next to the perimeter fence at Heathrow airport has proved unpopular with potential customers for some reason, so I have been called in to conjure up some positive publicity. As it is directly beneath the main flight path, I at first suggested painting huge advertisements for the special dish of the day and other attractions on the roof. Rather stuffily, the airport authority objected strongly to my suggestion, as they thought news of a plate of moussaka and chips for under two pounds might distract the pilot's attention. Eventually, my clients settled for the installation of a sealed time vault in the car park, containing a selection of bottled beer, a homemade steak pie, a video of the area and a copy of a suitable newspaper so that visitors to the space-port in the year 2196 will know what life was like in our time. The time-vault spoof is always a winner and extremely cost effective. All it takes to set up the photoshoot is a pile of earth and rubble, a spade or two and the brewery director and publican in hard hats, smiling and holding their wares to camera. That way, they get an extra plug in for company brands, and the story is guaranteed exposure as I change the name of the allegedly entombed newspaper to suit where the press release is going.

~

Having got our undeclared goldfish and bedding plants safely through the deserted customs checkpoint, we arrive at La Puce and visit the mill cottage to see how the restoration is coming along.

Outside, the sand pile is even higher and I make a mental note to launch Operation Desert Storm with all speed. Inside, we see that René is continuing to make an excellent job. The newly installed but ancient floorboards and other fixtures look almost as if they belong there. Bearing in mind how the mill was stripped bare by locals, perhaps the new items do belong exactly where they are, and have been reclaimed in the same way they were originally removed. If so, it has been poetic justice.

As soon as the mill is habitable, we will be able to vacate the farmhouse and let it out to recoup some of the cost of the restoration, which is running at three times the original cost of La Puce. This, we have found, is a reasonable equation for all improvement work on old French properties, even when, as with our efforts, work is theoretically done on the cheap.

As I open the shutters and set about airing the cottage, I

find we have already had uninvited guests. A small rodent is gamely attempting to climb out of the toilet bowl in the bedroom, and another lies dead on the carpet. Resisting the urge to quietly dispose of yet another mouth to feed, I rescue the survivor and flush the corpse away to avoid the emotional cost of the formal funeral my wife would certainly stage. I attempt to smuggle the creature out of the mill, but my wife's animal antenna is working at full strength. Within moments she identifies the beast as a newborn shrew, and it is set up for life in a cardboard box lined with my newest vest as she tenderly feeds it with milk through a tube fashioned from the inside of my favourite fountain pen. While she is distracted, I return upstairs and open our English-French dictionary at R for rat poison.

The rat is sleeping contentedly on my vest, so I suggest that we visit Bar Ghislaine for some top-up provisions. Rural grocery stores are dying in France just as they did a generation ago in the UK, and the reason is the same. Even the older villagers now make their weekly trip to the local supermarkets for the better prices and variety, and visit the local épicerie only for daily necessities.

As we arrive, Ghislaine waves at us through the window, then scowls at one of the Jolly Boys' Club members, who is using the open-air toilet next to the shop entrance. After adjusting his dress he pats his crotch with a proud proprietary air, and Madame Ghislaine responds by grimacing derisively and waggling her little finger in the air. Suitably chastened that my wife has also been a witness to his humiliation, he pretends not to see us and hurries back to more respectful male company.

As a concession to the chilly day, a single oak log smoulders in the cavernous fireplace, and the Jolly Boys' Club is in full session. Following the usual round of handshaking and polite enquiries as to the state of our livers, we are invited to join the party. This is a particular honour, as women are usually not welcome in rural bars, let alone when the daily debating school is in session. As in pre-war Britain, the ladies of Cotentin still let their men appear to be in charge when out and about, excepting certain obvious arenas such as the shop, church and, when the patron is pushed too far, the Bar Ghislaine.

Today, our panel consists of Mr Maurice, his nephew Alain, Marcel Bernard, René and Old Pierrot. Apart from his age, most things are indeterminate about Pierrot. Few people outside his small circle of intimates know what he used to do for a living, whether he is married or even where he lives, which is most unusual for any village.

The main subject for today's debating circle, we learn, is fuel. I call for a round of pastis from Madame Ghislaine as our entry fee. The two opposing camps divide into a preference for oak, which is harder to find but burns well and slowly, and beech for its warmth and aroma. There is also some discussion on the comparative merits of open fireplaces and wood-burning stoves, and a rumour to be spread that a newcomer from Cherbourg has bought a house outside the village and is having electric heating put in. He is either very rich or very stupid, as everyone knows that wood is free. Especially, I reflect silently, if it comes from someone else's land. We have lost several small trees from the copse this year, but our estate manager has told me that this is a necessary culling exercise to let the others breathe.

As the discussion becomes heated, René ushers me to another table to announce that he has at last located the perfect stove for the mill cottage. It is the property of a friend in a distant hamlet, and they have just concluded a deal at a very good price. The *poêle* is very old and impressive, and is thought to have been looted from a local manor house immediately after the Revolution. Naturally, there is no chimney pipe included, but that, he assures me, will be no problem, as every ironmongery and hardware shop in the region will stock suitable tubing for adaptation.

The price will be a mere 1000 francs, a fraction of the cost of a new reproduction model, and I will be buying history as well as completely effective and free heating for the rest of our days in Cotentin. To celebrate, I order another round of drinks, and René takes the opportunity to mention casually that he has ordered another trailer load of sand. This, he assures me, will all be used in creating the walkway of marble around the big pond.

Grasping the moment while virtually the entire complement of the Jolly Boys' Club is present, I decide to launch phase one of Operation Desert Storm. My friends will have noticed, I begin, that I have a very large hole next to the mill cottage where the machinery used to sit. Over the past year, I have consulted with all the experts on how best to fill it in. Both Henri the Tractor and Mr Janne have ruled out the idea of simply scooping up earth from elsewhere on the property and dumping it in the hole, as the surrounding walls would deter even the finest digger driver in the region. Has anyone any other ideas for a solution?

As I appear to wait for a response, I loudly remind René that we now have a huge surplus of sand, even bearing in mind his plans for the marble walkway. At this, Marcel looks up, his face aglow with inspiration. Why not, he suggests, simply put the mountain of sand into the hole? Given a year or so in the rain, it will settle much better than earth, and avoid the expense of a mechanical roller. I look impressed, then smile sadly. It sounds a very good idea, naturally, but because of the walls, every kilo would have to be shifted by hand. My friends all know how incompetent I am with shovel or spade. Furthermore, Donella, though strong for a woman, has little stamina. The proposal is impeccable, but the execution would take forever.

To a man, the Jolly Boys' Club volunteer. If we will provide luncheon and ongoing refreshments, they will gladly contribute the labour. The talk turns to past achievements with favourite spades and the most effective wrist actions. I order another round to celebrate the arrangement, and as Ghislaine arrives with the bottle, I catch René giving me a look of reluctant admiration. I am obviously learning how to get things done the local way.

~

Later on the same afternoon, after Ghislaine has evicted us, I am invited to make my first visit to the house of Mr Maurice. It is a particular honour to be allowed into any Norman's home, and especially so as a foreigner. Mr Maurice also whispered something about allowing me to look inside his wardrobe and try the contents. Even in my current condition, I am still alert enough to realise he is not inviting me to ease his collection of winter tights on, and have heard all about his special collection of calva. Mr Maurice's nephew Alain is to be the only other guest, as the surviving members of the Jolly Boys' Club have rather pointedly not been invited to join us. My wife has returned to La Puce to tend to her flock, and René has buzzed unsteadily off aboard his mobylette to make arrangements for the collection of the stove. I can't help feeling that there may be some sort of hidden agenda behind the invitation to share the secrets of the wardrobe.

Like most people in the region, Mr Maurice rents his house. It is located at the bottom of a winding track on the village outskirts, standing in a cluster of ramshackle old buildings, flanked by the usual mountain of firewood and collection of rusting car bodies. As we arrive, a handful of consumptive-looking chickens scratch determinedly in the dirt yard, while a three-legged dog investigates the remains of a long-dead cat. Inside, the one large room serves as bedroom, bathroom, kitchen and sitting area. A stack of World War II American ammunition boxes provide the main seating arrangements, and the chemical toilet is within comfortable range of the giant fireplace. An oak table, which any London antiques dealer would kill for, takes centre stage, bearing the remains of a hundred forgotten meals. As if distancing itself from its squalid environment, a magnificent eighteenth-century solid walnut wardrobe stands aloofly in the furthest corner. It is undoubtedly worth more than the house and the land it stands on.

I follow Mr Maurice to the corner and respectfully accept his invitation to open the doors of the *grande armoire*. And, on rough shelves made from yet more ammunition boxes, are crammed hundreds of bottles, flasks and sealed jars. They contain the fruits of our host's labours for more than half a century. Each holds a different vintage of calva, and each has its own distinctive flavouring. A true artist, Mr Maurice has allowed only his imagination to limit the range of fruit, vegetables and flowers marinating peacefully over the decades. Alongside a coffee jar containing cherry goutte, I discover raspberry, blackcurrant, chestnut and even sunflower varieties. The deeper I explore the depths of the aromatic armoire, the more unusual and exotic the combinations become, and I await our first tasting with interest.

After a brief lecture on the contents, age, history and ingredients of the top shelf, our host selects what looks like a specimen jar, wrapped carefully in a pair of black tights. I can't help thinking of the moment during our first encounter when my wife watched in fascination as Mr Maurice hitched his trousers and adjusted his seams. Later, she was quite disappointed to discover that several layers of women's tights are considered locally to be far superior to thermal underwear – and considerably cheaper.

The jar is reverently unsealed and the tasting begins. After an initial sip, I agree with our host that the flavour is, to say the least, interesting, and he explains that the hitherto secret ingredient is a very rare type of mushroom. Having dangled the bait, he and Alain continue to ply me with glasses of his special concoctions, each benefiting from the addition after brewing of fruit, flower, herb or even animal parts.

The afternoon wears on, and, as ever, I find that calva has

magical properties. My patois has improved to such an extent and density that my host seems to be having no problem in keeping up as I let rip with a stream of anecdotes and explanations about English cricket, the history and development of the British Pub (1216–1949) and the trouble with our royal family.

Like a scorpion, Mr Maurice chooses exactly the right moment to strike before I become so far gone that I am unable to speak. Casually, he returns to the subject of his mushroom goutte. Nowhere, he purrs as we move on to a particularly piquant sweetcorn vintage, can one find a finer variety of fungi than in a mature copse of mixed oak and beech in a wet soil, with the leaf mulch undisturbed for long years. As I attempt to nod sagely without head-butting the table, my host asks silkily if I am aware that I am the owner of exactly such a copse. Gamely trying to concentrate, I say yes, I do know that the copse at La Puce is such an unique occurrence. Is it not then a shame, he asks, pressing me to try a soupçon of the daffodil calva, that I am absent so often at exactly the time that the various fungi in the copse are precisely right for gathering, and that they should be wasted on the casual visitors who raid my land without any repayment?

I ponderously explain that this is precisely why I have come to an arrangement with Coco that he should have full gathering rights in exchange for our annual mushroom omelette orgy.

Topping up my glass, Mr Maurice points out that, as far as all sensible and informed critics are concerned, his nephew, Alain, is a far superior fungi collector than Coco, accomplished as their good friend undoubtedly is. Would it not be an ideal solution to continue the arrangement with Coco, but allot he and Alain alternate days of exclusive access to the copse? That way, both would be free to indulge their expertise and enthusiasm, I would continue to enjoy my yearly omelette, and would also receive an annual gift of a bottle of the finest mushroom goutte...

By this stage, I am beyond argument, and in seconds Mr Maurice has produced an official contract, which he just happens to have drawn up in case I might be in agreement. I sign away half the harvesting rights to my copse for all eternity, and the deal is celebrated in suitable fashion.

My only problem now is explaining the new arrangement to Coco, and finding my way back to La Puce. I eventually make my excuses and leave, bid an emotional farewell to the dead cat, and begin my unsteady journey home. Over the next hour, I rest frequently on the verge to take my bearings and reflect that, despite my triumph with Operation Desert Storm, I still have a lot to learn about the way business is done in my new hometown.

~

It is not a good time for René to call. Donella, who I initially mistake for the Grey Lady, has tiptoed in to the darkened room to say our estate manager is here and the stove ready for collection. We must, she says he says, go now lest it be lost to another anxious buyer. I am helped to dress and stagger into the yard, where René, an unknown accomplice and a very noisy tractor await. I ask him to turn off the flashing light, and climb up into the cab.

On board and bucketing on our way through the night, I recover sufficiently to ask why it is so important we pick up the stove at dead of night. My companion answers only half-sarcastically that his mobylette not being quite up to the task, the tractor is the only available and suitable vehicle, and it is booked for a session in a chicory field in the morning. Besides, the roads are clearer at this time. I can still taste the mushroom calva, and concentrate hard on gulping down the sweet night air and keeping my seat behind the driver's cab.

At last, we turn off the lane and lurch down an even more potholed track and stop. I fall from the grunting tractor as René takes a torch and disappears into the darkness. A little while later, he returns and silently beckons. We must, he cautions in a stage whisper, be as quiet as the night, as we do not wish to disturb the pregnant donkey in the ruined barn which looms up beside us. I consider questioning this out-of-character consideration for animals, but tiptoe on and fall over a piece of the stove, which is holding the door to the barn shut. Inside, torchlight illuminates our goal. It is certainly an impressive sight. Displayed to best advantage on a pedestal of concrete building blocks, the wrought-iron poêle appears almost as big as Mr Maurice's magic wardrobe, and every bit as decorative with its engravings, relief scrolls and curlicues. Presently, it is being used as a chicken coop, and René quickly evicts and silences the two incumbents by grasping their beaks and holding them firmly beneath one arm. Obviously, he is still concerned about the pregnant donkey's uninterrupted slumber.

It is left to me and my mystery companion to wrestle the giant stove from its pedestal and roll it to the tractor on some convenient lengths of metal piping while René attends to his chicken nursing. This done, we collect the doors, grating and other attachments from in and around the barn, heave the stove on to the trailer and depart, René admonishing the driver sharply to keep the revs low. As we near the end of the track, I ask why I was not required to pay the owner before taking the goods, a usually strictly observed Cotentinese tradition. It would not be fair to disturb him on such a small matter, he explains as if to a child, and I should know by now that all good farmers are soundly asleep at this late hour. I can settle for the stove when we arrive back at the mill, and he will pass the money on in the morning. We rejoin the lane and the tractor roars up the incline as I fancy I hear a dog bark in the distance, followed by an angry shout. René tells me I am mistaken. It is nothing but a fox, who as everyone knows, does his best business at night.

Back at the mill cottage, we unload the stove and stow it safely behind the sand mountain, René considerately covering it with a tarpaulin for protection against the night air. I hand over the 1,000 francs, and before leaving, he surprisingly volunteers to start installation work later this very day. He also suggests that I keep the deal to ourselves, as our rivals for the stove will be jealous and bad feeling could be caused by self-indulgent boasting about our bargain.

The driver, who has so far remained totally silent, moves to the back of his tractor to do some unseen business with René, and raised voices temporarily disturb the silence. The obviously disgruntled figure finally reappears, mounts and starts his tractor, and it rumbles truculently up the track and into the gloom. René disappears in the direction of his mobylette, and I think I hear a muffled squawk coming from beneath his voluminous poacher's jacket. I retire to the mill, contemplating the pleasures of chestnuts roasting on our magnificent stove by next Christmas.

Donella will be pleased with our latest acquisition, but I will not show it to her tonight, as she is on a badger-spotting vigil by the caravan, and would not wish to be disturbed. She is convinced there is a sett in the bramble jungle in the top field, and has shown me the alleged tracks. I suspect they actually reveal a convenient short cut to the big pond by season-ticket-holding fishermen en route from buying bait at René's caravan, but have said nothing.

I go to bed. It has been a long day.

6 MAY

René has been almost as good as his word. Less than a month after he promised to install it, the giant stove is in place, standing on a stone plinth against the wall at the end of the mill cottage, which will be our sitting-room area. Inside and with all its doors and fittings attached, it looks even bigger, but René says that we will need all the heat we can get when autumn comes. He has assured us that there are no ghosts on the premises, but takes grim relish in predicting we will need a bigger pile of firewood to see us through the dark days than Mr Janne, the undisputed local champion for yearly *fagot* consumption, uses at his rambling manoir. Apparently, the problem with our mill cottage is that the stone-block walls are more than a metre thick, and it will take at least a winter of constant habitation and blazing fires to infuse them, like ancient storage-heater bricks, with insulating warmth. On the upside, the mayor has told us that the building will stand forever as cows' milk was mixed with the mortar when it was built. This early damp-proofing device certainly seems to have worked.

As there was no chimney piping with the stove, I shall have to find some and do the job myself, but René says this will be no problem, as a common or garden metal drainage pipe will be ideal. I see that he has also left me to make a hole for the pipe through the gable-end against which it stands. It is even thicker than the side walls and I do not think that, excellent for smaller tasks as it has proved to be, my Black and Decker hammer drill will be up to the task. I shall visit *Boueve et Fils* tomorrow and buy a man-sized sledgehammer.

7 MAY

The fridge being empty, I breakfast off the remnants of last night's *pot au feu* and some bread stolen from the bird table in the yard. As I make my frugal meal, the ship's bell on the gatepost signals the arrival of the mayor, and I usher him in after his usual polite protestations about the condition of his boots and the early hour of the day.

Of all the men I have come to know across the years, John Chevalier is one of the most decent, gentle and content. His philosophy is as simple as it is wise, and he is greatly respected throughout the area for the quiet concern with which he fulfils his self-imposed obligations to the community and his small part of France. Devoted to the community and the continuance of its way of life, he spends more time at the tiny mairie at Néhou than at his farmhouse. Among a sea of paperwork and petty squabbling, he is an island of calm. Each weekday afternoon at three, he dons the mayoral suit with flared trousers he bought to celebrate the birth of his son, and takes his seat at the desk in front of the crossed flags of Normandy and France. For the next two hours, he will deal with a steady stream of villagers as he dispenses justice and practical advice, and strives to make sense of the latest European directive concerning the banning of dumping rubbish at village rubbish tips. Transparently in love with his wife, his work and his life, he is a happy man, far richer in spirit than the most successful Parisian bureaucrat.

As usual, there is much to talk about before we get down to the reason for his visit. First, we must reassure him as to our health, the general well-being of our Queen (who is also the Duke of Normandy) and how my friend Mr Major is getting on with running the country. As he enquires about our premier, he nods deferentially at the wall where a photograph of my mother and Donella with John and Solange hangs next to one of me apparently arm-wrestling with the leader of Her Majesty's Government.

Some years before, organising the re-opening of an East End pub in London after it had been set on fire by a disgruntled customer, I had hired the most convincing of the many John Major look-alikes available to pull the first pint. The event was not a runaway success, as the pub's locals turned out to be rabid socialists to a man, and we had to smuggle the look-alike out through the cellar before he came to harm. Before the near-riot, we had posed for a photograph together, which I had hung on the farmhouse kitchen wall. When a visiting French friend explained the joke to René, the news that I was a personal friend of the *chef* of all England went round the village like wildfire. René had either misunderstood my friend's bad (i.e. non-Norman) French, or deliberately neglected to explain that the man in the picture was not the real PM, a revelation that would naturally diminish his status as my estate manager.

The main reason for the mayor's visit, he explains after the formalities have been completed, is to ask permission to put his cows to graze in our mill garden later that day. A thoughtful and efficient farmer, John makes full use of every blade of grass he rents, and it is time to give the top fields a rest. He usually puts his cattle into the mill cottage garden at this time, but knows that we are working there and does not want to disrupt our restoration work, which he has thoughtfully forgotten to check for conformity with planning regulations.

When we bought La Puce, we were naturally pleased to learn that there was an existing grazing agreement with the mayor of Néhou. Although he recommended that we maintain the arrangement for all sorts of sensible reasons, Mr Gancel the notaire advised us that the property's change of hands meant we were entitled to terminate the long-standing agreement. If we wisely decided to carry on as things were, a suitable yearly fee and conditions would be negotiated and agreed, and a yearly contract drawn up, authorised, notarised, witnessed and signed by what appeared to be half the village. Already having learned that any involvement of a notaire is very time-consuming and expensive, I promptly typed up a lengthy and completely meaningless contract full of pseudo British legalese, added a first-class stamp, asked my local Portsmouth publican and two of his customers to sign it, and duly presented it to the mayor. The document, I explained, gave him full and exclusive use of the land till his retirement, and there would be no charge.

John was so visibly moved by my gesture, that I immediately felt bad about creating the fake contract. However, our verbal accord was known to the notaire and village, and therefore was just as binding. It was also a lot cheaper.

～

Having told John he was welcome to put his beef into the garden, we shake hands and he departs. I slither down the slope from the farmhouse and undress among the paint pots and cement bags on the first floor of the mill, ready to indulge in a long-awaited treat. I am to test out our new bath. Taking René and three other strong men to carry upstairs, it is still a talking point in the village, as it is not only a traditional English bath, but an English lord's traditional English bath. Of 1930's vintage, this cast-iron monster is oval, big enough for me to achieve maximum submergence, and is finished off with impressive ball-and-claw legs. Taking the air in rural Sussex one Sunday afternoon last summer, we had passed the gate to a gypsy settlement and seen the luridly painted monster, bearing a roughly daubed price tag of £30. Talking to the vendor, we learned that he had recently won the rights to strip and salvage all the outdated plumbing before a refit at nearby Cowdray Park, and the bath was just one of the redundant fittings. I had been told it came from a guest wing, but didn't dissuade René from painting word pictures at the Bar Ghislaine about the great English lord soaking in his bath with the odd chambermaid after a hearty game of polo with the Duke of Windsor and Wallace Simpson.

I am just about to dive in when Donella calls up the stairs to say that the cattle have arrived but are unaccompanied by either John or Solange. They are also eating her herb garden, and one of them looks suspiciously like a bull. It appears to be sharpening its horns on the stone wall behind the mill after having had the five-bar gate off its hinges with a few experimental charges. She is concerned that the herd may now wander unchecked into the water meadow and come to grief in the big pond. I reassure her that there are no bulls in John's herd but agree that a fall into the big pond could be dangerous, as the whole herd would doubtless be stripped to the bone in moments by the voracious Cray gang.

Pausing only to don slippers and my Superman dressing gown, I join my wife in the garden. I still do not know if the proposition that bulls find the colour red irritating is true, but my appearance has an immediate effect. The cow that Donella thinks is a bull promptly snorts, paws the ground, lowers its massive head and moves towards me at considerable speed. As I leap with unaccustomed rapidity into a convenient nettle patch, the whole herd thunders up the cart track to the road. Aware of the consequences of a ton or more of cow meeting suddenly with a car coming down the hill at ninety kilometres an hour, I attempt to keep pace, and we burst out on to the road at around the same time. Thankfully, the coast is clear, and I pursue the herd in the general direction of St Sauveur.

By great good fortune, the first vehicle to meet us in our headlong flight is the ancient van of Mr Janne, and even more fortuitously, he is sober. Within moments he has set up a roadblock and, after an admiring glance at my Superman dressing gown, authoritatively directed the alleged bull into one of his own roadside fields.

A long queue of traffic has now built up, and everyone takes the opportunity to show that, whatever their present situation and professional status, they have not forgotten their basic countryside skills. Smartly dressed men and women desert their BMWs and Mercedes, their inner peasant coming to the surface, and vie to show off their specialist herding techniques with an array of umbrellas, briefcases and handbags.

Eventually, all the cows have been ushered into the field, and the identity of their owner established. The herd belongs to an elderly lady living near the crossroads, and their rightful home is in a field alongside La Puce.

The fuss over, I return somewhat shakily to the mill, where I find the Cowdray bath, without the modern design benefits of an overflow device, has flooded the premises. Thankfully, little permanent damage has been caused, although the cows' milk mortar has proved its value as damp-proofing, and the ground floor is now a shallow swimming pool.

19 MAY

An eventful overnight crossing from Portsmouth. Sharing a cabin with our latest Real France package visitors, we all suffer a sleepless night due to the gymnastics which are taking place next door.

In the morning, we meet our noisy neighbours queuing for the toilet, and realise that we know the couple. Both are happily married, but not to each other. They explain, implausibly, that they were unable to book separate cabins and are on an urgent business trip. Over breakfast, my wife suggests that they must be in the bed-testing business.

We exchange stories about how we met our spouses, and I amuse our guests with the tale of my short career as a private detective. In between jobs, I had responded to an advertisement for a correspondence course to learn the profession, and managed to persuade a friend to lend me his tiny basement office in a Southsea terrace. All went fairly well until my first job, which seemed a run-of-the-mill affair, checking the fidelity of the client's wife. I studied my course notes and duly set up an observation post in the alleyway behind the house she constantly visited. Immediately after gaining concrete evidence of her adultery as she dallied with a large man over a convenient kitchen table, I fell off the dustbin, and was spotted, detained and rather unnecessarily assaulted by her partner before being handed over to the police. Fortunately, I was let off with a caution after my profession and intent was explained and proven. I was also cautioned by the desk sergeant to check up on my facts before taking on any more cases, as it turned out that the woman was happily married to the man who punched me, the scene of the action was their own house, and my client a stalker who had developed an obsession about her and deluded himself into believing they were married.

I met Donella early one morning shortly afterwards when she arrived for work at the more affluent premises above mine and caught me borrowing their freshly delivered bottle of milk. Rather than turn me in, she tended to my black eye, replaced the bottle, tidied up my office and was doomed. When I decided to cease trading as a private eye and get a more reliable source of income as a gravedigger, she came with me and has been bailing me out of trouble ever since.

~

We arrive in some style at the Café de Paris in a fearsome-looking Range Rover bristling with bull bars, winches and a row of spare petrol cans lining the roof rack as if on safari rather than in Cotentin. We are also towing a battered caravan, which was the main reason for our visit to Hampshire, and our return with Jean-Marie Guedeney and his English wife, Kathy. Jean-Marie is Burgundian, and the couple run a chain of sandwich bars in the Portsmouth area. As he has lived and worked in Britain for nearly twenty years, my friend's moustache is much smaller than the rural French norm, but his belief in Gallic superiority in every sphere save cricket and real ale remains undiminished.

As a guest under our special short-stay package, Jean-Marie will doubtless prove indispensable for any advanced negotiations with René on the new pond Donella is planning, but his main chore for the visit is to tow the caravan into the water meadow.

With the day hardly awake, the Café de Paris is nevertheless a hive of activity, and for a moment it seems we have walked into the film set of *Apocalypse Now*. Freddo, Pierrot and a motley collection of customers are going hunting, our host tells us, though the array of high-powered armaments has already given us more than a clue. As Freddo is introduced to our guests and makes a covert assessment of Jean-Marie's moustache rating, he explains that a fox has been sighted on the outskirts of the town, and the posse is getting ready to hunt it down and free the area's livestock, elderly residents and newborn infants from its threat. As a fellow

Frenchman, Jean-Marie is invited to inspect the arsenal, and we move to where a selection of rifles, bandoliers, hunting knives, nets and what looks suspiciously like sticks of dynamite is heaped carelessly on a table.

Freddo's toddler grandson is at this moment playing with a double-barrelled weapon slightly longer than he is, and my wife hastens to take it from him. Giving her a soft-verge look, Freddo stiffly assures her that he is not *stupide*. Though the *fusil* is loaded, the safety catch is firmly in place. Obviously, the child is too young to go on the hunt at present, but will be ready for action next year when he will receive his first rifle as a doting grandfather's birthday present. The patron then offers to shoot anything edible that comes into his line of fire for Donella's pot, but my wife says not to bother to kill anything especially for her, as she has brought some frozen turkey drumsticks across the water.

Approaching the bar and, I suspect, wishing to impress us, Jean-Marie orders our coffee and calva with machine-gun rapidity, but is served hot chocolate and pastis by Collette's mother. After I coach him in the necessary patois phrasing, he has another brief conversation with *Maman*, who congratulates him on his command of French, and asks what part of England he hails from.

~

At La Puce, we move our luggage into the farmhouse, then drive down the track to the mill, which is now barely visible behind the sand mountain.

Kathy alights from the Range Rover and immediately sinks to the ankles of her expensive high-heeled fashion boots. A town girl by birth and inclination, she has only visited Jean-Marie's ancestral home in Burgundy during the searing months of July and August, and has not encountered real country mud before, especially the Cotentinese variety.

Jean-Marie is obviously far more at ease. A keen off-roader, he spends his weekends looking for a challenge along the forest tracks of Hampshire, but has never seen anything approaching the promise of our land, even in a comparatively arid May. He becomes even more enthusiastic when he sees that the route to the water meadow runs steeply uphill through the mill garden after passing through a gateway only marginally wider than the caravan. And all this before meeting the real challenge of the permanently saturated reservoir field. Taken together with our attendance at the fund-raising soirée at the village hall this evening, the visit promises to be a most enjoyable and memorable one, he says, almost licking his lips in anticipation of both the meal and the mud.

Anxious to display his vehicle's capabilities without delay, Jean-Marie loses no time in starting his motor and skilfully manoeuvring the caravan to line up with the gateway. All goes well for at least ten feet, and then the back and front wheels of the all-terrain vehicle disappear in the rich Normandy earth. After a few moments of spraying the caravan and rear wall of the mill and settling even further in the mire, Jean-Marie refuses to concede defeat and announces it is time to bring his brand-new power winch into play. He finds a suitable tree on the riverbank, hooks up, and begins to pull the sturdy ash out by the roots.

As we stand at approximately eye level with the roof of the sinking vehicle, René arrives to welcome us, collect his bottle of duty-free scotch and savour the moment. I can see that he is particularly pleased that it is a British vehicle, which has fallen foul of good Norman soil, and even happier when he learns that Jean-Marie is from Burgundy.

After a while, as the stricken vehicle continues to sink, our estate manager tells our guest not to abandon hope, as he will go and fetch his mobylette. For a moment I think he proposes using it to pull both the Range Rover and the caravan into the water meadow, but he explains that a friend with a tractor is working just up the road. With the pooled resources of René, the tractor and Roland the spécialiste, all will be well, and Jean-Marie, his unfortunate vehicle and our caravan will be out of trouble.

~

While we wait for rescue, Donella provides our friends with wellingtons and suggests a tour of inspection of the rest of the terrain. I take the opportunity to visit JayPay and seek suggestions for a suitable regional dish to impress our guests at lunch tomorrow.

JayPay recently moved into a farmhouse less than a mile away, and has therefore become a close neighbour as well as friend. Up until a month ago, the family of eight had the grandest council house in the region, created specially from the former vicarage next to the church at Néhou. Apart from his status as general manager of the fresh meat and charcuterie section of a supermarket outside Bricquebec, JayPay is regarded as the most knowledgeable and formidable chef in the area. He also has been battling virtually single-handed to halt the annual fall in the village population. So far, a decade on, his tally is a mixture of six sons and daughters, all almost identical in their striking dark looks and sunny natures. As befits his accomplishments, JayPay's moustache is on a par with Big Freddo's, a subject, which is the focus of much dispute and the occasional wager between regulars at the Café de Paris and the Bar Ghislaine. The claim as to who has the biggest and best moustache in Cotentin (perhaps all France) has allegedly risked fistfights between the opposing camps.

JayPay carries his authority, responsibilities and giant moustache with equal ease. Apart from his work, countryside and reproductive activities, he somehow finds time to devise and create the regional dishes for regular fund-raising dinners at our village hall. This month's featured region is the Alsace, and the dish *choucroute*, an awesome collation of pickled cabbage and parts of the pig which most English people would not believe existed, let alone be suitable for consumption.

At their farmhouse, I park the car a safe distance from the attentions of the dozen or so bored dogs looking for a little sport, and call for a safe escort. Eventually, Madame JayPay appears wearing her usual combination of a resigned pout and cigarette. As we walk to the barn in search of her husband, she tells me she is more than happy with their new home, given that there are only four bedrooms. She would have liked more, just for the sheer pleasure of having one permanently spare and empty *chambre*.

Moving onto the subject of large families and the state's changing attitudes towards rural tradition and culture, she recalls an encounter with an official health visitor shortly before the birth of her youngest. The woman had not even borne a single child, but had presumed to give her advice. Even worse, the session had included a warning about the perils of smoking, and a severe admonition that Madame should at least stop the filthy practice while pregnant. This was a ridiculous proposal, as in earlier years she had hardly had time to light up between conceptions. Besides, the evidence is there for all to see, as her children are obviously healthier and happier than any mollycoddled town kid. Having often stopped to pick up her beaming offspring during their three-mile walk to and from school, I have to agree with her. Anyway, concludes Mrs JayPay, she had kept the woman quiet by promising to cut back on the Philip Morris, and is nowadays down to forty a day.

In the barn, JayPay, who obviously likes making things, is working on his new invention, an incubator resourcefully created from an old beer-bottle display cabinet and the heating elements of a redundant electric fire. Correcting my teasing suggestion that it will make a snug crib for the new member of the family, he explains that it is destined to hold and nurture up to four dozen pheasant eggs at a time. As Freddo and his fellow *chasseurs* seem to be running out of targets on their weekly hunt, he is setting up an intensive breeding programme to re-stock the local shooting range. As he gently cradles and strokes the tiny eggs in a massive hand, I once again reflect on this apparent ambivalence of attitude towards the miracle of creation and the pleasures of the kill.

In the lofty kitchen, we gather at a table marginally smaller than the landing area of an aircraft carrier and Madame JayPay does the honours with homemade biscuits and a bottle of *pommeau*. As she busies herself adding cigarette ash to the food cooking on the stove, I toast my friends' happy news and explain my problem. I have a visitor from Burgundy, and wish to surprise him tomorrow lunchtime with my knowledge of and expertise in our regional specialities. I know JayPay has a busy day ahead as he prepares to feed more than a hundred villagers at one sitting, but that, of course, is no challenge to someone of his capabilities, and I am lost for ideas.

My friend takes a ruminative sip of his liqueur, wipes his moustache thoughtfully, then calls for pencil and paper. It is almost as important, he says, to choose a suitable dish for the occasion, as it is to cook and serve it perfectly. Tonight, our friends will be dining on choucroute, so my special meal should redress the balance, and be more subtle and lighter in texture and taste. With another sip of pommeau, inspiration comes. In the short time at our disposal, he will attempt to school me in the philosophical approach and precise sciences involved in the creation of a truly perfect *salade Normande*, followed by scallops in white sauce. The salad will reflect the simple yet inspired approach the Cotentinese take to matters of the stomach, and the scallop dish will mark and honour the ancient pilgrim's trail passing by the kitchen door of La Puce.

For the next hour, I am slowly taken through the mysteries and rites of making a salad consisting of little more than a single lettuce leaf. The secrets of the scallop dish take longer to unveil. Spices are brought from the larder, wrapped in twists of brown paper, labelled, numbered in order of inclusion and placed before me. Apart from the simple recipe and method of cooking the dish, details of the precise vintage and origin of the dry white wine for inclusion are written down, and I am required to practise the correct method of crushing the garlic cloves with a fork a dozen times before my mentor declares himself satisfied. Finally, we come to the inevitable secret ingredient. Returning from a lengthy visit to the barn, JayPay presents me with an earthenware jug wrapped discreetly in newspaper. He has just drawn a little calva from the giant oak barrel where it has been maturing for the past eight years. It is not quite ready for drinking in truly sophisticated company, he says, but is more than adequate for inclusion in the dish. As he escorts me and my precious package past the slavering dogs, he explains that the oak barrel was a major factor in his decision to buy the house. There were many cheaper and bigger properties for sale, but none went with a lifetime's supply of vintage calva. Had the previous owner not died alone and with no heirs or even distant relations, JayPay would never have pulled the coup off. It just shows, he says sagely as I back carefully out of the yard, the good sense of ensuring continuity of life and possessions across the generations by having a reasonably sized family.

~

Back at the mill, I find that Norman know-how has triumphed over British technology and Burgundian driving skills. The caravan is sitting happily at the far end of the water meadow, and the Range Rover and its master are sullenly skulking behind the sand mountain. Roland and his tractor have returned to their labours, and René, as ungracious as ever in victory, has offered to give Jean-Marie some tuition in off-road manoeuvring on his mobylette. I calm a potentially explosive situation by suggesting a glass of good wine and a game of ludo, played to Burgundy rules.

It is now time to encounter the choucroute and we make our way on foot to the village hall at Néhou. Jean-Marie initially takes this as a further slight to his driving capabilities, but I explain that it will be a long evening, and we do not want him to join the ditch-of-the-month club after such a demanding and frustrating day.

The mayor is greeting guests at the door, and thankfully appears to have little trouble in understanding Jean-Marie's French. After bestowing a few compliments on the wine, food and agricultural practices of Burgundy, our thoughtful host ushers us in to take an *apéritif* before the festivities commence.

The hall is set with tables laid for more than a hundred, and many of the guests have already arrived. The women of the village have made a special effort to mark the occasion and are dressed in their party finery. Most of the men have changed into clean bib and brace overalls and brown gumboots. Old Pierrot has even put on his Sunday-best peaked cap.

We fight our way to the bar, which is in the capable and enormous hands of Mr Janne. He is dispensing the choice of pastis, bottled beer and wine at nominal prices and we drink generously to help the night's good cause, which is to buy new books for the school.

Everyone seems to be entering into the spirit of the event and determined to enjoy the evening. Married couples go out together rarely in the Cotentin, but when they do, they tend to get their money's worth. Though there is scant room around the sea of trestle tables lining the hall, the mobile DJ is doing good business, and JayPay's children are filling the floor on their own. Some couples are actually dancing together, though René has not yet decided to do his traditional whirling dervish act. Perhaps he is waiting for 'The Birdie Song'.

Alerted to our presence, JayPay makes an entrance from the kitchens, swathed in acres of white apron and a Michel Mouse T-shirt. Perspiration is rolling down his face and threatening the integrity of his waxed moustache, but he is obviously on good form. After meeting our friends, JayPay registers our status by showing us personally to our table and we see we have been given a most privileged position, equidistant between the toilets and the bar.

Following tradition, the names of the guests allocated to each table have been written on the paper tablecloth, leaving individuals to sort out for themselves whom they choose to sit alongside. I note that our party includes the entire Jolly Boys' Club, the mayor and his wife. It is time to choose the wine for the evening, and before anyone suggests a sausage competition, I order a case to be going on with. After another scrimmage and round of drinks at the bar, we take our places and the mayor makes a short address, welcoming all and making special mention of our foreign guests, particularly Jean-Marie and his wife.

As ever, the service and procedure are simple in the extreme, and the quality of the food unmatchable. Following a rehearsal on a mound of assorted smoked sausages and meats from around Europe, which for some highly illogical reason is called Plate of the English, we clear our palates with a shrimp and cream soup, and stand by for the main course. There is an embarrassing moment when the wine is tasted and declared unfit for human consumption by JayPay, who promptly sends it with a curt demand for a fresh case, but Jean-Marie handles the tide of apologies and explanations like a seasoned diplomat.

With freshly charged glasses, we toast the arrival of what looks like the component parts of a whole pig atop a mountain of pickled cabbage, and the meal commences. For the next half-hour, conversation falters as we set to in earnest, and the pile of bare bones beside each plate grows apace. Kathy and Donella do their best to keep up with the rest of the party, but surrender when second helpings arrive. After a cigarette and a lemon calva sorbet to aid digestion, we move on to a lightly oiled salad, which I suspect is the inspiration for my starter tomorrow lunchtime, deal with a selection of suitable cheeses, the best part of a loaf of walnut bread apiece, and then do battle with great wedges of apple tart in a layer of cream thick enough to ski on.

By now, the pace of even the most determined eaters has fallen off, and most of our table politely refuse JayPay's invitation to finish off the remains of the choucroute. René brazenly fills a carrier bag with leftovers for his dog, although we all know he hasn't got one.

As we sit and recover, the mayor tells me that work on the Patton orchard is nearing completion. An American tank has been installed in pride of place, the grass trimmed and a car park built, and now he is in search of a suitable boulder to carry a plaque detailing the momentous events that took place there during and after the D-Day landings. I tell him I shall shortly be phoning my friend Robert Simon at Cherbourg to order more gravel for the mill track, and promise to enquire about the possible location and transport of an impressive stone. Since we have been working on the mill, more than ten tons of quarry chippings have been laid on the ancient track, and all have been swallowed up by the mud. JayPay claims that we could ask the commune to pay for or provide the gravel as it is a long-established public right of way, but I feel this would only confirm my acceptance that it isn't part of our property. I look out of the window and sigh as I see that it has started to rain quite heavily since we arrived at the hall. It will certainly spoil our friends' visit if Jean-Marie is unable to move his off-road vehicle from outside the mill cottage without the return and assistance of Roland the Tractor.

As we retire to the bar, Donella tells me some unexpected good news. René has said he has finally struck a deal with a local landscaping specialist, and work on the new pond will start first thing in the morning. I say that I will believe it when it happens, as we have only been discussing the project for the past three months. I also consider asking her why we need yet another expanse of expensive water, but I already know the answer. The garden pond is even more overstocked with expatriate goldfish now, and the plan to create a new home for them by the stone bridge was a total washout. With the sinister Reggie and Ronnie Crayfish gang holding sway over the big pond, she will not transfer this season's baby poissons rouges there.

While I was learning the secrets of lettuce salad at JayPay's this afternoon, she enlisted Jean-Marie and Kathy's help in staking out an area the size of an Olympic swimming pool in the water meadow. She has also been in negotiation with René to discuss piping water through it from the river and out to the millpond to encourage comfortable conditions and optimum breeding. This time, she will be the sole designer, overseer and clerk of the works, and the new pond will be all the better for it. Surprisingly, she has found René most agreeable to her demands that he lay in piping to and from the pond, despite the extra work involved. She has been drinking, so I do not suggest that our estate manager would be most agreeable to any method of ensuring the fish in the new pond will be prolific in their breeding, and consequently justify a further issue of season tickets to the local angling community.

Other business conducted at the bar includes a discussion with the Jolly Boys' Club on making a start on Operation Desert Storm soon, and we seal the deal with another round of pastis before the mobile disco makes any further conversation impossible.

By one o'clock, we and our visitors are ready to give the villagers and their children best and retire from the action. Outside, the early morning air tastes as fresh as the lemon sorbet, and the rain has eased to a fine shower. We make our way home through the silent lanes to La Puce for a brief nightcap, and Jean-Marie confesses that his visit has been a revelation. Like the ten million Britons who visit his country each year, he had always honestly believed that real France was to be found only beyond the Loire valley. With England looming less than a hundred miles to the north, he had thought it impossible that such a truly Gallic culture could exist and flourish virtually in the shadow of the Isle of Wight. If it were not for the weather, food, drink, local customs, dress and language, he could almost be at home in Burgundy.

JayPay's Cream of Shrimp Soup

1. Make a white sauce, from butter,
flour and milk with seasoning (calva optional)
2. Sauté carrots, onion, celery and a lot of shrimps in butter
3. Add wine, thyme, bay leaf and seasoning and
simmer for one glass of wine
4. Strain the liquid into the white sauce, reserving the shrimps
5. Peel some of the shrimps and set aside
6. Crush the shells and the unpeeled shrimps,
add to soup and simmer for one cigarette
7. Strain soup, stir in cream and almost boil
8. Take from heat, add lots of butter, a dash of
calva and the peeled shrimps.

20 MAY

Having spent a surprisingly comfortable night in the mill while our guests use our bedroom in the farmhouse, we are awoken by the sound of birdsong and a tractor.

Looking through a convenient hole in the roof, I see that René and his lake specialist have arrived to break ground. We dress as they prepare themselves for the work with coffee and calva in our makeshift kitchen area, and I wonder exactly why René has actually turned up when he said he would. His lack of procrastination is becoming worrying...

After meeting a beaming and reassuringly competent-looking Mr Gilbert and his tractor, I watch the battered machine rumble into the water meadow and reflect on values on either side of the Channel. In England, Jean-Marie's Range Rover would be an enviable status symbol. Here a reliable tractor is far more desirable.

We assemble by the stakes marking out the perimeter of the new pond, and are joined by Jean-Marie and Kathy. They report on a blissful night in the farmhouse, and Kathy asks if we had come into the kitchen for some reason during the early hours. Donella and I exchange glances, but decide not to recount the legend of the Grey Lady in case our friends are considering visiting again. Since my dream – and after a night on her own in the farmhouse – my wife has become convinced that we do have a spectral presence at La Puce. Getting out of the bath and preparing for a peaceful night while I was on a solo visit to England, she was surprised to hear a series of bangs and crashes from the kitchen. Locking the bedroom door, she spent the night in some distress, and in the morning found that the kitchen door was firmly locked and bolted from the inside. Even René in search of beer from the fridge could hardly have got in and out of the house without trace, she concedes. If there is a fantôme on the premises, I feel sure that it is a benign presence, and just wish it would hurry up and lead us to the miller's gold before we run out of credit at Crédit Agricole.

Leaving Donella to enlarge on the dimensions, shape and style of the new pond with René and Mr Gilbert, I return to the farmhouse to telephone Robert Simon.

We met Robert and his wife Christiane soon after we bought our first wreck in Cotentin, and they have become valued friends. Apart from owning the largest building supply business in the region, they are both anglophiles, and we have mixed much business and pleasure with them over the years. We first met when I arrived in their yard and demanded the cheapest possible mass-produced materials for the job in hand, which was to tile the kitchen floor at La Puce. Robert seemed embarrassed at my directness, and suggested politely that I might perhaps consider using a far better quality, more durable, attractive and slightly more expensive tile, which would bring out the character of our ancient farmhouse. This, he said, was how a French customer would look at the project. To my shame, I continued with the English approach and pressed for quantity rather than quality. He then suggested we went to a nearby bar for a chat about how business was normally conducted on his side of the Channel. After three coffees with calva, he gave up trying to convert me, and suddenly remembered he had one pallet of tiles, which were seconds and a discontinued line, which could therefore be mine for half the normal price. Later, I found out that the handmade terracotta tiles were the best money could buy, and were a regular and popular item at the yard. Since then, I have tried to moderate my aggressive and very British attitude when looking for a bargain buy in France, but Robert and Christiane still continue to provide us with cost-price materials while finding excuses for their kindness.

After an exchange of pleasantries with Robert, I order yet another lorry load of stones for the track and mention the mayor's need of a big boulder for the Patton orchard. As ever, Robert comes up trumps. He tells me he just happens to have a special offer on chippings next month, and his lorries pass our door on their way to and from the quarry near Haye-du-Puits. If the driver stops off on his way to Cherbourg and we take potluck on the size of stones and the time they arrive, we will make a big saving. I tell him I do not believe the bit about the special offer, but will shamelessly take advantage of his indulgence. I send kisses to Christiane and go to investigate progress on the new pond.

In the water meadow, an altercation between René and my wife is in full flood. Donella tells me she has carefully described the size, depth and landscaping of the new pond, and stressed that she wants all of the earth piled on one side to make a raised bank where she can build another observation post. René insists that it will be better to heap the earth all around the perimeter of the pond as it is dug. Donella retorts that she is sure that it will be better for him and his spécialiste friend, as it is easier to dump the earth closest to where it has been excavated, and she does not want to have to use advanced climbing equipment to reach the water's edge at this pond. She is by now an old hand at lake building, and not to be trifled with.

Adjudicating, I say that, based on past experience, I have to admit my wife has some cause for concern. The last spécialiste employed by our estate manager had created the big pond by the simple principle of starting in the middle of the chosen site and working his way outwards. As soon as the shovel broke ground below the water level in the meadow, the hole in which he and his *tracteur* was sitting began to fill. It was then a race against time and the incoming tide, with the machine becoming more and more bogged down as it churned up great mounds of earth and deposited increasingly wetter bucketfuls to the nearest point it could reach. After the job was finished and the driver had swum back to the bank, another tractor had to be employed to pull his out of the mire. The result that greeted us on our next visit looked like a particularly muddy day on a Somme battlefield in the rainy season. But, I hasten to remind her, when taken to task about the state of our formerly enchanting water meadow, René had merely shrugged and said that nature would take care of it. The grass would soon grow over the mud mountains, and all varieties of reeds and wild flowers would ring the pond, while the ankle-turning clods of earth would eventually be broken down by rain and occasional visits by grazing cattle. He was absolutely right, and a year on the big pond looks as if it has been there since before the mill was built.

Donella is still adamant. This time, being on site, she wants the new pond to be perfect, and exactly to her specifications.

René, smiling grimly, promises to carry out Donella's instructions to the letter. The earth from the excavation will be positioned exactly as my wife desires, down to the last kilo. A little disturbed at the ease of our victory, I suggest we leave our workers to get on with it, and return to the mill for the unveiling of my speciality luncheon.

~

The Normandy lettuce salad and scallops in cream and calva have proved a great success. René tried a few mouthfuls and grunted reluctant approval, while Mr Gilbert had seconds and Jean-Marie said he was more than surprised with my performance at the oven. He, obviously like me, is not a chef, and there were some areas ripe for considered criticism were he not a guest at our table. But all in all, it was good... especially for an Englishman.

Cotentin Scallops in White Sauce and Calva

1. Take a lot of scallops from their shells and
remove the nasty bits
2. Test the calva;
3. Slice some mushrooms
4. Peel some onions and garlic. Chop the onions,
crush the garlic (NB with a fork)
5. Melt a lot of butter in a pan and add the scallops
6. After again testing, pour some calva into
the pan and set it alight
7. Add the onion and cook for one glass of
wine (my rate of consumption)

8. Dust with flour, stir and add some dry white wine
9. Add garlic (leaving out the fork), cinnamon,
clove, nutmeg and pepper
10. Fry the mushrooms in another pan and add to the scallops
11. Mix crème fraîche with an egg yolk and pour over
12. Stir for another glass of wine (do not boil).

Normandy Lettuce

1. Test some cider
2. Mix some with vinegar and crème fraîche. Season
3. Add lettuce
4. That's it.

As our guests are booked on the 5PM ferry from Cherbourg, we are in good time to drop in for a farewell drink at the Bar Ghislaine. I take an afternoon's worth of bottled beer to where René and Mr Gilbert seem to be progressing well and following Donella's directions implicitly. As I leave, René asks me if I am really sure that I want all the earth on one side of the pond, and, fortified with self-confidence by the reception of my speciality meal, I stand firm.

It is approaching four o'clock, and the Bar Ghislaine is heaving. Following tradition, virtually all the male attendees at the soirée choucroute have decided to take the day off and gather for hair of the dog. JayPay is deservedly the centre of attention, and receiving tribute to his performance in the form of unstinted praise and pastis in equal proportion. Our visitors are also enjoying themselves.

Proving popular with the Jolly Boys, Kathy is being schooled in some interesting patois phrases and expressions. When we arrived at the bar, she had refused any strong drinks for herself or her husband, and reminded him constantly of the need to allow good time for the journey to Cherbourg. Since Old Pierrot slipped a large goutte in her coffee, she has become much less concerned with the hour, and has already invited the entire Jolly Boys' Club to stay at her Southsea home later this year.

~

It is twenty minutes to five, and our guests have just left. Both seem confident that they will arrive on time for the ferry. Off season, departure times are elastic, but I think they are being optimistic, as even in Jean-Marie's Range Rover it is a good half-hour to Cherbourg, unless he is planning to go cross-country. However, they seemed unconcerned, and say they will return to continue the party if they miss the boat. Having waved them off, we decide to return to La Puce and the water meadow to check progress on the new lake.

Though yet empty, the pond looks perfect. Obviously of an artistic temperament, Mr Gilbert has brought Donella's vision to life. Naturally shaped and curving gently around the perimeter, the level falls steadily from the bank to a depth of precisely one metre at the centre, and all of the excavated earth is neatly piled at one end. Mr Gilbert has even used his giant bucket to tamp down the mound, which will soon provide an elevated picnic and observation area. The pipe which will be taking the overflow water to the millpond is in place and buried, and the trench from the river is near to completion. An empty-bottle count shows that René has been working at optimum rate, and he is about to bury the plastic piping which will draw fresh and constantly running water from the Lude. As he explains, the trick is to position the end of the pipe a few centimetres above the level of the river, then slope it steadily down towards its entry point into the pond. Finally, he will use one of the marble slabs to create a barrier downstream.

Unlike our plastic sandbags, his *gros barrage* will cause the water level to rise, enter the pipe and feed the pond. A moveable plastic bend fitted on the entry end of the pipe will control the flow, and the cunningly placed overflow pipe will keep the level in our new pond at precisely the desired height. Our only problem will arise from my wife's insistence that we pile all the earth on the far side of his otherwise impeccable creation. Apart from his unspecified prediction of impending disaster, all seems well, but to show off my engineering background I question him closely about the mechanical equations he will use to ensure the correct slope of the entry pipe from river to pond. Would it not be best to borrow a theodolite, hammer in some levelling pegs or at least fetch the spirit level and a ball of string? With a sigh, he pushes me out of the way, then opens and empties a bottle of beer in his usual efficient manner. Re-filling it from the river, he pours water into the pipe. Obeying nature's prime directive, it runs downhill and into the empty pond. The angle of slope is clearly correct.

I humbly open another bottle of beer, hand it to him and slink away.

~

Dusk is falling, and I am sitting beside our new pond. Just as René had predicted, the barrier has caused the river level to rise, and water is gurgling merrily through the pipe. Already, we have a foot of water, and Donella is contentedly splashing around in her waders, positioning tubs of plants and reeds transplanted from the big pond. René and Mr Gilbert have roared off on the tractor to catch up with festivities at the Bar Ghislaine, and peace has descended upon La Puce. Even better, nature is already taking a hand in stocking our new pond. A regatta of water boatmen have taken up residence and are sculling happily about on the surface as tiny mayflies practise touchdowns on the gently swaying tops of the water plants. A distant series of croaks tell us that word is spreading about a new and much more satisfactory display arena for Triple Salco and his troupe, and Donella is considering transferring at least a generation of poissons rouges to their new home.

It seems that news of a new habitat has also reached other sections of our countryside community. While the long Normandy twilight deepens, we hear a series of unfamiliar birdcalls, in particular the harsh and, to us, perplexing cry of a herring gull. It is not unknown for seabirds to come inland, especially when a plough or digger has been at work on the land, but we are twenty miles from the nearest coastline, and gulls are rare visitors indeed to our neck of the woods. Donella is at a delicate stage with a flag iris, so I am sent to investigate. On the ridge of the feed store alongside the grotto, I find a single starling is giving a perfect imitation of a gull's jagged screech. Over the next ten minutes, this Rory Bremner of the bird world runs through his repertoire of impressions until the arrival of our pet feral cat sends it ducking and diving away in search of a safer perch.

At the pond, Donella is extremely sceptical of my claim, and asks if I have been at the goat's cheese again. But I know what I saw and heard, even if it must remain yet another unexplained phenomenon of the magical and mysterious Cotentin.

21 MAY

The fish man arrives early to catch us on the hop, and we hide in the bathroom as he prowls around the farmhouse. In the absence of shopping centres in the depths of the countryside, virtually everything can be bought from the mobile vans, which regularly visit each village, hamlet and isolated household. There are weekly vans offering everything from charcuterie to the latest video recordings, and a three-piece suite and complete wardrobe of clothes may be had from the back of a removal lorry which fights its way down the narrow tracks of the hinterland each Thursday.

For all these convenience goods, prices are considerably higher than at the supermarkets and stores, but we try to patronise mobile salesmen whenever we can to help keep the system alive. Sometimes, though, they can be over-enthusiastic when it comes to closing a sale, and we were netted by the fish man during our first working visit to La Puce. Having discovered that the place was now owned by an English couple who found it hard to say '*non*' and didn't even know how to order any quantity less than one kilo, he became almost as regular a caller as the mayor. As we seemed always to be at the end of his run, he would take the opportunity of clearing his stocks by pressing vast and expensive amounts of mussels, oysters and fairly lively crabs into our reluctant hands, always with the injunction that they must be prepared, cooked and eaten at once. Finally, too embarrassed to make any more excuses about eating out that night, and unable to claim that we were just dashing off to catch the boat for Portsmouth, we developed a complex hide and seek routine to avoid his high-pressure sales pitch. He knows we are there when our car is outside, and we suspect he knows we know he is there and are avoiding him. At first, I would remove the striker from the gatepost ship's bell used to summon us from the fields, but he failed to get the message, and began seeking us out in the copse, water meadow or even the loft of the mill cottage. Nowadays we simply go to earth wherever we are at the time. His persistence has paid little dividend of late, but we believe he is actually enjoying the game as much as us.

～

It is just as well that my wife did not stock the pond last evening, as it is completely empty. Frogs, water boatmen and mayfly have moved back to their former lodgings, and the pots of reeds and other water plants sit isolated on the dry bottom of the pond like lonely cacti in a desert landscape.

Closer inspection shows that René's tombstone barrier has been toppled by the flow of the Lude, and the entry pipe is high and dry. Of more import is that the water already in the pond has drained completely away. Walking around the perimeter, we discover where it has moved to. The low bank where the pipe from the river is buried is now a bog. I raise René at his caravan and demand an explanation. He points out that, in some places, the land around the pond is actually lower than its bed. It has been a comparatively dry period, the ground is always thirsty, and water will always find the most convenient gathering point. This is why he wanted to surround the pond with a retaining ramp of sodden earth. We, of course, knew better. But there is no cause for concern, as he will replace the barrier later that day, and once the surrounding earth has soaked up enough water, the pond will fill and all will be well. Perhaps. We can of course hire Mr Gilbert to return and move the banking earth to where they both said it should be in the first place.

We sit and look at our expensive hole in the ground and the morass alongside it. Donella makes the best of it by considering its nurture as a natural marsh area, with a bridge to allow us to reach the caravan and big pond. I make a mental note to phone Mr Gilbert when we return in June after our next raiding trip across the Channel.

ELEVEN

Moving Mountains

2 JUNE

An uneventful crossing, except for an encounter with a travelling tarot-card reader and clairvoyant. We meet as she is taking lunch in the cafeteria, and, as business is slow, Donella is offered a special discount sitting. We discuss the reading afterwards, and my wife says she was very accurate. Mystic Margaret divined instantly that Donella is an animal lover with a strong and durable personality, who has suffered many years of having to cope with someone with a difficult and demanding nature. I point out that my wife spent the whole of lunch telling the woman about her menagerie at La Puce, but am quite impressed that she managed to detect the unseen presence of my mother-in-law. I am not impressed, however, with the prediction that my wife will shortly be going on a journey overseas, as the reading took place in mid-Channel.

After leaving the port, we stop off at Auchan, the giant hypermarket on the outskirts of Cherbourg. We are here to pick up the ingredients for the Desert Storm lunches, and my wife knows that the choice, preparation and presentation of each meal will be vital. The last time I saw her looking so apprehensive was when she encountered the bull in our mill garden.

As usual, Auchan is under siege, but we manage to find a parking spot within a kilometre of the main entrance. Donella inspects a shopping list the size of a toilet roll while I search for a ten-franc piece to release a shopping trolley from the thousands chained together outside the food hall. Some English visitors have discovered that a two-penny piece will fit into the slot on the handle, but as you only get your own money back when you re-chain the trolley, I don't see the point in cheating.

Inside, the aroma of freshly baked bread and newly expressed coffee mingles with the tang of reasonably fresh fish, garlic and Gallic perspiration. We pass a sprinkling of British buyers feverishly loading their trolleys with cases of wine selected solely by price, and I am reminded of a publican couple who visited us last year. Learning that Auchan regularly puts on ludicrously cheap special offers in the food hall as loss leaders, they stopped off on the return journey to the ferry to see if there were any suitable pub catering bargains. Noting a huge placard advertising the regional equivalent of Bayonne hams at around five pounds in English money, they loaded their trolley with a dozen. Having to fight their way through the checkout, hand over their credit card, load their goods and hurry to the ferry, it was far too late to return the hams when they realised that the price displayed had been per kilo rather than for the whole leg. What made it worse, was that there wasn't much call in their style of pub for the rather acquired taste of raw, smoke-cured meat, and they got constant complaints from the darts team that the stuff in their sandwiches tasted funny and was definitely going off.

~

At La Puce, we discover that summer has been hard at work in our absence. One of the great pleasures of our fleeting monthly visits in the past was the way the progress of the year would be so colourfully registered on our arrival. We would leave behind a white carpet of snowdrops in January, and return in February to a golden panorama of primroses. The following month, we would be met by daffodils and butterburs, with their bushy pink heads nodding discreet welcome. In April, we would find cuckoopint and early purple orchids waiting patiently alongside the cart track, and then a mass of bluebells and goosegrass would invade the copse to signal the end of spring and the approach of summer.

Today, we stop to enjoy the white clusters of elderflower and the tall foxgloves guarding the entrance to the track, where overhanging branches of beech, hazel, birch and sweet chestnut have been woven together by tendrils of honeysuckle to form a snugly arched progress down to our secret cottage. It is very good to be home again.

Outside the mill, we unload the three-piece suite, bed and dining table and I apologise yet again to Victor, our Volvo, reassuring him this should be his last really major transport operation. If all goes well with Desert Storm and the finishing touches to the restoration, we shall move into the mill later this month. Funds in our foreign reserves are at an all-time low, and the farmhouse must be let soon.

Since putting the farmhouse up for rent with an English agent, we have had some interesting replies and proposals. One middle-aged couple wanted to move in and take over the fields to keep goats and pay us in hand-woven mohair jackets. Another potential tenant with a ponytail and white BMW dropped in to suggest it could be profitable for both of us if he set up a cannabis-plant production factory so near to the ferry port. If asked, we could tell any visitors that blanched rhubarb was being raised under the black painted glass, and he would take charge of all growing, harvesting and transport arrangements. As Donella said, even the French police would know the difference between marijuana and rhubarb.

~

At the far end of the water meadow, the grass has turned bright yellow. Across the two acres, there must be ten thousand flag irises bobbing in the breeze. The land here is too wet for the mayor to regularly graze his cattle, and the meadow has remained virtually untouched for centuries, so the tall and elegant water-loving plants have taken over. Robert Simon has told us that flag irises are the model for the national emblem of France, originally adopted by Clovis, a fifth-century king of the Franks, but I am more excited about their commercial prospects as I start a head count. I have seen them in our local garden centre in the UK, where a small pot is more than a fiver.

I have reached a mental profit of almost a thousand pounds, allowing for packing, shipping and trade prices when Donella summons me to the small pond. It is still empty, and grass is already growing on the bed. My wife points out that if René does not do something about the tombstone barrier, we will soon have the most expensive dent in the ground in France. I consider reminding her whose idea it was to leave areas of the bank lower than the water level in this part of the field. Instead I come up with a plan to keep her mollified until I can have strong words with René. Fetching the long hose from the garden shed, I connect it up and turn on. Water begins to flow into the pond again, and my wife is content.

While the pond fills, I search the local centres of entertainment for our estate manager, and eventually spot his mobylette and distinctive American tank commander's helmet outside a bar in the hamlet of Valdecie. As ever, the Bar Pétanque is in the sole charge of Madame Françoise, a young widow whose husband died a few years ago. To help support her struggle to keep the business going, most of the local men visit the bar from time to time, but I see that René is alone in a corner, his glass of wine untouched. It is the first time I have seen him cry.

Madame Françoise quietly explains that it is the anniversary of the death of Papa Ribet, who now sleeps in the church-yard across the road. René comes here every year to explain how it goes for Mr Ribet's only son, and he has been ashamed to tell his father that he has lost his home and his wife, and now lives in a caravan. I decide that a discussion with René about the barrier is of minor significance, and leave him alone with his grief.

Pulling up at the mill cottage, I see an unfamiliar car parked by the sand mountain. It is a white Peugeot with leopardskin seats and at least three CB radio aerials. All these accessories predict a high moustache rating for the driver.

Inside, I am introduced to Hubert, who not only teaches English at a local school, but also speaks the language, which he is demonstrating in what appears to be an intimate *tête-à-tête* with my wife. I also note that his tightly fitting shirt is open almost to the waist, that it strains across his ample paunch, and that gold glitters among the thick matted hairs on his chest. Moreover, his carefully waxed moustache is bigger even than Freddo's. Judging from the bottle beside him, Hubert is on at least his second large malt whisky, and he is sitting in my armchair. He stands so that we may shake hands and measure each other up. I am pleased to see that though he is younger, I am an inch or two taller, and my belly is considerably bigger, which means a great deal in local terms of prestige.

During our somewhat stilted conversation, Hubert explains that he lives in the Val de Néhou, which is an isolat-ed and striking area of marshland outside the village, and has stopped by as he heard that we are losing fish to local predators. René's name is mentioned frequently, and my wife's expression tells me that I can no longer continue the deception that Trevor is only one member of a thriving trout colony. Hubert goes on to say that he has a friend who is a keen fisherman and likes to catch *gardon* purely for the sport. They are very difficult to catch, and the poorest family will not eat them as they are small and full of bones, so they would make ideal inhabitants of our pond. If we wish, Hubert can also ask his friend to provide a large and voracious *brochet*, which will keep the pond clean and under control. He is obviously not aware that the big pond is the Cray manor.

Making a mental note to look up both fish in the dictionary later, I thank him for his kind offer, and ask what the price will be. The quiver rate of his moustache points tells me he is offended, and he says that the fish would be a gift. His friend the fisherman, however, is quite fond of whisky. After looking sadly at the bottom of his empty glass for a long moment, our new friend shakes my hand, appears to think about breaking strict local etiquette and kissing my wife on the first meeting, then roars off, slithering up the track with the car windows open and Johnny Halliday singing 'Le Jailhouse Rocher' at full blast.

As the prickles on the back of my neck subside, I remark how short he was, and that he seemed to have been making himself at home with my whisky and chair. My wife tells me not to be so silly, that he was being extremely helpful, and that she found him quite charming. I go to check on the water level in the new pond, and consider growing a real moustache.

~

Though the hose has been going for a couple of hours, the bottom of the pond is barely wet. As I consider connecting up another hose, I am called away by the sound of a lorry coming down the track. Unless it is yet another load of sand, our latest batch of shingle has arrived.

Looking at the mountain of stone on the back of the bright yellow Brument-Clot company lorry, I see that Robert has been his usual generous self. Fortunately, the vehicle has a tipping device, so I ask Denis the driver if it is possible to drive slowly back up the track, raising the tipper and shedding shingle as he goes. That way, we will just have to spread it around a bit rather than having to make countless wheelbarrow trips to and from a pile that would almost match the sand mountain. I realise that this will take a considerable degree of skill, but Denis is Robert's best driver.

Rising to the challenge, Denis makes a twenty-point turn outside the mill, and sets off back up the track as I walk behind to direct operations. Immediately, I see that the slope of the track means that instead of a steady flow, an avalanche of shingle rushes furiously out of the open tailgate every time Denis operates the tilting device. Also, each time the front of the tipper rises above the level of the lorry cab, it comes into conflict with the tunnel of overhanging foliage. Before long, though the bottom half of the track is dotted with heaps of shingle as roughly per plan, the front of the lorry has become firmly wedged under a particularly strong oak branch. Denis explains that if he continues, either the tilting mechanism will shear, or we will lose a tree. I climb onto the cab with a completely unsuitable junior hacksaw, while Donella and Denis begin attacking the shingle piles. As my wife points out, it would have been a good idea to move our car up the track before unloading, as we are now cut off from civilisation until all twelve heaps have been levelled off and the lorry freed.

A couple of hours later, we have made a reasonable job of spreading the shingle unevenly along the bottom half of the track. It is six inches deep from the turning circle outside the mill up to the lorry's tailgate, but there is not a new stone beyond, as we cannot force the wheelbarrow between the banks of the track and the sides of the truck. In spite of his fatigue, Denis enthusiastically suggests that he return to the quarry for another load, which he can discharge on to the top half of the track from the road. That way it will cascade down and make up the level. He graciously accepts a coffee and a small advance on his tip, while we go for another inspection of progress at the small pond.

The bottom now appears to be fairly damp, and I do some quick calculations based on a distant maths exam involving the time taken to fill a bath with the hot and cold taps running at different rates of flow. To the untrained eye, it appears the pond is about the size of 200 baths, and a timing experiment with a pint glass and the hose followed by some long division and multiplication sums indicates that the water should be at a satisfactory level by the day after tomorrow.

Denis now appears at my shoulder, whistles loudly, does some brisk ooh-la-lahing after looking at the hose and the work it has to do, then asks if we realise that our water is metered at the road and charged for by the litre. I pretend to know this, and privately decide to cut down on baths over the coming year. Further bad news from Denis is that his lorry will not move. The obstructing branches of the oak have been removed, but there now seems to be some sort of mechanical fault. We return to the scene and scramble underneath his truck to discover that two of the three nuts and bolts holding the drive shaft coupling together have shaken loose in the struggle with the oak tree. They will now be buried somewhere under twelve tons of pea shingle. We retire to the toolshed to see if we can find some temporary replacements.

Some time later, and we are to be found lying under the lorry in a mélange of mud, shingle and tree branches. I am holding a nut fast with a pair of electrical pliers, while Denis is tightening the last bolt with an oversized spanner, the gap made up with a ten-franc piece. Eventually, as the blood from our skinned knuckles mixes with engine oil, grease and leaf mulch, the job is completed, and too exhausted to struggle from beneath the truck, we stay where we are and share a cigarette. Denis tells me that his real job is as a helicopter technician, and I tell him all about our former life across the Channel.

By now, our mutual adversity has meant we have advanced to pet-name terms. He is Den-den, and I explain that, to the villagers I am George-o, though within the Jolly Boys' Club I have the honour of being known as Mr Beerbelly. I now attempt to explain the origins and development of the Anglo-Saxon nickname, and run through a selection of common modern diminutives in England such as Billy, Chas, Daz and Shaz. To further illustrate the differences and difficulties that can be encountered by the foreign visitor, I tell Den-den about an artist friend called Conrad Barnes who visited us last year. When I invited him over to paint the restored farmhouse, he took it as a request for a tasteful watercolour, but was just as happy when we asked him to apply three coats of traditional powdered whitewash to the outer walls. In the Café de Paris to celebrate the end of his commission, the conversation had abruptly stopped when I had called his pet name across the bar. Later, Freddo had taken me aside to say that though the epithet was in fairly common usage in the market place, it was not a good idea to call my friend 'Con' in more refined circles, as it was the equivalent of comparing him with a vagina, only more so. I already knew that *connerie* meant a cock-up, so should have guessed that *con* would not be too far away in the slang vocabulary.

Prolonging our moment of quiet companionship, Donella passes us coffee as we lie beneath the lorry and exchange anecdotes and ambitions. As we talk, our undernourished squirrel stops by to see what is going on, and I notice what looks like an early ox-eye daisy growing from the bank. A relatively short time ago, I would not have imagined that life would find me stretched out beneath a lorry halfway up a mill track in Normandy exchanging intimacies with a former helicopter mechanic. All things considered, I would much rather be exactly where I am than anywhere on the M25.

Much later, and Denis has delivered his second load and gone, and another twelve tons of shingle have been spread evenly across the top half of the track. To save on water rates, I have bathed in the new pond, which has already reached ankle height. The water boatmen have taken up residence again, along with some curious ball-shaped creatures, which float on the surface for a moment, then drop like a depth charge into the comparative deeps. I have looked in the dictionary and found that the fish Hubert's friend is bringing are roach. I also now know that a *brochet-de-mer* is a barracuda, but reassure my wife that the fresh-water version is merely a pike. Nevertheless, she says we will refuse Hubert's kind offer of the predator king of the river, unless I am sure it will really be safe from René's customers, and particularly the Cray gang.

Far above, our kestrel is making his teatime rounds. He arrives each day in the morning and afternoon, and follows the same routine. Selecting a suitable part of the terrain, he will hover till spotting a target, then drop like a stone to pick up his takeaway. Birds of prey flourish in this area, and seem to be much respected for their hunting skills by those who would shoot a harmless starling without a second thought. René says that our regular visitor is not a kestrel but a *buse* or buzzard, and will often stop work to watch it go about its business. He seems to admire its freedom and dignity, and is obviously pleased when it strikes and finds a victim.

3 JUNE

It is René's birthday. We discuss a suitable present, and I suggest the two bottles of malt scotch and 400 English cig-arettes bought on our recent crossing. My wife says it seems rather unkind to speed him to an even earlier grave with such a gift. Besides, she points out, as René drinks to excess every other day of the year, he might want to have an inverse birthday celebration by staying sober for twenty-four con-secutive hours.

I stand firm and explain that, comparing the strength of the English cigarettes and the purity of the scotch with what our estate manager and the rest of the locals normally drink and smoke, our gifts could be classified as health products in Cotentin.

5 JUNE

I return from an early morning visit to the big pond to report on two amazing developments. We have a corn circle, and our frog colony is speaking patois.

Pressed for details, I explain that an almost perfectly round circle of flattened grass has appeared in the water meadow behind the caravan. It is roughly twelve feet across, and the surrounding grass is standing upright at its normal knee height.

Displaying her usual cynicism with regard to all matters supernatural, my wife disputes a visit by a miniature alien spacecraft, but says that foxes are known to create a flattened circle for cover when resting in long grass. When I remind her that, thanks to the local shooting clubs, foxes are slightly rarer than aliens in this region, she becomes even more excited at the prospect of her alleged badger tenants stopping for a picnic in the reservoir field.

When asked about the other phenomenon, I tell her of the extraordinary spectacle I have just witnessed. Arriving at the big pond, I came upon hundreds of lemon-yellow frogs actually playing leapfrog through the rushes at the water's edge. What's more, as they jumped over each other, rather than making their usual croaks, they were all shouting 'wheah', which, as every pretentious Briton with a home in France will tell you as he or she uses the word, is national patois for 'yeah'.

Perhaps, I suggest, this eccentric behaviour is the result of abduction and examination by my aliens, who, landing in the depth of night, have mistaken our frogs for the dominant inhabitants of this part of the world.

Perhaps, my wife suggests as if to a particularly unintelligent plank, the frogs are playing leapfrog because it's what they do at this time of year, and their excited cries are merely their mating song.

After consulting our wildlife library, I grudgingly concede that she may be right. However, I shall make a point of buying all the local papers tomorrow to see if there are any reports of other mysterious happenings in the neighbourhood.

7 JUNE

My alien-visitation theory has been destroyed. Making a closer inspection this morning, I found at least twenty cigarette ends in the centre of the corn circle, and an empty bottle of René's birthday scotch in the long grass at the perimeter. Faced with such evidence, I can only conclude that our estate manager went for a midnight walk with his gifts, returned to the wrong caravan, then spent some time walking round in circles before giving up and settling down for the night exactly where he was.

12 JUNE

A red-letter day. Our estate manager calls to announce I may from this day forward call him by his pet name, which is Néné. We may also now move on from *vous* to *tu* when addressing each other. It is the first time I have heard René's pet name, as nobody in the village appears to use it. He tells me that this is because they are not allowed to, but his father called him Néné. I tell him I am proud to be in such company, and that he should feel free at all times to call me Mr Beerbelly. Néné says nothing about extending these privileges to Donella, so I think she must still be on trial.

13 JUNE

Néné says he has found us a long-term tenant for the farmhouse. He has been approached by a most respectable friend currently living in a nearby village who has urgent need of new accommodation for himself and family of nine. The man is a good worker, and is free to tend the land part-time under our estate manager's careful supervision. He will not require wages, but will expect to occupy the farmhouse within the normal tied cottage arrangements which ensure free lifetime tenure. A further bonus is that our telephone will not be used as the family knows no other customers of France Télécom, and the heating and hot-water fuel bill should be low as they are a hardy bunch and do not bathe obsessively. I promise to discuss the proposition with my wife, and briefly do. Following her instructions to the letter, I return to his mobile home and politely but firmly reject my friend's proposal. Having heard my decision, I notice he returns to the 'vous' usage when we say our farewells. I assume it will also be back to René now too.

On arrival at the farmhouse, I find my wife thumbing through the telephone numbers of all the English settlers in the area so that she can determine who has recently split with whom, and will therefore be looking for a reasonably priced roof above their heads.

15 JUNE

John and Solange Chevalier appear at the kitchen door to say they have just moved their steers into the clearing in the scrubland alongside the copse. I immediately suspect a more formal reason for the visit, as both are in their Sunday-best clothes. When John accepts a small glass of whisky, I am even more suspicious. After a long conversation about the condition of the fields, hedges and gates and his fond memories of La Puce over the past thirty years, my friend announces that he has an important announcement to make. He is to retire this Christmas, after almost sixty-five years at his farm in Le Hequet. He and Solange will take a small town cottage next to the fire station in St Sauveur, and have just bought a new car to visit all the places they have never had the time and freedom to see.

It will be a wrench to leave the home where their children grew up, but it is compulsory to retire from farming at his age. Their son has a good job in the town and no wish to continue in the family tradition, so the rented farmhouse must go to someone else. He will miss La Puce and will, if I wish, help find a new tenant who will take good care of the land. He will be happy to have more free time, but will miss the feel of the earth through his hands and under his feet. I ask them to wait for a moment and go upstairs to my study. There, I take a piece of my headed notepaper, write upon it and add a first-class stamp. Returning to the kitchen, I ask them both to sign it.

The document, I explain, negates our former arrangements and is a contract for life, giving them full, free and exclusive use of the two main fields. John may wish to start a small orchard like Mr Margot over the road, or to grow some fine vegetables. He may prefer just to know that the land is there if and when he wishes to use it. I would be honoured, I say, if he will visit us often, and perhaps teach me how to live with and use the land one thousandth as well as he has for the past decades. He looks at the paper for a long moment, then gruffly clears his throat and rubs a hand across his eyes. For all the difficulties in language we have faced over the past years, we are now both, I think, in total accord.

I stand and wave as John carefully pulls out of the yard and heads off in the direction of Le Hequet, then go back to pour myself a large scotch. The mayor and his wife have been a constant and important factor in our lives since we bought La Puce, and I find the thought of their leaving unsettling. Perhaps I should be more like the people of the area, and accept life, death and change as an inevitable part of nature.

20 JUNE

Our newly shingled track is put to good use as the Jolly Boys' Club arrives in and on a motley collection of vehicles, comprising two mobylettes, Marcel Bernard's ancient Renault and a tractor with roof light flashing and klaxon hooting. Bringing up the rear is Michel, briefcase clasped under one arm and a huge shovel strapped to his crossbar. My friends are obviously in a festive mood and intend to make a day of it. We gather in the mill for a quick coffee and calva before beginning our assault on the sand mountain, and Michel takes the opportunity to pass round previously unreleased photographs of himself in various waiting rooms, hospital beds and operating theatres. As we admire a medical magazine picture of our friend sitting with a puzzled-looking man in a white coat, Marcel begins to unload a selection of period wheelbarrows, spades and shovels, and the debate begins as to who shall have which. My tiny Spear and Jackson edge cutter is the usual source of ribald remarks due to its small surface area, and René asks yet again if it is only the women who dig the gardens in England.

Before we get into another lengthy discussion on comparative techniques and shifting rates, I lead the way to the foot of the mountain we must move and explain my plan. Basically, we have around thirty tons of gritty sand outside the mill, and a pit more than eight feet deep between the renovated part of the mill and the original gable wall. If we move one to the other, the unsightly hole will vanish. When the sand has settled, I will lay slabs, repoint the remains of the side walls and the massive gable, and create a patio area. Over the coming months and years we will build a stone archway where part of the side wall has fallen down, and fit a heavy, much-studded oak door with huge hinges contrived to creak satisfyingly each time we enter our peaceful retreat. In the centre of the patio, we will build a perfectly proportioned ornamental fishpond, with water pumped to and from the millstream, and illuminated by an underwater spotlight. Strings of tasteful fairy lights will be draped across the old gable-end, and giant earthenware pots will line the restored walls. When all is done, we shall have a secret garden of order and tranquillity, contrasting satisfyingly with the natural wilderness all around. But every journey, I remind them, starts with but a single step. And that step awaits us now. Before we take it, I thank all my friends for their efforts in the long days ahead as they labour so hard to help Madame Donella and I make our dream a reality.

My eloquent description is met with a smattering of applause, a shuffling of feet and a long silence as my friends consider the amount of work and expense involved in building a formal and useless garden in the middle of thousands of hectares of traditional farming land. They are too polite to comment, except for René, who loudly queries the point and purpose of fitting a gate when there is not even a roof to deter the most incompetent burglars. He also questions the sanity of buying and installing a water pump when we will have several thousand litres an hour cascading into the millpond a few metres away as soon as he has borrowed Mr Pigeon's source. He falls silent, however, when Donella brings up the subject of the tombstone barrier he has yet to fix, and turns his attention to organising the workforce into suitable teams and shift patterns.

～

In spite of recent experiences, I am still amazed at the way my friends deal with a challenge which would daunt a gang of much younger and fitter Irish groundworkers. Economical with movement and seemingly casual in their steady attack on the sand monster, these men with a combined age of several centuries fill a wheelbarrow to overflowing with no more than a dozen swings of the shovel, and take it in turns to push it along a scaffolding plank and into the pit. They rest often to straighten backs, spit on hands and mock their companions' efforts, but then return to the task with renewed vigour. In barely an hour, they have made a noticeable impression on the sand pile, and have established an easy rhythm. At this rate, we may even complete the operation before darkness falls. We have been lucky with the weather as the morning sun is warm upon our backs, and René is actually threatening to take one of his coats off.

I am ferrying armfuls of cold beer from the feedbag larder in the river, and Donella is preparing lunch in the mill as an old Citroën van with a corrugated tin roof rattles down the track. The inhabitants step out, and an orgy of hand-shaking, cigarette lighting and bantering commences. Hubert has arrived with Jackie the fisherman, and we gather round the back of the van to unload a dozen sloshing dustbins. Hubert explains that his friend has been out early, and the bins are full of roach and other small fish which will be at home in our ponds, with no fear of human predators. He looks deliberately at our estate manager as he says this, and I begin to believe I may have misjudged him and his motives on our first meeting.

Our fleet of wheelbarrows are taken out of service, loaded with the bins and the long trek to the big pond begins. In a touching gesture, Hubert invites Donella to launch her replacement stock into the waters, and I notice how he thoughtfully steadies her with a thick arm around her waist as she leans out from the bank and releases the silvery cascades. Recovering from the shock, the fish gather in a precise formation and dart off to investigate their new home. Donella announces that luncheon is ready, and we retire to dine outside the mill.

~

The long lunch has gone even better than my wife had dared hope. Except for René, who is rarely seen to eat in public and is rumoured by his critics to live almost entirely on alcohol, all our guests have praised the excellence of the *repas d'affaires*. Donella has excelled herself, especially with the main course, which was young pigeons in farm cider. Marcel is particularly pleased that she has used his cider in the ingredients, though René makes a formal complaint about our incessant waste of JayPay's best calva on cooking, when Mr Janne's newest bottling would have served adequately. The case of burgundy left by Jean-Marie has been declared first rate. I have presented Jackie with a bottle of twelve-year-old malt in appreciation of his gift, and he has insisted that it is immediately opened and shared by the company. The extra-strength Somerset cider I have brought to the feast has been declared more than fit to drink, and the river larder is running low on bottled beer. Hubert has contributed a brace of his precious bottles of special reserve calva, and Marcel is moved to admit that it almost matches his best vintage for smoothness.

As we bask in the early afternoon sun, I sense that we are being watched, and Donella points to where our skinny squirrel is looking enviously from a sycamore tree by the entrance to the copse. The remains of our meal has also attracted the attention of the bird community, who become ever bolder as they dart to pick up morsels of baguette, Mrs East's homemade Normandy apple tart and Safeway's extra-fruity Dundee cake. I look at my watch and the sand mountain, and decide that we have done enough for the day; it would be wrong to disturb the moment and break the mood of quiet contentment.

Jackie, however, has other ideas. The talk has turned to past feats of labour, and he is stung by the Jolly Boys' consensus that the youngsters in the region don't know the meaning of hard work. Having finished off the malt whisky, he claims that he and Hubert can shift as much sand in three hours as the JBC has achieved in the whole morning. René is very happy for him to try, though Hubert seems none too pleased at having been volunteered without consultation. But the wager is struck, and the contest is on. With the senior members of the workforce making themselves comfortable around the pile and Michel as referee, the relative youngsters set to with barrow and spades.

Sharp comments on style, stamina and short barrow loads

fly as fast as Jackie's spade, and Hubert loses several buttons on his shirt as he strains to keep pace with his partner and push the monstrous loads up the sloping scaffold plank. Rather than slow down, the pace quickens as the moments pass, and as the deadline arrives, the tally of barrow loads is only narrowly in the veteran team's favour. Hubert blames the English wheelbarrow for its poor design, turning circle and overall manoeuvrability, but Jackie concedes defeat more graciously. Of one accord, the entire workforce now joins in a final blitzkrieg on the rapidly diminishing pile. We toil solidly for a long hour before I call a halt for coffee and cigarettes all round to get our breath back.

As we relax, another visitor arrives. The Travers family have owned the fields around La Puce since before the Terror, and there is talk locally of noble blood. This is not uncommon in France, especially in the case of an unmarried mother in the family tree after 1780. The theory goes that the hundreds of male aristos who escaped Madame Guillotine fled to remote parts of the country, changed their names but not their leisure pastime of impregnating local peasant girls. Ergo, any trace of illegitimacy at about the right time enables the descendant to lay claim to noble ancestry. A relative of my wife recently traced the maternal side of her family back more than two centuries and, to the delight of the village, found that Donella is distantly French, and that an ancestor in Guigamp had not been married on the birth of her son in 1792. The villagers are naturally disappointed that her aristocratic lineage has been marred by the Brittany connections, but some French blood is better than none.

Mr Travers is said to be a millionaire. His tractor and other important personal possessions are not the trappings of a wealthy man, though this factor, as in any rural area, could be evidence for or against the allegation. After reserved greetings all round and a perplexed frown as he obviously wonders why I and half the village are burying tons of perfectly good sand, we get down to business. He has come to tell me of a serious problem. One of my trees has fallen into one of his fields, and represents a great danger to his cattle.

Leaving the workforce to see off the remnants of the sand mountain, we go to investigate. Climbing the steep slope leading from the ford across the river up to where his elevated fields run alongside Hunters' Walk, I see that we have lost one of the giant beech trees lining the western boundary between La Puce and the rest of France. The ownership of these trees has always been a point of contention, as René explained when we first took possession of the property. They line a steep bank rising to Mr Travers' land, and the precise position of their sprawling and exposed roots determines to whom they belong. If they are wholly visible as far as the bottom of the bank, the particular tree under examination is mine. If the roots surface from more than halfway up the slope, they belong to my neighbour. If somewhere in-between, we each own a vertical half of the tree.

As far as I can make out, the law as it is understood and agreed locally is similar to the regulations regarding party walls in England ever since the Great Fire of London. Broadly, the owner may do what he likes with his side, providing it does not affect the integrity of the other side. Even Norman farmers have not found a way to cut a tree vertically down the middle and leave their neighbour's half flourishing, but there is a cunning device commonly employed by those seeking long-term firewood supplies. Leading me to a nearby field during an early lesson in *bocage* feud tactics, René had shown me where great slabs of wood were missing from the trunk of an otherwise healthy oak. The excuse had been to create a flat surface on which to staple a length of barbed wire marking the division of properties. In fact, said René, it was done to kill the tree. Eventually, the great oak would die from the massive wound and crash to the ground. The neighbour could then claim that it was a natural death and take his share of the wood.

Closely examining our fallen beech, I see that nature rather than malice is the guilty party. The core is rotten, and it has obviously succumbed to a recent southwesterly.

Removing his greasy cap and lowering his head as if paying his last respects to the deceased, Mr Travers declares himself greatly distressed by the fall. There is now a large gap in the bocage, he explains, and his cattle could force their way through and fall to their doom down my bank and into my river. Something must be done.

I accept responsibility but have by now learned a little about negotiations of this sort. I look resigned, walk about a bit and make a few heavy sighs. I will, I say, ask René to organise a tractor to tow the tree away in the morning. Then he will repair the gap with barbed wire. This will cost me a great deal of money, but I am willing to pay to avoid any bad feeling between us. The tree will, of course, provide me with firewood for the whole winter, but at quite a price. From his expression, I can see that my ploy is working.

Mr Travers puts his cap on and takes it off again for a while, and continues to regard the tree like a detective at the scene of a particularly messy murder. He then examines the corpse intently, kicks it, rips off a piece of bark and crumbles it in his fist. It is obviously, he says, very dead and will burn away in seconds. It will make for very expensive firewood. He has a better idea. If he asks his son to bring the tractor and drag the tree across the gap, it will serve as an adequate barrier. I will not be put to the great expense of employing René nor risk being sued when he doesn't fit the barbed wire for months and a cow falls to its death. Would this, *p'tet*, be a suitable solution to our mutual problem?

I consider the offer for the obligatory ten minutes and agree. We shake hands on the deal and I return to the mill, pleased at how well I handled the encounter. I don't remember ever seeing any cattle going in to that field, and they would have to be driven past the door of the mill to reach it, but nevertheless feel satisfied with the outcome. I have, after all, just taken on a rural Norman negotiator of Mr Travers undisputed class and come away with the shirt still on my back.

At the workplace, the sand pile has gone, and so has the hole in the ground. The team is celebrating quietly at the table in front of the mill, while Marcel fixes the sticky lock on our new front door, using a broken sickle blade as a screwdriver.

Once again I wonder at the contradictions in the Cotentinese character that the day's activities have so clearly exampled. Notoriously close with their money, they will use all their country wiles and ways to win an argument or preferably an extra few francs. But, when a friend has need of their help, they will labour all day for a meal and a few bottles of beer. In the countryside, as René often remarks when not pricing a job for us, time is cheap and good friends are valuable.

Desert-Storm Pigeons in Cider

1. Ask someone who knows how to dress and truss some formerly young pigeons
2. Brown them in some hot butter, then season and add thyme and bay
3. Pour some calva over, and set it on fire
4. Cover and cook for half an hour, then keep warm
5. Add farm cider to the meat juices and boil for half a cigarette
6. Add some more butter away from heat
7. Pour juice over pigeons and garnish with slices of baked cider apples.

Mrs East's Apple Tarte

1. Mix some yeast with warm milk
2. Add liquid to flour, melted butter, oil and salt
3. Rub together till workable, then leave
for two slow glasses of wine
4. Butter a tart tin and line with the pastry
5. Peel and thickly slice some apples, leaving
out the core and seeds
6. Mix more flour with ground almonds,
caster sugar, cinnamon and butter
7. Flavour with calva
8. Arrange the apple slices in the tin and
cover with the almond mixture
9. Bake for another two glasses of wine, and
serve with crème fraîche.

I JULY

Today is a big day, as we officially move into the mill cottage. It is Sunday, and we are to host a small soirée for the friends who have helped us complete the restoration. We have still to find a tenant, but we start out early for Bricquebec to pick up supplies for this evening's celebration.

The PMU betting shop is busy when we call in to see if we have won the Lottery. It still seems strange to see people drinking cold beer and pastis at bacon-and-eggs time, but we are adapting well.

Our next stop is the Café de Paris, where Freddo is enjoying the start to his most profitable and therefore favourite weekly session apart from market day. He interrupts a story about his latest hunting expedition to ask if I would like a few dozen trout for the soirée. He has been out with Pierrot. In the square outside, the usual couple of farmers haggle over another tatty ewe as it stares myopically from the back seat of an even more dishevelled saloon. Meanwhile, the town youths are performing their Sunday early morning ritual of screaming by on souped-up mobylettes for the entertainment of spectators at the tables surrounding the square.

At the bar, René and Mr Maurice are enjoying a Sunday outing with Bernard, Madame Ghislaine's partner. Otherwise handsome, he bears the constantly harassed frown of someone knowing he should not be enjoying himself, and that his partner will ensure he will pay the full price for his pleasure. I call for a round and check that my friends will be arriving in good order for our soirée. Along the bar, a large *gendarme* is already on his second bottle of Freddo's specially imported muscadet, and looks set in for the day.

I remark to our host that the policeman looks a little unsteady on his feet, but Freddo says it is all right, as he has his official motorcycle outside for the journey home. As usual, the talk concentrates on yesterday's sports results, whose car was seen outside whose house in the early hours, and who nearly won the National Lottery. It is very like a Sunday lunchtime session in any pub in Britain, only a lot earlier.

2 JULY

It is a little before three in the morning. We are sitting beside the new pond, which is full to the brim and holding its level now that the surrounding land is waterlogged. René has still not fixed the tombstone barrier, so we have no running water, but my wife is working on him. As I break out the tomato soup while trying to hold the torch steady with my teeth, she is tempting some newly domiciled roach with the remnants of the buffet from the party, which has only recently concluded. The legendary Cotentin wind has gone to bed, and the surface of the pond is as smooth and shiny as silk.

The soirée has been an unqualified success. Our guests did their duty and trooped around the mill, admiring the stained beams and whitewashed walls, horse brasses and giant bath. Most were obviously wondering why an apparently sane couple would spend so much time and effort on creating a home from what had been a cattle byre for the last fifty years, but were far too polite to ask. Luckily, nobody expressed familiarity with the stove, and Madame Christian the Goat has invited us to visit her for an intensive training course in its proper maintenance and use.

René has promised to fix the barrier later today, and find us a chimney pipe so that we can have a test run on the stove before the winter. Madame Ghislaine has presented us with a wall plate which roughly translates as 'Welcome to our home; it's not much, but it's ours. ' Marcel shyly presented a box of light bulbs from a past delivery, and Donella was deeply moved to see that he had painstakingly painted each one with coloured sheep marker to make fairy lights for our secret garden.

The highlight of the evening was the mayoral cutting of a ribbon across the door. John seemed in an unusually reflective mood all evening, and eventually took me to one side to say he will be retiring earlier than originally announced. He will leave his farm at the beginning of September. There seems no point in staying on till Christmas and the official retirement date, and he has much to do. Taking my hand, he thanked me for my friendship, and said he hoped that our business relationship has been to my satisfaction. With my permission, he would continue to honour his obligations to La Puce, and keep the hedges trimmed and the gates in good order. Perhaps, as we have already discussed, I would be kind enough to allow him to visit every week to continue our friendship. I reminded him of our contract, and promised there will never be another tenant in the top fields in his lifetime.

~

As we sit and watch the mist above the water swirl and dance in the torch beam, there is a flash of silver and a satisfied splash. All, apart from constant money worries, is good within our little world. The endless cycle of nature moves on, and our first proper summer at La Puce is approaching full bloom.

13 JULY

A stimulating and unusually interesting morning crossing, as we fell in with other serial French property restorers. Like us, visiting property owners all seem to be taking part in a competition to determine who can carry the most heavy and dangerously placed loads. Normally, Victor, our capacious Volvo estate, is clear winner, but today he was comparatively lightly burdened with a second-hand greenhouse, two dozen paving slabs and a selection of giant earthenware plant pots from the Philippines. They are shipped over by a taxi-driver friend who owns half a house in Manila, and spends his holidays in the jungle overseeing the manufacture of exotic pottery turned on old car wheels. The samples are destined for the yard at Brument-Clot, and if they sell we shall split the difference with Robert and Christiane Simon. Every centime we can make will help prolong our time in Cotentin.

On this crossing and in the dangerous load competition, we were hopelessly outclassed by a fellow traveller in a Lada camouflaged with more than two dozen stripped pine doors hung carelessly over the windows as well as balanced recklessly on the rackless roof. We struck up a conversation on the car deck, and learned he is a former policeman from the Home Counties who has hit upon a winning scheme to subsidise his pension and the upkeep of his house in Brittany.

Finding out to his cost that a new and bland lightweight interior door at his local *bricolage* cost around £100 and that nearly all French properties described as in some need of restoration don't have them, he now runs a booming export business. Every month, he scours the demolition sites and skips of affluent southern England, salvaging discarded doors and taking them to a dip and strip centre, from where they emerge interestingly distressed and free of their layers of gloss paint.

Our enterprising new friend then ships the doors over and sells them through his regional freesheet publication to other Britons at half the price of a standard and inferior French door. Business was so good, he confided, that next month he would be bringing over a complete vat and the necessary chemicals to set up operation in his back yard, with British couples coming from far and wide for strip'n'swap parties. Before parting, we added his contact details to our list, and retired to the bar to consider the value of stealing his idea for Normandy, sited at La Puce. Better yet, we could reverse the process, as half the solid-oak craftsman-built dining tables in our region are disguised beneath sheets of starburst plastic veneer and layers of greenhouse paint. Stripped and cleaned up, they would fetch a small fortune in any English antique shop.

In the bar, we fall into conversation with a number of own-ers, marked out by their weather-beaten faces and charac-terful working clothes. Normally, we expatriates studiously avoid each other on French soil, but the boat is always a good opportunity to exchange useful information and anec-dotes. As usual there is a classic *fosse septique* bore, and, before we can escape he whips out a folder and starts talk-ing us through his collection of snapshots of each step of the installation of his septic tank in the Charente. Thankfully, before getting into full flow, he is roundly trumped by a jolly couple who casually mention that, as their house was sited in the Auvergne, they had to use dynamite to blast through the volcanic crust and make a suitable hole for their tank.

The operation went precisely to plan, except that the blast blew all the windows out of the house next door, which belongs to their mayor. But there was no comeback, as it had been he who had set the charges. The explosion, they add, finally beating the bore into sullen submission, also disturbed a coven of hibernating whip snakes, which immediately went into a frenzy of precipitous mating.

The anecdotes now evolve naturally into a general discussion on the problems of sewage disposal, as virtually every owner will at some stage have to confront the issue. Experiences and tales told over the years have led me to suspect that a great many owners who fondly imagine that they have an efficient drainage system may have nothing but a very expensive hole in the ground. Our case seems typical, with the installation of the plastic tank taking place in our absence, and the only evidence of its existence being a lot of disturbed earth at the alleged site, plus the assurance of René that he had fitted the largest, most sophisticated and therefore costly tank available. So far, we have had no obvious problems, but each spring a crop of the most exotic and evil-smelling plants appear above the tank's alleged resting place. Donella looked them up in her Culpepper and thinks they may be stinkweeds, but they seem far too large and are, anyway, the wrong colour.

~

Arriving at Cherbourg, we make straight to La Puce and discover that we are landlords, and that the sand mountain is back.

René is bearded in his caravan, and tells us that he ordered the new load at a special seasonal discount, and there will be barely enough to construct the reinforced cement terrace outside the mill which we need to put a respectable distance between the building and the moles which tunnel in the front garden like crazed prison camp escapees. He will start work on the *terrasse* later that day, immediately after he has finally fixed the barrier. He also informs us somewhat resentfully that Madame Lynn and Charlie the dog have taken up residence in the farmhouse.

Until recently, Lynn Wooster and Graham Braye were our

nearest English neighbours, and had spent two years painstakingly restoring a large house just outside St Jacques-de-Néhou. Unfortunately, there has been a parting of the ways. The house is now in danger of being repossessed and Lynn has been left homeless. After arriving to employ his skills in treating and preserving ancient timber, Graham's business has failed, the debts have mounted, and he is now living elsewhere. It is a familiar but always tragic story, and one which haunts us every day.

The irrepressible Lynn and Charlie had been getting by ever since as agents for English owners in the area. For the past few months, she had been living a nomadic life, cutting grass, receiving and cleaning up after paying guests and generally giving absent owners peace of mind. As she was weary of living out of her car and we are now settled in the mill, Donella had come to an arrangement where Lynn will take over the farmhouse at a modest rent. All parties involved except René are happy with the arrangement, especially Charlie, who now has a ten-acre back garden.

Our estate manager seems to think that Lynn has been moved in to spy on him, and he does not get on with Charlie. I attempt to mend bridges by presenting him with his monthly bottle of whisky, and he unbends enough to offer me a drink and ask if I have heard the rumours about the mayor's retirement. Already, he says, there have been enquiries from local farmers about renting the fields at La Puce, and he is negotiating for the best price and terms. I explain that I have told the mayor that we will not be replacing him, but that I would like René to start thinking about stocking the remaining fields with our own animals. He shows immediate interest, and we sit overlooking the water meadow with a notepad and pencil to begin discussions on how I can become the only farmer in the Cotentin to make a profit.

~

This afternoon, we are to visit Haye-du-Puits for our regular browse at the Bonnes Affaires depot. With the complete absence of second-hand shops in the region, the depot is an exchange centre for everyone with household items to sell and those in search of a bargain buy. We are in need of a bedside table for the mill, though will probably return with a carved walking stick or art deco clock with a missing pendulum.

Before leaving, we take our traditional walk around the land to see that all is well. The tombstone barrier is now almost horizontal on the river bed, but a build-up of snagged tree branches, silt and other debris has formed a makeshift dyke, and water is trickling through the pipe into the new pond. I reach the bank in time to secrete a dead roach before my wife stumbles upon it, and looking around, she is pleased with the way nature is reclaiming its own. Already, healthy grass is growing on the earth banking and the weeds and water plants are flourishing. Triple Salco is performing a demanding sequence of exhibition dives from the cairn of stones in the middle of the pond, and wild flowers discovered flourishing in our Slough of Despond include bogbean, spotted orchids and arrow-headed water plantain.

We walk up to the Travers' field by the ford, and I see that our fallen beech tree has disappeared. In its place and keeping the non-existent cows from danger is a neat line of barbed wire nailed to gaping wounds on three other beeches. I make a mental note to drive past the Travers home on the way to Haye-du-Puits and see if I recognise any recent additions to the gigantic woodpile there.

Madame Lynn and Charlie are not at the farmhouse when we call, and we decide to move some tools and gardening equipment from the bikeshed down to their new home at the mill. A low and totally unrestored stone building opposite the farmhouse, the bikeshed has two ancient oak doors, each riddled with what we originally took to be the advanced stages of attack by giant woodworm. Further investigation showed that they had merely been used for shotgun practice over the years, presumably in the absence of any living or moving target. Above each door is a massive stone lintel which has been cunningly set at average-forehead height. During our relatively short time at La Puce, the rough stone slabs have claimed at least a dozen victims, and a livid scar above the eyebrows has become a membership badge for our Real France package guests.

Although René has reminded us on many occasions of the good money we could demand for bed and breakfast facilities in the bikeshed, we decided from the start that it should remain exactly as it has been for the past two centuries. Everything else at La Puce has been replaced or restored, and we wanted to have just one area left as it was, at least partly to remind us of what we had achieved elsewhere. The beams inside are rotten, there is no power, the floor is baked earth, the tiles leak and the stone walls are mostly held together with ivy, but it is full of charm and character. It is also home to a family of voles, so Donella would not countenance improvements anyway.

This time remembering to duck, we push our way inside and find that someone has fitted a carpet. Closer inspection reveals that this is actually a healthy growth of blanched grass. A well-gnawed seed sack shows that the vole family has been busy, and the dirt floor and damp atmosphere has provided a perfect environment for an inside lawn that any British gardener would be proud to claim. In one corner and nestling comfortably on top of my plumber's tool bag, we find the tiny nest. Without even putting my case to Donella, I resign myself to the expense of a new set of stilson wrenches, and we tiptoe out, leaving the property in the hands of its contented tenants.

~

The depot at Haye-du-Puits is busy, with a score of locals picking through the sometimes bizarre and always wildly contrasting selection of items, which today include a kingsize divan in leopardskin finish, with loudspeakers set in its sheepskin-bound headboard, jostling for space with a genuine nineteenth-century solid-mahogany Napoleon bed. Apart from the bedside table and against all the odds, I am hoping to find a length of stove piping, complete with brackets and bends, but settle for an Edwardian parasol in mint condition which seems a snip at 100 francs. Donella likes a chandelier made from an old wagon wheel, but it is full of worm. During our tour of inspection, we meet a pleasant English couple who are looking for a front door for their cottage on the coast. I give them the telephone number of the Brittany dip'n'stripper, and they respond by promising to keep an eye out for lengths of stove piping. We visit a nearby café, and Donella drinks half a cup of lemon tea before confiding that it tastes a little weak, even by Cotentinese standards. I look inside and see that the metal teapot contains nothing but hot water and a slice of lemon. Donella does not want to make a fuss and says the surly patron must have forgotten to add the teabag, but I am not so sure. As we leave, he says something to the barmaid, who giggles, but I do not leave a tip so have the last laugh.

~

On the way home we stop off at Boueve et Fils and have some luck. In the ironmongery section I find a single elbow bend, and a metal Chinese hat which Mr Boueve the elder assures me will protect the open end of my chimney pipe from the worst downpour Cotentin can provide. When I ask about piping for the stove, he looks at me as if I am a madman, and explains that it is high summer. Stovepipes, like mushrooms, will appear in the autumn. I think I will have to visit the bricolage in Valognes. It is a twenty-mile round trip, but the nearest thing to a good DIY shop in the region, and I want to have the stove up and running in good time for roasting the first chestnuts from the tree by the wooden bridge.

Rolling down the track, we are amazed to see that René has made a start on the terrace in front of the mill. He has already staked out the area with split logs held in place by sharpened branches, and introduces me to a friend and his wheelbarrow, who are scaling the new sand mountain the hard way. Eric, René tells us, is the star football player for AFC Negreville, but is otherwise temporarily unemployed and homeless, so is moving in with our estate manager till he can be found new lodgings. Though without a home, Eric owns a metal disc grass cutter, which makes him a man of some substance. He will clear the farmhouse garden in a trice, and his rates are most reasonable.

Other important events have unfolded, and René has a favour to ask. A relative of Christian the Goat is to be married next week, and the couple need somewhere to spend their wedding night. There is no suitably romantic room for their nuptials in the immediate area, and the hotel at Bricquebec charges a fortune for a night in the bed, which Queen Victoria allegedly used. All the village knows about the lace-trimmed marriage bed in the guest bedroom at La Puce, and we would win many friends if we would allow the young couple to spend their first night together there. René will see to all the arrangements, and we will hardly know they have been there. I promise to clear it with Madame Lynn, and after asking René not to cut any more branches from the chestnut tree by the wooden bridge, we leave them to their labours.

14 JULY
Our main task for the day is to clear the big pond. Although the nearest trees are twenty metres away, the fierce autumnal winds continually blow dead leaves across the water meadow and on to the surface. Over the winter months, they sink and form a layer of sludge at the bottom, making the water murky and unattractive. Now we have more than one fish to look at, we intend to tackle the problem with an old

country trick told us by René. All we have to do is sink bales of barley straw in the pond, and somehow, they will attract all the suspended detritus. Although I don't understand the physics involved, it's worth trying. If it works we will be able to follow and perhaps frustrate the exploits of the crayfish gang during this hot period, when they are at the height of their murderous activity.

Alongside the caravan, we find the barley straw, which René has purchased on our behalf. Disappointingly, it is not woven tightly in rustic string netting, but sealed in modern plastic bags. With due reverence and respect for our boat squatters, the upturned dinghy is moved for the first time this year and prepared for launching.

Having shifted *La Puce d'Eau* (aka The Water Flea) from her winter resting place, we are disappointed to see no more evidence of our lodgers than a series of small, perfectly round holes about an inch across. I think my wife was hoping to see the interior of a neatly kept little house, complete with miniature chairs gathered around a cheery fire like an illustration from *The Wind In The Willows*, but she is at least content that some wild creature's family has been taking advantage of the shelter.

It is a moment's work to push the craft down the bank and scramble aboard. Donella throws me the first of the barley-straw bags, and I paddle out, anchor at a suitable position, and push it over the side. At once, I detect a problem. There is air trapped inside the plastic covering, and the bag bobs happily on the murky surface. Offstage, a frog croaks encouragement as I lean over and stab at the bag with my single oar, but merely send it skimming away to the far bank.

I call for my wife to fetch a screwdriver, then I pursue the runaway bale. Eventually, I manage to puncture the tough plastic surface, and the bag settles fractionally lower in the water. By now, Reggie and Ronnie and a number of their gang have crawled up from the depths to see who has come on to the manor without their permission. A huge, brilliantly blue emperor dragonfly also arrives to settle on the prow of The Water Flea and enjoy the spectacle. On the far bank, there is a movement in the rushes, and I see that even the feral cat has joined the crowd. Determined to have my way, I pursue the bag around the pond, spurred on by an excited medley of croaks, grunts and squeaks from my audience. Poking, slashing, stabbing and cursing, I finally make a big enough hole to insert the large stone I have been using as an anchor. The bag promptly rolls over, and the stone drops out of the hole.

An hour or so later, all six bags have been torn apart, and their contents have spread themselves around the surface of the pond so that it looks like a strawberry patch protected from the frost. Donella has also found the heap of netting sacks meant to contain the straw where René had left them behind a fresh molehill under the caravan. I paddle wearily back to the jetty, cutting a temporary swathe in the straw surface. At least the leaves will not be able to sink this autumn, and I have made a new friend in Douglas the dragonfly, who has followed my career with fascinated bemusement around the pond all day.

Outside the mill, we find a cow up to its knee joints in freshly laid concrete, and René setting about its hindquarters with a scaffolding plank. The cow's owner is vainly trying to wrest the plank away from him. Though his farm is two miles distant, Mr Sorrell owns a small field on the other side of our stream, and exercises his right of way to it every summer. There has been bad blood between the two men ever since I commissioned René to enquire about buying the field, and Mr Sorrell broke the unwritten rules by coming directly to me to negotiate. He is, according to the locals, an aspirant candidate for the Euro Green party, which would account for the way he seems to leave his land entirely to nature, and is so concerned about the welfare of his cow.

Mr Sorrell now joins René and his cow in the wet cement, and the tug-of-war for possession of the scaffolding plank heats up. Entering the fray, Donella and I manage to calm the situation down. The cow is persuaded to leave the future terrace and stand in the ford for a hose down, while René and Mr Sorrell are invited into the mill to settle their differences over coffee and a large scotch. The situation becomes much more amenable when Mr Sorrell sees the picture of me posing with the John Major look-alike, and I promise to ask our premier if he can put a good word in for my neighbour before the Euro elections.

19 JULY

The day is not going well. Donella has spent the morning on the big pond with a garden rake, but has only succeeded in moving the floating barley straw around the surface. She is most concerned that the covering will cut off sunlight and air to the fish, so I have been delegated to oxygenate the water.

Lacking an electric agitator as used by the professional trout-pond owners, I park The Water Flea in the middle of the pond, then swirl the oar around as if hand blending an enormous batter mix. René has assured me that this will introduce bubbles of air into the pond, but it is very hard work and I become giddy as the boat reacts to my eccentric paddling and spins round on its axis. Douglas the dragonfly has not left my side, and the frog troupe has reached hysteria pitch. Resting from my labours, I see Christian the Goat striding across the meadow towards me. By the set of his shoulders I can see that he is not a happy man, and he loses no time in passing on the bad news. One of his animals has been found lifeless in the dry stream by the wooden bridge, and Christian has no doubt that the guilty party is Charlie the dog. I offer to buy him a replacement, but Christian is inconsolable. The goat was a favourite with his children, and they are too wise to be fooled. We agree that I will visit his home that afternoon to discuss what is to be done, and he leaves without shaking my hand, which is a bad sign.

A little later, Madame Lynn appears in some distress. She

has also received a visit from Christian, and there have been harsh words about the alleged goat-worrying incident. This was immediately followed by the arrival of René, who had called to discuss accommodation arrangements for the wedding on Saturday. As she explains to us, she is quite happy for the couple to take over the master bedroom for the night, but is somewhat perturbed by the six old mattresses René has brought and positioned around the house. The wedding party is going to be much larger than expected, he says, and has claimed my permission for them to find shelter at La Puce. Since he left, several strangers have called at the house with their luggage, and checked that they will be sure to get the full English breakfast they have already paid for. I promise to investigate, and promptly return to the comparative peace of the big pond.

My reverie is disturbed by three small boys with large fishing rods. They ask me how the trout are biting, and I ask them why they wish to know. They explain that, as season-ticket holders to the pond, they wish to complain to the management – i.e. Mr Ribet – about under-stocking. It has been a long time since they caught anything except the occasional roach, a species which, of course, is virtually inedible. I apologise for the poor sport, and promise to speak to my estate manager about upping the fish quota.

21 JULY

The wedding has taken place, and the grand concourse through Néhou has been voted one of the most memorable for years. Following tradition, the party has spent the afternoon driving slowly round and round the village, with horns sounding continuously. Apart from a confrontation with a small herd of cows and a new member for the ditch-of-the-month club, there have been no major incidents. The best man chauffeuring the bride and groom, as tradition also demands, drove the lead car. Rather than a string of tin cans trailing from the back bumper, it had an old-fashioned besom broom fixed to the roof. At the reception in the bar at Néhou, I compliment Madame Ghislaine on the magnificence of the wedding feast, and ask if she will give me the recipe for the apple dumplings, which are not at all like my mother used to make. She does not see the joke, and questions how they could be, as my mother has only recently become a visitor to the Cotentin? She starts writing it down anyway. As she composes, I tell her about reading of old plantation marriages in the French-speaking southern states of America. The wedding ceremony involved the couple stepping over a broomstick to confirm their union, and I wonder if there is any connection with today's display and procession of the old-fashioned broom.

Madame Ghislaine snorts at my fanciful notions as she refills my glass, and says that the besom strapped to the car is actually a symbol to show who is really in charge of a French marriage, and also that a broom has been bought and is ready for offensive action if necessary. It might not appear so to the outsider, she adds while directing a look, which could open a mussel at Bernard, who is dallying with a pretty bridesmaid, but in Cotentin it is the women who wear the real trousers. I know what she means, and it does seem that the more belligerent and swaggering the man, the more he lives in fear of his wife. The boasts in the bar, the aggressive style of driving and the braggadocio all seem to be in direct contrast to what probably goes on behind closed doors.

Today, however, all the couples at the wedding feast are on at least outwardly cordial terms, and dressed for the occasion. There is hardly a pair of working boots in sight, and all flat caps have been left at home. And the men look just as smart. Obviously avoiding a confrontation over the mattress-rental affair, René is said by Christian the Goat to be putting the finishing touches on the marriage bed and settling the happy couple in at La Puce.

The mayor has already made two speeches, one involving a very complicated but obviously earthy joke in patois I could not follow, and Hubert is filming the occasion on his new video camera. As the shadows from the gravestones in the churchyard opposite lengthen and before we settle down for the evening, I tot up my intake for the day, and suggest to my wife that we would both be better for a slow stroll back to La Puce.

Night begins to fall in earnest, and bedding Victor down outside the bar, we take the short cut across the open fields behind the village. After four years, we now feel well known enough to risk the journey across someone else's land, and anyway all the owners are at the wedding feast. In the distance, car horns start up and fade away in the direction of the farmhouse where René and Lynn await the paying guests' arrival, and we are alone in the tranquillity of a perfect summer evening. Beyond a wire fence, a cow lifts its head and regards us incuriously for a moment before returning to its business. A magpie has hitched a ride upon the back of a sheep in an adjacent field, and we both automatically bid it good day for luck. The bats are swooping low, and the full moon makes strange figures beneath the trees as we make the journey last.

The lights are blazing at La Puce as we arrive through Mr Margot's orchard. René is showing an elderly couple how the security lamps work by driving his mobylette in and out of the yard, and some local children are happily shying stones at the fairy lights around the patio. Madame Lynn has sensibly retired from the fray and left the revellers to it. Before following her example, we see a flickering light in the bikeshed and look inside to discover three mattresses laid out on the grass carpet. The vole family will have company tonight, and René has proven his point about the value of our guest annexe.

Down at the mill, all is tranquil. We take a torch and flask of minestrone soup and set off for the big pond. It is a clear night and a distant chorus of croaks indicates that love is in the air in other parts of our estate. There will be work to be done in the morning, with guests to see off and the farmhouse to be reclaimed, but for now, it is time to say goodnight to the more permanent residents at La Puce.

Madame Ghislaine's Apple Dumplings

1. Peel and core some apples
2. Put some cinnamon and butter in the holes,
and cook in a slow oven
3. Mix flour, butter, salt and a little water to make a dough
4. Make the dough into a ball, then flatten with a rolling pin
5. Repeat (4.) several times, then leave dough in a cold place
for one glass of wine
6. Roll out the pastry and cut out circles large enough
for wrapping apples
7. Place apples on dough circles
8. Mix some redcurrant jelly with calva and pour over apples
9. Wrap apples in dough circles
10. Brush dumplings with egg yolk and criss-cross
pastry with fork
11. Bake for two glasses of wine, then flambé with
calva at the moment of serving.

2 AUGUST

7AM: It is far too hot to work, so I persuade my wife that we should down tools and go on safari. Instead of working as usual on one small corner of the land, we should spend a whole day exploring every square yard of it. We can take provisions, and draw up a route map which will take us to the furthest corners of our empire, ending up at the big pond for a campfire supper and sing along before sleeping for the first time in our fully-equipped caravan. We will even take pads and pencils, and sketch every wild flower and tree on our journey, which will include tracing every inch of the Lude's winding way through our territory. Quite simply, I am proposing an adventure and expedition in the footsteps of Darwin, Cook and Livingstone.

My wife agrees after reminding me that at ten acres, La Puce is hardly in the league of the uncharted African interior, and goes off to boil some eggs. From the cooker, she vetoes the idea of sleeping in the caravan. We shall sleep under the stars, she says. It will be cooler, and we might even encounter the badger family out taking the midnight air.

8AM: Suitably equipped, we start our long journey by crossing the wooden bridge, pausing for me to paint a word picture of the mighty torrent, which will thunder down from the water meadow and into the millpond when René has diverted our neighbour's distant source. Arriving at the bottom of the sloping farmhouse garden, we set up camp alongside the goldfish pond for our first rest break. As we take stock, we see that our imported studs have been hard at work, and count over twenty tiny black infants vainly trying to swallow bemused insects at least twice their size. I pour the coffee and discover we have forgotten the sugar. My wife says we must improvise. She remembers from her Culpepper that there is a wild flower which can be used as a sweetener, similar in appearance to deadly nightshade. I tell her not to bother to forage in the hedgerow beside us. If we become desperate, I feel it would be much safer to fight a bumblebee for its nectar.

Much refreshed, we continue our journey and tramp through the grasslands and up the stepping-stones to the vegetable patch, where it is clearly evident that my wife's plot is doing far better than mine. When the April snow threatened my early potato crop, Donella became more and more possessive of what was originally agreed to be my sole province, and the situation became so bad that we decided to call a truce and establish his'n'her plots. To ensure fair competition, we have both been planting seeds from the same packets at the same time, and there will be a grand vegetable show and weigh-in next month, with the mayor and Solange as judges. It is clear from surface appearances that her crops are already doing considerably better than mine. I still expect the potato section to be a walkover in my favour, however. For the past month, I have been making late-night visits to pull up, inspect and carefully replace samples from her neat rows of Maris Pipers, and they do not seem to be doing at all well. I shall take a chance and leave mine permanently buried until the day of judgement.

From the vegetable patch, we return down the slope to the wooden bridge, and lower ourselves down the knotted rope to where the sunken millpond gently stagnates in the shadow of the ancient gable-end wall. I have already cleared out more than a ton of rubbish, which included the rusting frame of an old bike and, even in this isolated location, the inevitable supermarket shopping trolley. The ten-franc piece was missing from its slot, so I suspect that René is the culprit.

We stand for a moment looking at the curved scar and gaping axle hole in the wall towering above us, and try to picture the mighty wheel working at full flood. Down here, the centuries fall away and it is not difficult to hear wooden cogs turning, great stones inexorably grinding, and cart wheels rattling on the track as the miller schemed and sweated to skim off a few more sous to join his secret hoard.

Back in the present, we shoulder our baggage and pick our way across the rocky surface of the dry river bed to the stone bridge. For the first time, we go under instead of over it, admiring the smooth symmetry of the arched roof above us, with not a centimetre showing between the hundreds of perfectly dressed and squared blocks of local stone. Built to take the weight of no more than a cartload of grain, it has withstood the test of our twelve-tonne lorry loads of gravel with ease.

Beyond the bridge, we enter swamp territory. While we regularly clear the entire length of the Lude, we have left this section of the course of the dry river alongside the copse untouched. Over the years, fallen trees and branches have slowed and swelled the trickle from the water meadow, and now it forms an interesting and foul-smelling soup, its surface covered with dense weed and rotting vegetation. It makes an ideal breeding ground for a vast variety of insect life, and we often see quite large lizards basking contentedly beside its stagnant depths. René has warned us that here there be water snakes and other varieties of deadly poisonous serpent, but we think he exaggerates.

We climb out of the dry river so as not to disturb the gently bubbling primeval ooze before us, and rest awhile in the heart of the roadside copse. For the moment, there are few species of fungi on display, but in a few weeks the fairy ring will appear close to where we sit, and Coco and Alain will be in serious competition for the choicest and most valuable specimens from the season's crop.

Pressing on, we leave the copse and journey to where the Lude leaves our land and passes beneath the D900 on its way to St Sauveur and the open sea. We wade across the clear waters, and take on the acre of wild scrubland that not even Christian's most hardy and rapacious goats dare to confront. Ferocious attacks with our plastic picnic knives having no effect, we bypass the hundreds of vicious bramble shoots waiting to feed upon our unprotected legs and climb back into the Lude. Making steady progress, we soon cover the 200 waded paces to the stone washing chute and, ignoring the ford to Hunters' Walk, splash along the stream under a tunnel of hazel, larch, birch and beech branches to the grotto. We are weary, and there is no better place for lunch.

1PM: Replete, we sit and watch the cascade tumbling into the wide basin built to avoid flooding when the miller had filled the reservoir field, opened the miniature lock gate and sent the Lude surging back en route. The artificial and stone-lined basin is not, of course, a real grotto but, roofed with branches and cool and tranquil on the hottest and most frustrating of days, it is a place of magic to us.

2PM: From the grotto, we cross the mill garden to the herb patch, then on to the middle pond. Triple Salco summons his troupe to put on a special display, but we apologise and move on. We have far to go before the day is done.

Carefully edging over the dizzy heights of Tombstone Bridge, we emerge on to Hunters' Walk, and see a flash of tortoiseshell and teeth as our feral cat disappears with something furry wriggling helplessly in its mouth. My wife does not know whether to be dismayed at the loss of a resident, or pleased that the cat will dine well this afternoon.

We stroll along the avenue of giant beech trees, stopping for a moment to pay silent tribute at the spot where, years ago, we saw the last living grouse in all Cotentin. A little further along, we pause to wonder at the Hobbit Tree, a long-dead and skeletal oak that still stands firm against the Manche wind and local woodpile builders despite being almost completely hollow. The track rises steadily, till we come to the end of our terrain and stand to look at the miles of empty fields beyond. It is a suitable place and time to take high tea, and we settle down upon the corpse of a fallen giant, which will see us warmly through the coming winter. Providing, that is, I can find a chimney pipe for my period poêle.

4.30PM: We re-cross the Lude and squelch our way across the water meadow, my wife pointing out the wealth of wild flowers as I count the flag irises and multiply each yellow splash by five pounds sterling. A rustic bridge conveniently created by a fallen maple leads to the overgrown and long-redundant cart track where my wife is convinced Badger

Hall is located. My suggestion that, with a bit of luck, we may see Mr Toad arrive in his yellow waistcoat and motor-car does not amuse, and we climb the sloping field to the road and the eastern boundary of La Puce. I try to spot the likely location of Mr Pigeon's source, and my wife says I am more likely to see the Toadmobile. She believes that the spring does not exist, and is a ploy by René to keep me sweet.

Deciding not to disturb him, we leave his mobile home behind and soon reach the field next to the farmhouse, where Charlie the dog is in search of rabbits. I tell him he is wasting his time, and he bounds off in search of other diversions. After pausing to exchange the time of day with two of the mayor's steers, we wave to the balcony and a sunbathing Madame Lynn, and move on to count the wealth of tiny young apples in our orchard. Anxious now to reach our destination, we briefly inspect the well, walk down the farmhouse garden slope and, ignoring the wooden bridge, climb the ancient retaining wall to return to the water meadow. Now we are nearly at our goal, and it is but a few steps to the big pond and journey's end.

5PM: The heat of the day is still firmly upon us, so we decide to leave bags and bedding packed, take our ease and enjoy the sights and sounds of a high-summer afternoon in, on and around our own golden pond. The entertainment starts with an aerial attack by a squadron of close formation swallows. Flying in from the sun, they wheel off individually to swoop down on the pond, re-fuelling with delicate dips of beak, they skim the placid surface. From sheer exuberance and just to show their skills, each pulls out of the low altitude flight path at the last moment, coming closer to a head-on collision with the caravan roof on each sortie. In the wake of the adult wing comes an inexperienced juvenile, who consistently misjudges his speed and angle of elevation and splashes down heavily before gamely limping away to gain height for another attempt. As if irritated by this display of youthful impetuosity, the black duck crashes free of the long grass on the islet and, quacking sourly, lumbers away to the relative peace of Hunters' Walk.

While all this is going on, I spot a friendly dragonfly that appears to be helping an injured colleague from one clump of reeds to another. I then see that there are dozens of couples, all gamely piggy-backing through the air: my wife patiently explains that they are mating, and it is quite normal for them to do it at this time of year, in broad daylight and very publicly. I point out that Douglas the emperor dragonfly, who has come to sit with us, is obviously above that sort of thing. She says he may well be of British extraction, or just hasn't found a mate big enough to cope with him yet. If he, of course, *is* a he.

The *hirondelle* wing continues to make raiding passes on the big pond, and far above them, our buzzard arrives to see what all the fuss is about and study the teatime menu. On the far side of the pond, a single finch has ventured on to the landing platform of the bird table and is sorting through the remnants of our high tea. The Dundee cake is finding favour, and he has sharp words with a grey wagtail come to join the feast. As if to show who is boss of the big pond in pecking order terms, Trevor suddenly rears from the water, snaps up an unseen morsel, and is gone with a twisting flash of pink and silver, and a slap that resounds across the water meadow. Annoyed at the disturbance, Reggie and Ronnie Cray and at least a dozen members of their mob emerge from their front doors and crawl menacingly through the shallows. They are obviously in search of a suitable victim so they can demonstrate who is really in charge. After our long trek, I am sitting on the ramshackle jetty with my booted feet dangling in the water, and the Cray gang obviously decide to make an example. They swarm up the bank, and Big Ron digs a lump the size of a gobstopper out of my hi-impact water-resistant welded seam sole as if it were butter. I rapidly withdraw my feet and placate the gang with a large piece of camembert, and then become aware of a dead frog drifting into view from behind the island. It looks poignantly human stretched out flat on its back, like a lifeless frogman. I try to distract Donella's attention but she has already seen it. Just as I am preparing to console her, the creature draws up both knees, then almost casually straightening its legs, goes skimming at least a yard across the still water. It rests there a while, then repeats the process, in the manner of an oarsman in no hurry to make his way through a lazy afternoon on the river. Whatever naturalists might say about the error of relating animal behaviour to human activity, this frog is definitely sunbathing on its back and enjoying, like us, a carefree day away from the everyday worries of its own small world.

Now that Trevor has taken the lead and defied the Cray gang, roach begin popping up all around the pond, delicately breaking the surface to feed, then disappearing with hardly a ripple. On the far bank, the action is hotting up as news of the beano spreads, and more and more birds flock to the feeding table. We spot great and blue tits, bullfinch, goldcrests, a reed bunting and a tiny wren unconcernedly rubbing shoulders before a rustle in the long grass sends them careering off to the safety of the hedgerow. The feral cat is hungry again, and looking for a suitable dinner companion.

8PM: The feeding frenzy is over, and calm has returned to the big pond. The sun seems to have enjoyed our company so much that it is reluctant to dip below the bocage lining the far end of the water meadow. Donella is deep in *Tales of the Riverbank*, and I am gathering wood to make our campfire, impatient for flickering flames, long shadows and thick bacon sandwiches.

10PM: At last, the dusk is stealing in to clear the way for night, and the bats appear. Where they spend the day we do not know, nor why they stay so little time with us. Perhaps, like early evening pub-crawlers, they are doing the rounds to find the most lively and inviting place to settle for the night. My fire is going splendidly, and I turn my mind to the mystery, which has baffled philosophers, scientists and boy scouts alike for centuries; exactly why does bacon smell and taste so much better when cooked in the open air?

11PM: We are about to turn in when a shadowy figure looms out of the darkness. It is René, come to see why we are reduced to cooking on an open fire. We persuade him to stay and finish off the cold bacon sandwiches, but he is more interested in the emergency rations of canned cider cooling in the shallows by the jetty.

1AM: René has gone, and we are preparing to bed down beneath the stars. I have learned more about my friend in the last two hours than in the three years we have known him. Drawn out by the intimacy of our situation around the fire and at least half a gallon of extra-strength cider, he talked longer and more candidly than during any heavy session in the Bar Ghislaine. He has still not revealed much about his past life, but it has obviously been a hard one, and he has had to live off his wits since he was a child. Towards the end of our conversation, I sensed that he would have liked to unbend further but, like the wild creatures all around us, he seems ever wary of revealing himself to a potential predator. Perhaps we will get on better after this encounter.

Despite the warmth of our meeting, the campfire sing along was not a success. It is very difficult to translate the words and meaning of such classics as 'Ging Gang Gooley Gooley' and 'Green Grow The Rushes-O' to a Norman in a water meadow at midnight, especially after several cans of strong Somerset cider.

2AM: Like most of the other residents at La Puce, we are settled down for the night, and have made ourselves as comfortable as possible with the materials to hand. Moved by the romance of the moment, I bring up the subject of the dragonfly dances this afternoon, but my wife is not responsive. She says that the ground is too hard and the stars too bright, and we are within sight and sound of René's mobile home. Just because she loves animals, she is not going to act like one. I bid her a gruff goodnight, roll over and try to find a comfortable gap between the molehills.

3 AUGUST

We have seen a wonderful sight, and one so rare in these parts that even René is impressed. As if to confirm that he has finally approved of our work, a most important and exotic visitor arrived this morning as we sat at the big pond, recovering from our night in the open.

Scouting for dead wood to start our breakfast fire, I saw a blur of colour among the elder trees by the river. Then a small bird with a large beak burst from the foliage and flew straight to perch on the feed table, where he ignored the scraps and crumbs for the common breeds, and focused his attention on the water. After a moment, he darted through the air, swooped, struck and made off back to the trees, a tiny sliver of silver glinting against his rainbow coat.

A kingfisher has come to La Puce.

4 AUGUST

Our social calendar for the rest of the month is full to overflowing. It is the week of the St Anne Fair at Bricquebec, closely followed by our village fête, and we have been invited to spend a long weekend in Burgundy. It is the height of the ferry tariff season, so we shall give our monthly raid on England a miss, though our finances are at a very low ebb. Bad news has come from Robert Simon, who says that they haven't sold a single Philippino pot from our vast range. He politely suggests that Normandy may not be ready for the eastern ethnic look, and his customers are more interested in plasterboard and roofing tiles than strawberry planters thrown on a genuine ex-Manila-taxi-wheel rim. I report the latest entrepreneurial catastrophe to my wife, who as ever looks on the bright side. We will, she says, at least not have to buy any patio pots for our secret garden when it is finished, and they will make ideal nurseries for preparing the baby goldfish for life in the big pond.

7 AUGUST

We arrive on the outskirts to find Bricquebec like a busy Friday evening at Junction 12 of the M25. The traffic is at a standstill, so we park by the hole in the fence at the funeral director's yard, and I try not to look at the familiar slabs of marble stacked inside as we set off on the mile walk to the square.

When we first visited the town on a market day, we were surprised at just how many local people would turn out to tour round a handful of stalls and see a variety of farmyard animals go under the hammer. Today, the centre of Bricquebec is busier than Portsmouth's Guildhall Square on a naval payday. Every metre of every pavement has been taken up with stalls involved in breakneck trading regardless of what they are selling. Mountains of carpets, furniture and farming tools vie for space and attention with stalls laden down with hundreds of varieties of cheese, and we even see an English couple doing a roaring trade in pirated videos of recent Hollywood blockbusters. This is particularly remarkable, as they will be in English, and I also know that some of the frantic buyers have no video machines on which to play them. Wherever there is a scrap of space, business is being done, especially by the Moroccan street dealers hardly visible beneath armfuls of rugs, scarves, leather jackets, alleged Rolex watches for fifty francs, and, as they proclaim, real gold jewellery for just ten francs.

Whole caravans of boiled sweets of every colour, size and flavour compete with candy floss, ice cream and wet fish stalls, and every corner has at least two *merguez* spicy sausage hot-dog stands trying to keep up with demand. Butchers from across the region have abandoned their shops to plunder the rich seam of customers looking for a whole lamb or pig, jointed, cooked or even on the hoof as the customer prefers. An escaped hen from the poulterer's wagon unwisely seeks refuge under the skirts of the fried-chicken-and-*frites* stand, and even the trestle table selling winter underwear and bobble hats is under siege.

At the heart of the square, it is even busier, as a complete funfair is in full swing. We fight our way through the bois-terous hordes eager to pay to be giddily swung, dropped, suspended upside down and whirled round in a cacophony of deafening tinny music and klaxon hooting, and see that there is little chance of popping in to the Café de Paris for a quiet drink with Freddo. Every bar in sight is packed with revellers; each has thrown up a temporary counter and awning of canvas, scaffolding poles and rough planks which are even busier.

Freddo told us that at least fifty thousand people would visit the fair over the three days this year, and we thought he must be exaggerating. Now we see he has underestimated, and he and his staff of ten will probably serve that many customers in the Café de Paris alone. Officially starting on a Saturday morning, the Saint Anne Fair is supposed to close at two each morning and re-open four hours later throughout the three days, but in practice it just keeps going. After a long exposure to his favourite daytime tipple of *kir*, Freddo once told us that he and Collette make enough money from the three mad days each August to take a long recuperative holiday in the Auvergne immediately afterwards, and put more than a little aside for the retire-ment house they are buying outside Bricquebec.

Giving up our efforts to get within shouting distance of the bar, I reflect that he will probably pay for the roof of their new home in the next couple of hours. As we try to escape from the maze of fairground rides, tents and stalls, I collide with a large young man who is pointing a pump-action twelve-bore shotgun at me. Reaching for my wallet and preparing to tell him to take what he likes, I see that he is actually a customer at the nearby shooting range, the front of which is knee-deep in empty cartridge cases. The man is obviously intoxicated with the frenetic atmosphere, drink or both. I duck beneath the barrels, grab him round the waist and swing him in roughly the right direction. As we stand and watch, we see that the stallholder has cunningly appealed to the Cotentinese love of firing off shotguns at large, preferably immobile and very close-up targets. The object of the challenge to the customers' marksmanship is to hit a dinner plate less than ten feet from the firing position. Given the spread of the cartridge shot and the closeness of the plates, it would be a greater test of skill to miss them. At fifty francs for four goes and the prize for success a cheap baseball cap with *le champion!* stencilled on the peak, the stallholder is actually hiring out the guns at a tidy profit rather than staging a competition. I now also understand why I have already seen at least a hundred men proudly wearing this normally rare type of headgear.

Keeping low, I take my wife's hand, resist the blandishments of at least three Original Astrological Consultants to the President of all France, and finally burst from the fairground maze to collide with a pretty girl in traditional Dutch costume, who happens to be riding a boneshaker bicycle while carrying a tuba. Helping her to her feet, I see that she is not alone.

Behind her stretches a long and wobbling line of young men and women, all in costume, steering ancient bicycles with one hand and playing a trumpet, drum, fife or xylophone with the other. The clogs they are wearing further impede their ability to maintain forward velocity and balance. Thinking quickly, I grasp the girl, tuba and bicycle and manage to drag her out of the path of her colleagues, thus avoiding a massive pile-up. I hand over the dented euphonium while the procession wavers past, then all is explained as my wife points out a poster proclaiming that the high point of the fair takes place every day at 3PM, when Bricquebec proudly presents a special display by the Only Dutch Cycling Formation Band In The World.

Agreeing that little else could top our recent experiences, we cautiously make our way from the display area and return to the tranquillity of La Puce. Whatever is on offer at the *Grande Fête et Méchoui* at Néhou this weekend, I feel it is bound to be something of an anticlimax.

14 AUGUST

Actually, it looks as if the village fête is going to be quite a lively affair. We arrived at the field beside the church in good time for the open-air mass, followed by fairly orderly and good-natured queuing for the ladies-only portaloo. It was then time for me to make my traditional return to La Puce for our forgotten plates, knives and forks as these are not provided for the méchoui, which is the localised version of a North African lamb barbecue.

Now, the fête is in full swing, with every villager having dutifully turned up to support the occasion and provide another boost for the schoolbook fund. There is even a rumour that there are some heavily disguised spies from St Jacques in attendance, but this, of course, is a compliment, as they would only be here to see how things should be done properly at their miserable fête.

In one corner, JayPay and his team of volunteers labour in the fierce heat of the afternoon sun, turning whole lambs on spits above improvised oil-drum barbecues, while Mr Janne and Bernard are coping with the steady flow of customers at the temporary bar set up by Madame Ghislaine.

While not as sophisticated as the amusements on offer at the Bricquebec fair, the stalls lining the hedgerows have their own simplistic appeal and are marginally safer for spectators. Most consist of rolling, lobbing or throwing *pétanque* balls at pyramids of tin cans, while the main attraction is a lucky dip with a top prize of a full and virtually unused tractor spanner set. Every member of the Jolly Boys' Club has been roped in to help; even René has been delegated to sell raffle tickets for the Grand Draw, but I notice that Madame Ghislaine follows him round to take charge of the money. As he tears us off a strip, my friend gives me a stage wink, loudly declaring that he has been working since dawn and his mouth is as dry as a dead cow's udder. My wife having kindly offered to take over the ticket sales, we retire to the bar for an apéritif before the méchoui is ready.

An hour later, and we are at the head of the jostling queue for a huge slice of lamb, garnished with Normandy green salad and a bucketful of chips. As we steady our plates and stand by to fight off rivals for the delicious outer cuts of seared, crunchy skin infused with JayPay's secret marinade of herbs and spices, he ceremonially unsheathes his weapon. Holding the giant carving knife up to the sun, he squints at the glittering blade, but is obviously not happy with what he sees. As we salivate like dogs waiting anxiously for their dinner to be put in the bowl, he turns to his well-worn whetstone and hones his knife in the manner of a priest preparing his implements for a very special service. Finally, after much examination of the blade and consultation with fellow specialists on the team, he makes the final, crucial test. Rolling his sleeve and exposing a massive and densely hairy forearm, he draws the blade carefully from sweaty elbow to wrist. Holding it once again towards the sun, he runs a sausage-like finger and thumb delicately along the blade, then holds up a thick tuft of damp hair to the crowd, from whom is heard a reverent murmur of admiration and approval. At last satisfied, JayPay wipes the knife casually on the seat of his trousers, confronts the nearest lamb and carves a thick wedge from its saddle. My wife and I exchange glances, then simultaneously step aside to let the person behind us have the honour of bagging the first slice.

Dusk is approaching, and the fairy lights fetchingly draped across the water bowser by the portaloo are twinkling brightly. The mobile DJ is working his way up to 'The Birdie Song', and René is dancing with my wife. Filming the day's activities and indiscretions for posterity, Hubert frowns almost possessively as he records our estate manager's attempts to teach Donella a dual version of his whirling dervish routine. René has already disgraced himself by hijacking the tractor train ride and taking the carriageloads of village children on a much more exciting route through the field of cattle maize across the road. As René is gently but firmly led off the floor by my wife, the DJ blows loudly into his microphone and announces the draw for the raffle is about to take place. Shyly mounting the platform, Solange Chevalier reaches into the feed bucket held by Madame Ghislaine and produces a ticket. René nudges me heavily in the back as my wife's name is read out to polite applause. As René was for some reason entrusted with writing the names on the back of all the tickets, I am relieved to see that there are no other prizes but the plump Chinese rabbit with which my wife is presented.

Later, I spend a pleasant ten minutes at the bar with our mayor, who tells me he has heard from Robert Simon that a suitably large and impressive boulder for the Patton orchard has been located, and will be picked up and delivered free of charge by a Brument-Clot lorry in the coming weeks. I say I am more than pleased to have helped, thank him for a wonderful day, and go to collect my wife, who has just presented the large and cuddly rabbit to JayPay's youngest daughter. She is obviously delighted, and runs straight to her father to show off her unexpected gift. As JayPay holds the creature up by the ears and prods its stomach, Donella smiles fondly and says they are probably discussing what best to feed it on. I agree, but secretly wager that he is telling her the best way to cook it.

We prepare to leave, and see René behind the water bowser with a young woman. He is obviously drunk, and concentrating blearily on the unaccustomed practice of taking some notes from his wallet. He gives them to the girl, then sees us watching and hurries her away into the darkness.

About to drive from the field, we bump into Charlie the dog and Madame Lynn, who is looking particularly radiant. She tells us that she has met someone special. Bathing at Carteret, she struck up a conversation with the man on the towel next to hers, and they got on so well that she agreed to a dinner date. He is not young, but kind, charming and sophisticated, and the proprietor of two biscuit factories and a grand manoir at Carentan. We congratulate her on forming a new relationship, and as I encourage Victor over the bumpy terrain, I remark how glad I am that Lynn has met someone new. Fate was indeed kind, I philosophise, to place two lonely and obviously such well-suited people side by side on a crowded beach. My wife is silent for a moment, then observes that Fate was particularly kind in ensuring that Lynn's neighbour was not only lonely, charming, kind and sophisticated, but also the owner of two biscuit factories and a grand manoir.

I reflect on the complex workings of the feminine mind as we pull out on to the road, then my heart sinks as we are flagged down by a large gendarme swathed in leather, and wearing the standard menacing sunglasses under his visored helmet, even though it has long been dark. We are not two miles from home, and I had thought it safe to go beyond my normal driving ration of two bottles of beer. French policemen persecute all drivers, but seem to take a special delight in harassing the British motorists who contribute millions to the nation's economy each year. Clutching at straws, I take several deep breaths and waggle my tongue frantically around my open mouth as the figure approaches with the familiar cocky strut, leans down to my open window and removes his helmet and sunglasses. I then realise it is the boozy bobby, and that he has been drinking far more than me. He pumps my hand, crisply salutes my wife, and asks if we have had any more temporary guests in the ditch outside our farmhouse. He also asks if our special emergency supply of calva is still in stock, and remarks pointedly on how chilly the night air is after such an agreeable day. I let out a huge sigh of relief, give him time to find, fall off then re-straddle his mobylette, and we create another local legend by becoming the first villagers to receive a motorcycle escort home from the annual Néhou fête.

20 AUGUST

The mayor calls to say that the Patton stone will arrive next week and asks if we are free to attend the delivery so as to mark our involvement in the project. Regretfully, I have to turn his thoughtful invitation down, and explain we are going to spend a few days seeing how life in Burgundy compares with Cotentin. I wish him well for the ceremony, and remind him that he is judging our vegetable show next month.

27 AUGUST

We set out for our visit to Jean-Marie Guedeney's ancestral farm in a village not too far from Dijon. Though he was not born there, the property has been in his family for generations, and now that his parents have passed on, he has bought the farm to save it being sold to strangers. He has phoned from England, told us where to find the keys, and said he would be grateful if we could look the place over and give him the benefit of our experience in restoring interesting old French properties.

The trip goes well, except when we become stuck on the Paris ring route, which is like our M25 round London, only the standards of driving, road surfaces and signs are even worse. The stretch past the capital is supposed to take no more than an hour to complete, but at one stage we begin to think we will be on it forever. The night descends, we stop and change seats at my wife's suggestion, and I do not ease the situation when we see the Eiffel Tower three times from different sides of the river and I suggest she should think about a career as a Paris taxi driver. By midnight, we have thankfully left the lights and sights of the capital behind us, and arrive in the Valley of the Windmills by dawn.

30 AUGUST

Apart from the extreme heat and the complete absence of mud, we feel almost at home. In some respects, though, Burgundy is not as French as we are used to. The condition of property and age of the cars suggests that the locals generally enjoy a better standard of living, and Dijon is far, far grander and refined than we are used to with Cherbourg as our main town. There is even an Indian restaurant. We spend the morning visiting museums, exploring the narrow streets with their picture-postcard half-timbered buildings, and window-shopping at individual greengrocery shops in the market place which would make the food hall at Harrods look poorly stocked. There is a sophisticated café-bar on every corner, and each has a huge selection of filled rolls displayed in the window, with a hatch to serve the crowds on the pavement. This is obviously how Jean-Marie got his idea for his baguette shops in Portsmouth.

In the afternoon, we visit Jean-Marie's birthplace, an imposing four-storey stone building perched next to the church in an elevated village with panoramic views for miles across the rolling countryside. The house is up for sale, and I make a note to tell Jean-Marie in case he wants to buy it as well as the farm. Even within commuter distance of Dijon and as attractively positioned as it is, it will probably fetch no more than a scruffy terraced house in Portsmouth.

We take photographs of the graves of Jean-Marie's parents before we leave. His mother and father are buried alongside each other in the family plot, with a lovely view overlooking the valley. The polished marble and freshly cut flower displays show that the plot is regularly given loving attention by other members of the Guedeney family. On the way back, I remark on how well the relatives care for gravesites in every cemetery, and we rather morbidly discuss our preferences for a final resting place. Donella says she would like to be buried at La Puce in a biodegradable cardboard box, so that her body can help enrich the land as quickly as possible. I say she is only thinking of giving her vegetable plot a further advantage over mine, and that I would be happy with a cremation, and for my ashes to be scattered by the pissoir outside the Bar Ghislaine. That way, I would never lack company, and would be able to eavesdrop on so many interesting discussions.

Exhausting the subject of death and burial, we stop at a bar outside Jean-Marie's village and take an ice-cold beer on the terrace. Not for the first time, I notice how easily the Burgundians understand my French. Either they are more used to foreigners, or too polite to give the blank stares and mystified shrugs I still receive on occasion in my home region. As we drive back to the farm, we see a dead hare in the road and I suddenly realise that my friend Douglas the emperor dragonfly will probably not be around when we return to La Puce. I must remember, my wife says comfortingly, that he found a mate before we left, so has served nature's purpose. He will have had, in dragonfly terms, a long and happy life, so should not be mourned.

3 I AUGUST
It is my wife's birthday. We are booked in for a special meal this evening at an auberge highly recommended by Jean-Marie. I call him to tell him of our adventures so far, and tactfully remind him that he has not sent a birthday card to

Donella as I had suggested. Totally out of character for such a normally polite man, he rather testily says that the French do not suffer from the English obsession for sending a greeting card on every occasion from sickness to passing the driving test. Soon, he hazards, we will start posting a card to tell friends we have had a particularly satisfying piss.

As we dress after a lazy day sunbathing in the garden, the phone rings. It is either Jean-Marie to apologise for his tetchiness, or a problem at home. I have left the number with Lynn in case any problems arise, but have asked not to be bothered unless it is something important.

I walk into the cool hallway and pick up the phone.

It is René, and I realise that it is only the second occasion that we have spoken on the phone. Before I can ask what the problem is, he tells me.

John Chevalier is dead and Solange is in hospital.

Néné thought we would want to know.

TWELVE

'Life is but a Passing Shadow'*

We have driven home through the night, and go straight to René's caravan. He tells us that our friend had been at the Patton orchard to take delivery of the memorial boulder, and was waiting at the entry to the D900 when a lorry went out of control. The driver suffered a heart attack, and John had no chance to take avoiding action. It is said that the lorry driver may be a relative of the Chevaliers. The impact was on John's side of the car, and he must have died instantly. Miraculously, Solange is barely injured, except in her mind. René offers us a drink, but we say no and go and sit by the big pond. I cannot help thinking that John was at the junction at that exact moment because of the chain of events I had set in motion. If I had not made enquiries about the stone, he would not even have been there. If I had been there for the delivery, we might have talked for a few vital extra moments or he might have shown me round the orchard. Whatever happened, he would not have been sitting patiently at the junction when the lorry appeared around the bend.

* Inscription on a sundial at the manor house of the Sire de Gouberville et du Mesnil-au-Val, the author of an unique journal of sixteenth-century life in the Cotentin countryside.

My wife does not try to reason with me, and knows it is best to leave me with my thoughts. I spend the night looking at the water and remembering John Chevalier.

5 SEPTEMBER

The single bell at the church in Néhou has been tolling slowly all morning. It sounds completely different from its relaxed Sunday tone, or the nagging insistence with which it calls workers in the fields to attend the evening angelus.

We walk towards the village centre and join the gathering stream of people, all wearing their church clothes. I have no black tie, but my wife has made an armband from an old pair of charcoal grey trousers and sewed it to my jacket. It is the first time she has worn a hat since her father's funeral.

We pass the field where our mayor opened the village fête so recently, and I see that the water bowser and fairy lights are still there. The field is full of cars, and more are parked along the verges and outside the Bar Ghislaine, which is shut for the day. A gendarme in full dress uniform is directing traffic to an overflow-parking field beyond the church, and two policemen on motorcycles sit at either side of the broken gate. They have taken their helmets and sunglasses off, and are almost respectfully ushering the steady flow of vehicles inside. Already, there are at least twice as many people in Néhou as live here.

Although the ceremony is not due to start for more than an hour, the church is full. A large crowd is gathered around the main entrance, where the mobile DJ has set up his loudspeakers to relay the words of the service. There are some familiar faces, but also many strangers, some in military and civil uniforms of very high rank. A row of benches has been placed by the open graveside, which are already filled with older members of the commune, who sit silently looking at the neatly kept rows of marble slabs bearing the names of their friends and relations.

More cars continue to arrive in the narrow lanes than the village has ever seen, or will likely see again, and Néhou has its first traffic jam. The gendarme panics and puts a whistle to his mouth, but a very senior officer in a *képi* festooned with gold braid hurries to stop him and take personal command of the situation as the dignitaries arrive. We had known that John was well respected in the area, and it seems that other mayors, high-ranking Manche officials and important figures from all across the département have come to pay their personal tribute. While we wait in the crowded cemetery, men in uniform and wearing extravagant emblems and regalia of office move swiftly among the gravestones, nodding here, exchanging a few words there, and shaking hands with everyone within reach. Next to where we stand in the shadow of the church tower, a senior army officer pauses to pump the hand of a surprised and embarrassed chauffeur with a uniform even more splendid than his own.

There is a murmur from the crowd, and we see a procession making its way slowly along the middle of the lane from the distant parking field. At its head, young children carry huge bouquets and arrangements of flowers bigger than themselves, and at its heart is Solange. She is supported on either side by Mr Janne and her only son, and she is totally distraught.

The mass of people parts silently to make way, and she is gently led through the doors and into the dark interior of the church.

Overhead, the bell falls silent, and a single crow flutters back to its roost.

The service begins and the people around the door press forward as if to show that they would join the congregation if there were room.

For two hours we stand stiffly in the hot sun, listening to the words and music coming from inside the church and echoing harshly from the loudspeakers on either side of the porchway. None of those outside join in the hymns or responses made by the unseen congregation, but most make the sign of the cross across their breasts at what must be the appropriate moments. Eventually, we begin to shuffle forward into the cool porchway, and a few men slip away to relieve full bladders on the low churchyard wall before we enter. They make no attempt to hide themselves, and there is no disrespect in their action.

Inside, we move slowly down the aisle to where the coffin lies in front of the altar. I take the brush from the elderly woman in front of me, and following her actions, dip it into an urn and sprinkle a few drops of water across the casket lid. I have not been to a French funeral before and did not know what to expect. I am disappointed that the coffin is closed, and I will not see my friend's face for the last time. As I hand the brush to my wife, I see Solange leaning heavily on Mr Janne's arm.

Our eyes meet, but she does not see me.

Outside the church, and unsure what to do next, we stand and nod self-consciously to friends and neighbours. There is little conversation and no tears, but their faces show that they know what we have lost.

~

The interment is over, and we walk home with Christian, his wife and her mother, who tells us she was christened at the church, and will soon make her last visit there. She is nearly ninety, and it is more than three miles to the family home beyond the crossroads. Perhaps, she says, it would have been easier to stay at the church and wait her time.

10 SEPTEMBER

It is raining softly as I walk through the gates and stand at the foot of my friend's grave. The flowers are still fresh, and completely cover the marble slab. There is a photograph of John on the headstone, showing him as he was earlier this year and always will be in our memories. I make myself comfortable, and begin to tell him all the news about the village, and how his fields at La Puce are in good form as the summer leaves us.

13 SEPTEMBER

We return to the church for the christening of a new member of the commune. It is a boy, and he is to be named Jean.

Afterwards there is a celebration at the Bar Ghislaine. I expect it to be a sombre and subdued affair, but all the guests seem in good spirits. I disgrace myself when one of the Jolly Boys' Club makes a black joke about our commune population standing still as we have lost one and gained one in the same month and I take strong exception. JayPay calms the situation down, and when I apologise for my manners but question the taste of the *plaisanterie*, he merely shrugs, lays a huge arm around my shoulder and steers me towards the bar to explain something I must understand.

As I would have seen from the funeral, everyone in the commune loved and respected John Chevalier for who and what he was. There will never be another like him, and his passing was properly marked with a ceremony which will be talked about all over la Manche for years to come. That is the mark of his greatness. We have all lost a dear friend, and grieve for his wife. Unlike elsewhere in what is supposed to be civilised and modern Europe, Solange will not be forgotten and left to face the future alone. But life and death is commonplace in the countryside, and must be accepted as inevitable. Last week we mourned the death of a dear friend and good man. Today we celebrate life. The accident was a terrible tragedy, but it happened and nothing can change that. Now it is time to think about birth, not death. Life, as even the English would probably say, must go on.

I nod acceptance of what he says and accept the glass he offers me, but still feel angry at the world. No matter how long I live among them, I don't think I will ever really understand these people.

14 SEPTEMBER

The top fields at La Puce seem strangely shabby and untended when I take my morning stroll. Already the grass is getting very long, though I am probably imagining the level of neglect and decay I seem to see around me. René says he has found a farmer willing to put a couple of his horses in to keep the grass down, and it will save the expense of paying someone to cut it. I agree. It won't be the same, but at least there will be some life around the place.

I tell myself to buck up, and go to see how Trevor is getting on with the binful of young trout I secretly bought at Valdecie and tipped into the big pond when my wife was not around. With luck, she will think that Trevor has had an immaculate conception, or that they are a hybrid result of his liaison with a roach. She needs cheering up, and, as Jean-Pierre said at the christening, life must go on.

I 5 SEPTEMBER
The swallows have flown. I shall miss their joyous aerobatics around the big pond, and their departure is another reminder that the year is dying.

René says that, before France's Age of Reason (which naturally preceded that of any other European country), ignorant peasants believed that swallows hibernated in the mud at the bottom of rivers and ponds. Now we know that they winter in Africa, but I like the idea of them sleeping contentedly beneath the surface of the big pond, waiting to burst forth and welcome the sun and summer of another year.

I 7 SEPTEMBER
I am particularly pleased with myself today. I dropped in to the Photo-Kwik shop in St Sauveur this morning to pick up a roll of film, and the manager told me Helen Patton has engaged his services. He is to fly over the grand house at Néhou and take some aerial shots now that the restoration is complete. As he will be going past La Puce, I asked if he will take some photographs of our terrain while he is up there. We negotiated for a few moments and a satisfactory

deal was reached with regard to extra fuel, time in the air, photographic plates and additional artistic output. I handed over 300 francs and left, feeling I had pulled off a major coup.

It will be nice to have some panoramic pictures to show the extent of our estate. As we struck the deal, I considered asking the photographer if he has any specialist infrared equipment, which could detect and show buried metal, but don't want the word about the miller's gold to get out; he is a notorious gossip.

19 SEPTEMBER

René calls at the mill to say we have a problem. A plane has been circling the water meadow this morning at a very low altitude. He recognises it as the one the photographer at St Sauveur hires for work, and is concerned that he has been paid by the government to take some spy pictures and catch René working while he is supposed to be unemployed. He makes me promise not to tell the Social Security that I am paying him if a snooper arrives. I tell him not to worry, and that I have commissioned the shots of La Puce. He is dumbstruck at the thought of my spending money on photographs of grass, and says he could have taken some from the top of the giant cedar tree in the orchard which would have been just as good for half the price.

21 SEPTEMBER

I awake in the early hours, certain I am having a heart attack. There is a band of steel round my chest, and the pain is excruciating. I rouse my wife and ask her to phone the emergency services. She claims not to be able to remember the number, and reminds me that we do not have the card which would enable us to claw back medical expenses under the relevant EU agreement. It would cost a fortune to have me hospitalised, and besides, it is only indigestion. How anyone of my age could eat that amount of pork crackling at lunch followed by black pudding for supper and expect to get away with it escapes her. She fetches a bottle of *cidre bouché*, pops the cork and for once encourages me to drink it all down quickly, and straight from the bottle. The ice-cold fizzy liquid does the trick, and I bring up vast quantities of trapped air for the next hour. I start to feel much better, and the cider has its usual effect of making me feel amorous. My wife sends me to sleep on the sofa bed so she can get a few hours rest, and reminds me we have a heavy day ahead of us, as today is when the results of our long-running vegetable competition will be revealed. I lie awake for a long while after remembering that the contest was to have been judged by John and Solange Chevalier.

~

We have spent a hard morning in the vegetable patch, and are resting from our labours in the cool of the mill cottage. So far the day has not gone well for my side of the line dividing the his'n'hers plots.

Compared with my wife's mountains of runner and French beans, mine are but foothills. Her beetroots are pétanque balls compared with my marbles, and the sprouts do not even invite comparison. Despite my midnight sorties to unearth, inspect and unintentionally retard her main crop potatoes, her overall yield is at least twice that of my miserable pile.

In a sulk, I go to the bar to find sympathy in male company. Jacques Laiznay is there, earnestly treating his liver complaint. Jacko explains that he has been entertaining former fireman colleagues from Paris for the weekend and needed to take a healing infusion of *suze*. This exotic liqueur is based on the gentian flower and is, to my taste, absolutely foul. It has a revolting, sickly smell and bitter taste redeemed only by being extremely alcoholic, but the locals swear by its medicinal and restorative properties for internal problems. As most of their internal problems spring from excessive drinking, I think its main benefits are of the hair-of-the-dog variety. All the local men seem to be complete hypochondriacs, with a most peculiar logic dictating their dietary regimes.

The attitude seems widespread, and not confined to the masses. I once had lunch with a very senior officer in the Le Havre Chambre de Commerce, and he suggested we went to his favourite restaurant on the quayside, which specialised in dishes from his Alsace birthplace. After poring over the menu for a long while with a worried frown, he rejected my suggestion of a crisp white wine in favour of a purifying bottle of mineral water, and explained that he was on a very strict diet. His doctor had just broken the news that his cholesterol level was off the scale, and given him a small booklet detailing the comparative ratings for all meat, poultry and fish, together with items and dishes that must be avoided like the plague. After consulting it in tandem with the menu, he firmly turned down the oysters, and looked aghast when I even suggested a lean steak. Luckily, his favourite choucroute was the midday special, and not included as a specific dish in his booklet, so he contentedly ordered then devoured the groaning platter of fatty pork on pickled cabbage with ferocious dedication.

Hearing about my kitchen-garden defeat, Jacko commiserates and says it is a known fact that only women can coax any size of vegetable out of the dense soil in the area, and this is said to be because they have had so much practice in the challenge of extracting cash from their husbands' pockets. All the serious and professional growing is done by men in the sandy soil on the coast, where the carrots and leeks come as big as a stallion's business equipment. I take comfort from his remarks and he suggests we order a whole bottle of suze and treat our maladies for the rest of the afternoon. I agree, with the proviso that I can have lots of water in mine without risking our friendship.

Black Pudding and Apples

1. Peel, core and slice some apples
2. Fry them in butter, and season
3. Oil the pudding, prick the skin and grill
4. Arrange the ingredients in a casserole dish and heat
5. Just before serving, flame with a generous dash of calva.

23 SEPTEMBER

I am convinced my wife's telepathy with the animal kingdom is developing apace. On the way to Bricquebec this morning, we swerved to avoid an elderly mongrel standing placidly in the middle of the road. I stopped, and Donella ran back to warn other drivers while I approached the dog. Before I could see if it had a collar, it ran off and disappeared through a gap in a hedge. My wife wanted to set up an emergency roadside observation post in case it returned, but I assured her it must belong to someone in one of the roadside houses, and had gone home.

Privately, I am amazed at the charmed lives of the pets who reside by the D900. Like their owners, they seem to lack any degree of road awareness, and wander about the highway without a care. I have never seen a driver actually aim at an animal unless it is generally considered edible, but nobody seems to take any drastic avoiding action if a dog or cat chooses to get in the way. Strangely, dead pets in the road are even rarer than squashed hedgehogs or rabbits, and that is saying much. Last year, I was taking our bank manager for a soothing lunch at Carteret, and somehow managed to miss a suicidal pheasant that obviously saw no point in going on now that he was so totally alone in the world. Rather than compliment me on my driving skills and humanity, my passenger seemed quite upset that I had missed such a rare opportunity to bag some free food without even being put to the cost of a shotgun cartridge.

~

Later in the evening, I hear a noise outside and go to investigate. Opening the front door, I see the dog waiting patiently on the edge of the circle of light from our porch lamp. Her animal antenna working at full strength, my wife pushes past me with a bowl of food that she just happens to have prepared earlier, and the dog eats ravenously. It refuses all her invitations to come inside, but is still there in the morning, waiting for the breakfast gong. Donella seems not at all surprised at its appearance, but I am astounded. How it knew where to find us after our brief encounter four miles away is almost worthy of an entry in the *Guinness Book of Records*. My wife decides that she will call him Lucky, and I agree that this is a very apt name. He has no collar and was probably dumped by the roadside now that he is too old to hunt well, but Donella says that she will call the gendarmerie tomorrow to ask if anyone has reported a missing dog. I nod my approval of this responsible attitude, but privately place a small wager that she will find lots of things to do well away from the telephone for the foreseeable future.

24 SEPTEMBER

Donella has started on her latest harvest run to try and outwit the human scavengers who are always with us at this time of year. After the late spring and long, hot summer, the terrain at La Puce is providing an unusually abundant crop of uncultivated nuts, berries and fruit.

Earlier this month, there was a massive haul of blackberries and elderberries, and it is hard to move freely about the mill cottage for jars of jam, jelly and pickle, while plastic bins of gently fermenting and bubbling potions line every available shelf and standing place. My wife has even been looking thoughtfully at our giant bathtub as an ideal vessel for a major brewing of her special hedgerow wine. It will be interesting to see what our cider and calva specialist friends make of Donella's inventive blends, as homemade wine seems unheard of here, and would probably be seen as a gross infringement of France's sacred monopoly on alcoholic fruit juice. None of our friends will believe that the southern counties of England produce some very drinkable whites, and Jacko Laiznay looked at me as if I were a simpleton when I asked him why Normandy did not have its own wine. He explained slowly and clearly that we were living above the Loire, and it would be madness to even attempt to emulate the activities of those who create the finest wines in the world. He then went on to remind me that I, even as a settler, should realise that our area does indeed produce, export and consume vast quantities of its own inimitable beverage, which is called calvados, even though it was invented in the Cotentin. I can't wait to see his face when we present him with a rich and fruity rhubarb and apple hock from the stony southern slopes of *Le Val de la Puce*.

And my wife is particularly pleased that our animal charges will have such a rich harvest to choose from this year. The hawthorns have been particularly prolific, with their brilliant and firm red berries fighting for a place on the branch, and the sloe berries are full of potential for next month, as long as the locals don't get to them first. They are much prized in the area, and are added in modest quantities to help bring out the flavour in farmhouse calva. A huge harvest of hazelnuts is threatening to break the branches of the trees alongside the river and around the grotto, and thousands of crab apples have appeared among the oak bocage at the end of the water meadow. The locals like to use them for an especially piquant sauce. I have also never seen so many truly enormous acorns, and it will be a shame to see them go to waste – though the texture is firm and crunchy, they are far too bitter for any use I can think of. Perhaps I shall go over René's head and attempt to barter with Mr Pigeon, with our acorns given to his pigs in return for the rights to his source.

Across the Lude, Hunters' Walk is now boasting as many

beechnuts as stars in the evening sky. They are quite sweet, but fiddly to open and get at, and the only application for them I have heard of is to flavour chewing gum. Anyway, Donella says the skinny squirrel will need them all to see him safely through the winter. According to my recollection of country lore, all this fecundity shows we are due for a hard winter, but when I asked René, he just sniffed and said all it shows is that we have had a good summer…

Blackberry and Apple Confiture

*1. First, pick your blackberries and apples before they are stolen**
2. Simmer the cleaned blackberries until soft, then mash
3. Chop the apples and repeat the process, using fresh water
4. Mix the fruits, add the same weight in sugar, stir and boil to setting point
5. Add a dash of calva before putting the jam in jars.

Green Tomato Fool

1. Scald two pounds of green tomatoes briefly, then put them into cold water to make it easy to remove the skins
2. Chop and stew until soft with one pound of sugar and a little nutmeg
3. Sieve and add sugar to taste
4. When cool, stir in half a pint of cream and a good whack of calva
5. Serve cold.

---

* Make sure you pick your blackberries before the beginning of November, when, as they say in Cotentin, the Devil pisses on them. I'm not sure of the exact date but, as they also say in Cotentin, you'll know when he has by the taste…

La Puce Cider Apple Chutney

1. Simmer some chopped apples and onions in
a pan with a small amount of vinegar
2. When soft, add a pint of still cider, sultanas, pickling spice,
ginger and salt, then keep simmering till a pulp results
3. Stir in plenty of brown sugar until mixture thickens to a
satisfying texture, and seal and store in jars until
you can no longer resist trying it.

25 SEPTEMBER

While my wife is busy with her foraging, I decide it is high time to sort out the stove chimney-pipe situation. It is still far too early for roasted chestnuts, but I can't resist the idea of a test run. Although we are in the midst of an Indian summer, it is becoming noticeably chilly in the mill cottage in the evenings, and I want to be sure we'll be snug and warm for the winter.

Valognes is advertised locally as the Versailles of the North, though I have not yet heard a Norman claim it was built before its Paris namesake. Ten miles or so to the south of Cherbourg, the town lost many of its beautiful old buildings and much of its charm when the Americans flattened the town during the D-Day landings. The authorities literally stuck the remnants of the ancient church on the walls of the ugly post-war replacement, but it hardly makes up for the loss. The streets and areas by the river, where the eighteenth-century bourgeoisie houses and civic offices survived, only serve as a poignant contrast with the ugliness of the new buildings, but show what the town must once have looked like.

Apart from a respected university, interesting cider museum and some good restaurants, Valognes also boasts some reasonable bricolage shops for the rare Norman DIY enthusiast. Having exhausted their possibilities, I turn my attentions to a farming hardware store on the outskirts of the town. If all else fails, I know I can buy some proper stack pipes and joints at the specialist stove shop in Cherbourg, but have already discovered that a few yards of heavy metal tubing and some designer brackets would cost more than I paid for the poêle itself.

At the store, a terminally disinterested young assistant pretends not to understand my French for a few minutes till I use my best patois to compare his moustache with the hairs round a cat's arse. I realise immediately that I have gone too far, and smile to show that it was just a joke, and he disappears huffily to the warehouse. Returning no more than an hour later, he says yes, they do normally carry that which I seek, but are out of stock until tomorrow morning. I promise to return, and leave him looking thoughtfully at the reflection of his moustache in a sheet of galvanised iron.

While I am in the area, I decide to make a brief pilgrimage to Le Petit Bijou. The Little Jewel looks even more enchanting than when we regretfully sold it to Jeanne and Val. We will always wonder how different our lives would have been if we had refused their offer; but it is good to see that the old place is in such caring hands.

After my sentimental journey, I stop off at a restored mill on the Bricquebec road which now trades as a restaurant specialising in finding as many ways to fill a crêpe as there are flavours of calva in Mr Maurice's wardrobe. As I take my ease by the duck pond, I try to spot any parts of the restored mill which look as if they could have come from La Puce. I could never prove any claim to prior ownership, but Maurice's nephew Alain has a big van, and I hear he is not averse to the odd commission that needs to be undertaken after dark.

26 SEPTEMBER

At the agricultural store, I am greeted by the same assistant, this time wearing a blank stare and a clean upper lip, which proves he remembers my visit of yesterday only too well. After I ask him how many twenty-stone Englishmen with real whiskers and a smattering of patois he sees during the average year, he sullenly concedes to recall my order, and does his usual disappearing act. On his eventual return he is wearing a smug expression, and reports that the piping I seek has not yet arrived, though has been promised for tomorrow. Or, p'tet, the next day or the day after that. Fingering his naked lip, he asks me what I would like to do about the situation, and I refrain from telling him my real desires. Instead, I say I will phone each day until the tubing has arrived, and will ask for the man without the moustache on every occasion, which will probably be just before he is due to leave for his lunch. Then, we can have a long chat about the progress of the situation. He looks more concerned than when I insulted his moustache, and immediately promises to see what he can do to ensure that I am not inconvenienced for too long.

3 OCTOBER

My persistence with the assistant at Valognes has paid off. The length of shiny metal tube now leans against the gable-end wall where it will be fixed to take the smoke from our stove up to the open air above the roof of the mill. But before that can happen, and in order to connect the piping to the stove, a large hole must be knocked, at knee height, through the wall. Although it is more than a yard thick and the stone blocks look extremely hard, I am disappointed in the progress that my wife has made, despite the help of the brand new bolster chisel and lump hammer I bought her at Boueve et Fils yesterday.

Taking over to show how it should be done, I spend the next two hours penetrating a further inch, then rest while I consider further options. Calling on the Jolly Boys' Club to rally round and stage a similar joint operation to Desert Storm would, I feel, be asking too much of even their generosity of spirit. I briefly consider emulating the standard method for installing septic tanks in the rocky crust of the Auvergne, but don't like the idea of letting René loose with a bundle of dynamite and fuse wire.

After a few reflective prods at the wall with the bent chisel, I ask my wife to look up the French for pneumatic drill, then in the phone book for the number of the nearest tool hire centre.

4 OCTOBER

We are through. After wearing out two 'everlasting' chisel bits, the voracious *marteau-piqueur* has fulfilled its purpose in life. I wait till the dust settles, then peer through the hole to where my wife looks back at me from inside the cottage like a trapped miner seeing rescue finally at hand. She starts clearing-up operations, and has already earmarked the mountain of debris for use in a new rock garden. I commence fitting a piece of the tubing into the collar at the back of the stove, and find that my friend at Valognes has had his revenge. The pipe is far too big.

~

I have used the lump hammer to persuade the pipe to fit in to the stove. I have also slotted a short piece through the hole in the wall, and used the elbow bend, Chinese hat and some ingeniously adapted hanging flower basket brackets to complete the job. We now have a most characterful and rustic chimney pipe, and all we need is some newspaper, kindling wood and logs to bring our period stove alive after its years of humiliation as a chicken coop. I just hope it will provide adequate heat.

~

The stove is getting even hotter. In the last ten minutes the wooden beam directly above it has begun to smoulder, and the plastic frame around the picture of me arm-wrestling with John Major has melted. Our fireside chairs are now at least ten feet from the source of the heat, and we are stripped to our underwear. The real problem is that everywhere beyond the direct blast range is comparatively cold. In winter, we will either roast in front of the blaze, or freeze away from it. I lob a few more immature chestnuts at the distant furnace and ponder a solution. It would be nice to site another poêle at the other end of the cottage and have stereo stoves to even up the temperature, but the chances of getting our hands on a similar model through René's contacts, without being shot at or ending up in court must be slight. I shall seek out Alain and see if he knows where I can come honestly by a similar stove, but one that is much, much smaller.

5 OCTOBER

The Bar Ghislaine is quiet, and Mr Maurice is sitting in his usual spot, as usual alone and looking ruminatively at a large glass of suze. I often speculate as to why, with a far greater stock and range of alcoholic beverages in his wardrobe, he chooses to pay to spend his afternoons in the bar. My wife thinks it is because he is lonely, and, given his continual experimentation with ever more exotic flavours of calva, just hasn't got room at home for the amount of medicinal suze he needs to get through each day. But he seems more subdued than normal, and when I join him at his table, he says little in response to my polite enquiries as to his health and wardrobe.

When I ask about Alain, he takes a drink, fiddles with his tights, and then explains that Alain is dead. He was involved in a crash on the Bricquebec to Valognes route last week. The funeral is tomorrow, and of course I and my wife are welcome to attend. He has not seen René since before the accident, and would be grateful if I could pass on the details of the interment if I see him.

I offer our condolences, but say, if he will excuse us, we will not attend the service. As I leave after a suitable period of keeping him silent company, Mr Maurice says that he is sorry that I did not get to know his nephew better, as he was a good boy. It seems unfair that someone so young should be taken when he is still here at his great age; it is not natural. Our arrangement with regard to the picking rights in the mushroom wood are now, of course, void. I return home and tell my wife the news. She will write a letter to Mr Maurice, but is relieved that I have not committed us to attending the ceremony. We have both had our fill of funerals at the little church in Néhou.

～

Later, I call at the mobile home to tell René about the accident and funeral. He and Eric are both drunk, and seem disinterested. René says he will not be going to the ceremony as he is too busy, and asks abruptly for money to buy materials for breaking into Mr Pigeon's source. I respond in an equally blunt manner that I cannot see why he needs money at this stage, as all it will take to start is a couple of spades and some hard work. I will pay when the job is done, as usual. Perhaps if they drank less and ate more, they would be in better condition to take on the work. Eric looks as if he is considering taking offence, but obviously thinks better of it.

I leave them sitting sullenly among the squalor and go back to the mill. I do not like the look of René lately, and he seems resentful of me. I don't know if Eric is a bad influence on him, or the other way round. Either way, they are not good for each other – or me.

8 OCTOBER
The situation with René is worsening. He seems to spend most of his time nowadays sitting in the mobile home and drinking cheap wine with his friend. If there are any shopping errands or demands for money from us, Eric is sent to make them.

This evening, things came to a head when our self-appointed gardener appeared at the door, saying that he and

René needed money for food, and I must pay something off our bill for his work. I didn't invite him in, but asked that he explain what he had done on our behalf and how much he thought we owed him. Leaning heavily against the door frame, he gave me a crumpled sheet of paper, and said that René said there were many hours of work that he, Eric, had done which had not yet been paid for. The paper was covered with what I recognised as René's handwriting and calculations, and appeared to show that Eric had spent hundreds of hours keeping the farmhouse garden in trim.

I laughed incredulously, tore the paper up and said that he was paid immediately after last cutting the grass in the garden, which was more than a month ago. Since then we had neither asked him to cut another blade, nor seen any evidence that he has done so. He looked at me without malice as I told him I would be grateful if he would remove his machine from my shed, and take it and himself from the premises. He shrugged and turned to go, but I caught his arm and escorted him to the toolshed behind the mill. I watched as he returned to the mobile home to pack his things and leave, then asked my wife if she would make the journey to Boueve et Fils to pick up some new locks for the tool and bikesheds.

14 OCTOBER

We arrive at Bricquebec for shopping, followed by drinks with Hubert and Madame Audouard at the Café de Paris. My entrance is marred somewhat by Freddo, who calls over loudly that I should avoid drinking milk as the pub cat is loose on the premises. I take this to be a jibe at my moustache, which I have been deliberately growing while keeping the rest of my full set closely trimmed.

As we settle in the corner, I sit opposite Hubert to avoid close comparisons with the huge growth on his upper lip, and take grim satisfaction in noting that Freddo sends Madame Collette for our order rather than putting himself within the judging zone. We enjoy a leisurely conversation, during which I have a mild disagreement with our teacher friend about the comparative merits of our two languages. He says that while English is useful for ordering hot-dog relish or landing aircraft at an international airport, French is a pure and original language which has not been overly diluted or defiled with foreign words and expressions. I counter that, unlike some cultures, we have always had the self-confidence to absorb and adapt suitable words from foreign countries, especially those we have conquered, colonised and civilised. This gives a variety and subtlety of communication which is, in all modesty, unique.

As a former magazine editor, I can assure him that any article I have written in French needed to have at least one third more words and therefore room on the page. Any language, I conclude, which has to call a simple typewriter 'the machine which writes mechanically' must be constructed by and for a race which prefers to hear its own voice rather than getting to the point. This, in my humble opinion, is the situation and position. Hubert now politely refers me to the fact that every one of the words in my native tongue ending in 'ion' has been lifted directly from the French, and I have just used three of them in one sentence. There are hundreds of other examples where we have had the good sense to use their language rather than our own. I should also remember where I am sitting, which is in the country and region that virtually taught the English to speak after 1066.

As Donella sees that I am about to move on to a detailed tally and description of English away wins after that long-distant home defeat, she suggests we change the subject. Hubert immediately complies, and asks me how I am getting on with René. I explain that our relationship has not been too sound lately, and he tells me that he must be honest, and that many people in the village think that I am too gullible as far as he is concerned. I may think I am doing the Fox a favour by opening the gate to the chicken run, but we will both be the losers if I continue to invite him in. As I ponder over this oblique parable, we make our farewells on cordial terms, and are invited to dine *chez* Audouard the following evening.

15 OCTOBER

A dramatic and distressing confrontation has taken place at the Bar Ghislaine. We had met with our dinner host so that he could show us the way to his isolated home in the Val de Néhou, and René staggered in to join us at our table without an invitation, which I could see annoyed Hubert.

Seemingly very pleased with himself, our estate manager called loudly for a round, and ostentatiously pulled out a thick wad of notes to pay, both of which actions are most unusual. We tried to make polite conversation for a while, but René was obviously in a cocky mood, and several times looked blearily across at my wife, laughed at some private joke and grunted something in a rapid patois which was obviously coarse and caused Hubert discomfort.

As we stood to leave for the dinner party, Hubert asked if we were happy with the horses in the top field, and I said that they were doing a good job in keeping the grass down, and that we were pleased that René managed to find them. Hubert appeared puzzled, and said that it was he that had arranged with a friend for them to be put there. Looking at René, he loudly asked if we were satisfied with the rental agreement of 1000 francs for the year, which was a fair price. Especially when paid in advance.

There was a long silence, and Madame Ghislaine and the other customers began to pay keen attention as René tried to brazen the situation out before lurching to his feet, pulling a handful of notes from his wallet and throwing them on the table. I asked him why he had not passed the money on to us before, and he at first protested his innocence, saying that he had not seen us for more than a week, but Hubert quietly said he knew the money was paid over even before the horses arrived more than a month ago.

Normally, I would have covered the situation by taking the money and making some excuse about René already having mentioned he had it. But I was very angry. I reminded him loudly that it was my specific instruction not to let the fields out as this was my small way of showing a lasting sign of respect for our mayor. I had allowed him to take advantage of me for a long time, but now he had insulted the memory of John Chevalier with his petty greed. His father would be ashamed of him.

Nobody spoke for what seemed a long time, and René looked at me as if I had struck him. He left his drink and the money on the table, and pushed his way through the door. We listened to the furious buzz of his mobylette fading away in the distance before settling the bill and leaving.

~

The meal at the Audouards was a sober and awkward affair after the incident at the Bar Ghislaine. We left early, and returned straight home. There was a light burning in René's mobile home and I thought about going to see him, but decided against it. I said to Donella that I must have hurt him deeply, and I had broken our special relationship by speaking to him like that in front of other people. My wife said I was too soft, and he deserved to be shown up for what he is and that this would also show the villagers that we are not totally gullible. And besides she had already counted the money he threw down, and it only came to 600 francs, not the 1000 he charged Hubert's friend.

~

Midnight, and I am woken from my slumber by a series of blood-curdling screeches from the direction of the water meadow. I wake Donella and remind her of the ancient Norse legend of Helquin the Huntsman. I have heard the old locals talk of how he still leads the battalions of Hell across the night skies, all carrying coffins upon which ride the ghosts of the damned, filling the air with their pitiful cries of terror and remorse. She turns over and goes back to sleep after reminding me that we now live in the countryside, where owls are quite common. Or perhaps, she adds, it is merely René mourning the loss of his 600 ill-gotten francs.

16 OCTOBER

René has gone. All that remains to remind us of his tenancy in the top field is a cardboard box overflowing with empty bottles, two long gouges to show where the tow tractor arrived and left early this morning, and a broken gatepost. Obviously, the driver was not Roland the spécialiste. I am saddened more than I would have thought. In their different ways, René and the mayor have played a huge part in our lives over the past three years. We shall just have to make our own way in the future now that both have left us.

17 OCTOBER

Another unexpected departure. Lynn calls at the mill to tell us she and Charlie are also leaving La Puce. Her friend Yves has made an arrangement with his wife and rented a house for Lynn on the hill overlooking Carteret. It has all happened so quickly. The couple will be married when Yves' divorce comes through, and Lynn will move into the manoir as soon as is decently possible.

We congratulate her on her good news, and promise to keep in touch. We are very pleased that she has found happiness. But Lynn's good news means we must start looking for a new tenant very quickly, as the rent for the farmhouse is a vital part of our survival plan. I shall also miss Charlie the dog, but I suspect Lucky will be pleased to take over as sole proprietor of the woods, fields and streams at La Puce.

19 OCTOBER

To cheer ourselves up, we decide to go on a mushroom-gathering expedition. It is a good time to choose, as the copse is full of fungi, and Coco is away organising next year's festival of traditional English-skinhead music at St Sauveur. We spend the first hour wandering around and trying to decide which of the bewildering variety to pick, and which we should leave. We have got *The Big Book of British Fungi* with us, but the differences between those said to make delicious eating and the deadly poisonous types seem slight.

Donella scoffs at my caution, and says we should pick them all, and take it in turns to try a little of the ones we think are safe over the coming weeks. That way, if we make a mistake, only one of us will suffer, and we will know in future which types to avoid. Besides, by taking the poisonous ones as well as the edible varieties, we will save any of the animals in the copse from making a mistake.

I put my foot down and suggest a better idea. We will pick them all, but wait until the morning, then take them for analysis by the chemist at Haye-du-Puits. Even the most knowledgeable locals take advantage of the service, I point out, even if only because it is free.

In the evening, we dine on a thick and delicious stew, made with our own vegetables, which is very satisfying. I believe my wife was joking when she suggested that we use ourselves as guinea-pigs for testing the mushrooms from the copse, but recalling a painful experience with a marsh pepper ragoût of her creation, I sift carefully through the ingredients on my plate while she is not watching.

20 OCTOBER

We arrive at the *pharmacie* in Haye-du-Puits, and are surprised to find a long orderly queue shuffling patiently towards the counter. We are even more surprised when two people ahead of us offer their places. I wonder at this unaccustomed courtesy, then realise why none of the customers is eager to be served. It is a homeopathic chemist's shop, and all the people here seem to have unusual, often dramatic and therefore particularly interesting things wrong with them.

The customers are hanging about as long as possible to see what the others have got, so as to have something stimulating to discuss over dinner tonight and in the market tomorrow. Also, in complete contrast with the usual situation when money changes hands, those who have been forced to the counter make no protest about the charges for their nostrums and potions. They hand over large notes without question, and take the small amounts of change as gratefully and respectfully as if receiving Holy Communion.

We make speedy progress to the front of the queue, and soon stand in front of the chemist, a severe man in a pristine white coat, the pockets of which bristle with pens, thermometers and slivers of wood for depressing customers' tongues regardless of malady. The *apothicaire* seems disappointed when he finds we have no exotic rashes to show him, and that our only fungal growths are confined to the two Safeway carrier bags we carry. With an impatient flick of his head, he summons an assistant, and he and the customers immediately lose interest in us as the next client is pushed to the counter for diagnosis of something hopefully more demanding than a kilo of mushrooms.

The young assistant takes the bags to a curtained cubicle next to the shop door and disappears to examine our crop. We wait long minutes to hear the verdict, then I grow impatient, sidle over and peep through a chink in the curtains to see how he is getting on. I return to my wife's side and explain in a whisper that he seems to be looking each of the varieties up in an illustrated publication very similar to *The Big Book of British Fungi*. This does not fill me with confidence, and I am quite relieved when he returns to say that he cannot, alas, recommend that we eat any of them. Some may be safe, but it is best not to take a chance, as all are rather unusual and even rare. My wife reaches out to take the bags from him, but he pulls them smartly away and says he will dispose of them for us.

Outside, I remark on how thoughtful for our safety the

young man was. Obviously fearing that we might ignore his advice, he had kept the bags so we would not be tempted to dice with death. She is not convinced, and prefers to suspect that he is under permanent instructions from his boss. If everyone who comes for advice is told that their fungi are inedible and has them all confiscated, no member of the staff need ever pick or buy a single mushroom again.

21 OCTOBER

Our main activity this evening is an official visit to the Bar de la Place in St Sauveur to inspect the new owners. We have avoided going there in the past, and dubbed it the Fun Factory because the previous owner was so miserable. Even the townspeople found the place depressing and the service and decor appalling, which is saying something in rural Normandy.

Now that Mr Heureux has departed and new owners taken over, the bar is packed with customers who, like us, want to have a look at how things have changed. It is said in the village that the middle-aged couple now behind the bar are foreigners from Mayenne, but they must already have heard of our consumption rate as the husband immediately rushes over and shows us to the only vacant table. I order a beer and a pastis and reach for my cigarettes, and our host promptly whips the non-fumeur card from our table and places it on top of the jukebox. He returns with our drinks in moments, and tells us they are on the house, which indicates strongly that he is indeed from another part of the country.

A little later, we are joined by Jackie from the Dungeon and Madame Nellie, who have come to wish the newcomers well. They do not seem unhappy to see the size of the crowd, which includes many of their regulars, and I know they know the honeymoon is unlikely to last. The locals are treating the event as a special occasion and as an opportunity to take a look at the new hosts. The free beer would also have overcome any sense of loyalty to their regular haunts, but they will not all be back in the Bar de la Place tomorrow. When the takings dip to its normal share of the business that the five bars in town can sustain, the new owners will begin to know whether they have made a wise move.

The evening wears on, and as I start to explain to Jackie that it is the anniversary of the Battle of Trafalgar, Madame Nellie tactfully changes the subject by asking if we had heard that Guy the slaughterman is dead. He was only in his early forties, she says as my wife and I exchange glances, and though he was such a big and powerful man, his heart was not strong. We return with Nellie to take a simple supper of *croque-monsieur* and chips, and Donella and I talk in low tones about this latest demise. Scaling up the figures to allow for the difference in population, I work out that this would represent nearly one hundred Portsmouth people we know dying in a couple of months. We may have opted for what seems a healthy and relatively stress-free life, I observe, but it seems a rather short one, especially for men. Is this the real reason Donella was so keen for us to spend a whole year in Cotentin?

My wife smiles affectionately, wipes a tendril of melted cheese from my burgeoning moustaches and says that now I am learning to take such a philosophical attitude to life and death, I am obviously beginning to adapt to our new environment.

25 OCTOBER

It seems there are some advantages to René's departure. Though I am missing his company, this will be the first year we shall be able to get our hands on our own apples. We spend the whole day harvesting, then most of the night wrapping and storing those we cannot use before the end of the year. I am as fond of apples as the next man, but my wife is eyeing the giant bathtub again, so I think I will call Hubert in the morning and offer him a hundredweight or so for professional DIY calva production.

27 OCTOBER

I narrowly avoided an encounter with a drunken hornet this morning. René told me last year that they like to feast on rotting apples at this time and, after a long session, can become totally intoxicated. He sounded quite envious. As I took shelter behind the bikeshed, the beast zigzagged unsteadily off in the direction of the water meadow. If he disturbs the Cray gang as they settle down for winter, there could be big trouble on the waterfront tonight.

Boiled Leg of Lamb from Yvetot

1. Simmer some carrots, leeks, turnips, onions and a bouquet-garni for at least three glasses of wine, then add salt and a generous helping of calva
2. Rub the leg of lamb all over with garlic
3. Put the lamb in the stock and cook in oven for another three glasses of wine, basting occasionally
4. Make a roux with flour and butter, and thin it down with some of the stock, and continue to cook it for a leisurely cigarette. Away from the heat, add crème fraîche and capers
5. Serve your lamb on a long platter, garnished with the stock vegetables and the cream sauce.

4 NOVEMBER

The Indian summer is over and the land is closing down for the winter. The days are short, the legendary Cotentin wind is working itself up to a suitable fury for the long dark months ahead, and someone has turned the heavenly shower mixer from warm to cold. Most of our bird and animal lodgers have packed up and bedded down or gone to more hospitable quarters for the winter, though I can't imagine where they will find them. Nobody in the village has heard of or from René but, for us at least, his memory lingers on.

This morning, I found the larger of the top fields being

turned into a quagmire by a tractor in the control of a complete stranger. Quite politely in the circumstances, I asked him what he thought he was doing; he retorted that he knew exactly what he was doing, and that if I didn't, he suggested I get a good pair of spectacles or a book about farming. My nose should also have given me a clue as to the enterprise, which involved digging a great deal of *merde* into the ground to give it back some of the life which had obviously been drained from it for so long by an uncaring farmer.

From then, the tone of our conversation went downhill, and we almost came to blows before he explained that he had a verbal contract to work not only this field but all the others, and if I had a problem, I should consult the owner, Mr Ribet. After taking the golden opportunity to tell him that a verbal contract is not worth the paper it isn't written on, I explained the true situation vis-à-vis ownership, and gave him his money back, plus healthy compensation for his wasted pig manure.

In spite of the situation, I have to admit to a sneaking admiration for the Fox's negotiating skills. I had to repay the farmer much more than I would have thought a fair rent for the fields would have fetched.

5 NOVEMBER

More fireworks when my wife discovers some strange horses in the big field. I reach for my wallet and go to negotiate a settlement with their owner...

11 NOVEMBER

No temporary tenants have appeared in the top fields this week, so it looks as if we are free to walk through them without upsetting anyone.

13 NOVEMBER

We have heard from Hubert Audouard that René's friend Eric is happily working at the cider factory in Brix. As my wife says, it is not surprising that he is happy in his new location and situation, which seems along the lines of holding regular meetings of Alcoholics Anonymous in a pub.

We often pass through Brix on our way to and from Cherbourg, and sometimes stop to enjoy the scenery from the bar in the square. The village is at one of the highest points on the peninsula, with striking views almost to each coastline when the legendary Cotentin mist is having a rare day off. With its huddle of neat grey-stone buildings, narrow streets and tiny church, it somehow reminds me more of the Highlands of Scotland than northern France, and according to our historian friend Robert Simon, there may be a good reason for this impression. He has told us that, in ancient patois, Brix is pronounced Broow. This was the name of the eleventh-century seigneur of the village and a large chunk of the top end of the peninsula, who was so helpful in 1066 that William the Conqueror gave him most of Scotland as a small thank-you present. From there came the title of his direct descendant, Robert the Bruce, or de Broow, King of the Scots in the fourteenth century. I hope it is true, and if it is, the story may go a little way towards explaining the similar reputations for parsimony of Normans and Scots. Another indicator towards some enduring affinity is that Scots visitors seem particularly welcome in Cotentin, and the locals seem to be more at ease with their guttural attempts at French than many Britons are with the Scottish version of the English language.

HISTORICAL NOTE

Some years after Robert Simon told me about the legend, the heart of the Bruce was unearthed during an archaeological dig in Edinburgh, and an excited article in a French newspaper confirmed the Brix-Broow story. I thought about passing on the news to the remaining members of the Jolly Boys'

Club, but decided against it as they would inevitably point out that, as they had always claimed, Scotland as well as the rest of Great Britain is actually the rightful property of Cotentin…

15 NOVEMBER

To Carteret to say another farewell to Lynn and Charlie the dog. They are packing when we arrive, and will soon be off to their new home at Yves' manoir in Carentan.

Helping Lynn with the removals is a friend who has had a traumatic and unusually busy emotional life since her arrival on the peninsula. She tells us over drinks of an embarrassing encounter shortly after she moved in with her latest French boyfriend. Having split with her husband six months after settling in the area, she had discovered that the legal complexities of dividing mutual domestic possessions are even more convoluted than in England. During the process of separation, she had found the assistance of the local bailiff or *huissier* invaluable in helping her relocate some of her possessions to the home of her new lover, and from there to her next male friend and *ménage*.

After parting with him and starting a more serious and hopefully longer-lasting relationship with a separated but still married man, she found that the law of France required graphic proof of his adultery before divorce proceedings could begin in earnest. Accordingly, appointments were made, and two policemen arrived apologetically on the doorstep at a suitably early hour, accompanied by an official witness. He made careful note of the dressing gown and tousled hair of the householder, then went upstairs to cough discreetly and enter the bedroom. He came through the door just as Lynn's friend sat up in bed, arranged her flimsy nightdress and steeled herself to be officially recognised as the Other Woman. Their eyes met, and she saw that the official witness was none other than the bailiff who had been so helpful in her three last romantic disentanglements. After a polite conversation as he, the police officers and the current lover took coffee at the bedside, the huissier declared himself completely satisfied as to the circumstances. Before leaving, he gave her an admiring glance and handed her his card, with a reminder that he was only a telephone call away, and his rates were very reasonable if she decided to continue her magnificent progress through the bedchambers of the peninsula.

16 NOVEMBER

The election of a new mayor of Néhou has taken place, and we meet at the unofficial reception in the Bar Ghislaine shortly after the announcement. He seems a decent enough chap, but it is the general opinion that he will never replace John Chevalier. I think we should give him a chance, but my wife is not an admirer, as he won on a hunting and shooting ticket. For the past months, graphic posters reminding the commune of the need to be ever vigilant against any threat to their rights to kill have been plastered all around the village. There was quite a fuss when someone went round scrawling 'murderer' all over the candidate's features, but the culprit was never found. At least, the word was written in French, so the finger of suspicion was not pointed at anyone living at La Puce, but I know my wife's handwriting when I see it.

20 NOVEMBER

Even colder today. It looks as if the country tale about the abundance of berries in autumn signalling a long, hard winter may not be such an old chestnut. I am now spending at least an hour every day trying to maintain the level of the woodpile behind the mill. It is a perfect example of the law of diminishing returns, as the more effort I put in to ensure a comforting and respectable size, the more it seems to shrink as Donella makes raids to feed the endless demands of the giant stove. I cannot believe we are using this much wood, and am beginning to suspect we may be keeping half the houses in the village warm. After scouring Hunters' Walk for the last scraps of dead wood, I suggest we go to town and look at the price of electric fires.

It is market day at St Sauveur, and a miserable affair. The small band of hopelessly optimistic traders have deserted their stalls and are huddled together around the brazier at the merguez stand, which is the only place likely to do any business today. The wind rushes furiously through the streets in search of victims, and we take refuge in our favourite butcher's shop. Behind the counter, a young man is carefully making Catherine wheels from long tubes of white pudding, and seems mildly amused when we ask if our gentle giant is on holiday. He has been dead for almost a week now, and Madame has gone to live with her sister on the coast. The new butcher has taken the business over and hopes we will continue to patronise the premises. When I ask how our friend died, he merely shrugs and holds his fist to his nose before returning his attention to the boudin blanc. We go for a calming calva at Madame Nellie's, and are relieved to see that she and all the regulars seem in reasonable health.

25 NOVEMBER

We visit Cherbourg for our regular brush with civilisation, and to buy modest Christmas presents for our friends and neighbours.

Instead of eagerly looking forward to the monthly trip, we are finding it more and more difficult to make the effort. When we first moved over, I would often come up with excuses to visit the town and savour the bustle, noise and traffic, but since then have become increasingly acclimatised to life in the countryside. As the winter sets in, we are less and less inclined to venture even as far as Bricquebec. We will, however, force ourselves to make the journey, if for no other reason than the joy of showing the town a clean pair of heels as we hasten back to La Puce.

We lunch at a bar near to the ferry port, which specialises in real English chips and offers British television to homesick day-trippers. As we eat, a pretty blonde weather girl in a pink suit hands over to a stern blonde woman studio presenter in a pink suit who hands over to a severe blonde woman reporter in a German storm trooper's mackintosh to talk to an even grimmer female MP about how awful it is to be a woman in a man's world. A couple at the bar are having difficulties asking the patron for a bottle of HP sauce, and I offer to help translate their request. I then tactfully explain that they may be better advised to ask for things in English, as most of the bar staff speak it quite well, and can have difficulty understanding their own language when used by a foreigner. It is often best, I advise, to simply mime and point, relying on body language and making spoken communication unimportant. I take the example of my brother, who has developed an infallible technique. On a recent visit to a bar with us, he acknowledged the barmaid with a crisp *'bonjour'*, then ordered a hot chocolate, lemon tea and two beers by simply pointing at the bar pumps, using fluent sign language and repeating 'bonjour' continually. After getting exactly what he wanted, he said that he had developed the skill over a number of years, and now believes he can convey any message or meaning anywhere on Earth simply by using a subtle range of inflexions and stresses on a single word of the host language.

27 NOVEMBER

It has been raining liquid ice for two days, and we have been competing to see who can get closest to the stove without becoming part of it. Having counted the wormholes in the main beam for the hundredth time, I take to reading the old newspapers in the kindling box. There is an absorbing article by a British writer about Gilles Picot de Gouberville, who was the seigneur of Mesnil-au-Val in the sixteenth century. With plenty of time on his hands, Gouberville kept a diary between 1549 and 1562, writing between ten and thirty lines every day. According to the modern-day editor of his work, Gouberville used the phrase 'I did not leave the house' 3310 times in the thirteen years. While I understand exactly how he must have felt, I hope that my work will offer some rather more interesting observations on daily life in the Cotentin to readers in the twenty-fourth century.

29 NOVEMBER

I tire of my daily battle with the woodpile, and persuade my wife that we should spend the afternoon in the Bar Ghislaine and take advantage of the free heating. It must be remarkably cold, as there are two smouldering logs in the giant fireplace. I notice immediately that Mr Maurice is not in his usual position, and Ghislaine breaks the news we are already expecting, but hoping not to hear.

She tells us that he was at Marcel Bernard's house two nights ago for supper. They walked out into the yard to say goodnight, and as they shook hands, he looked up at the night sky, commented on how clear, bright and *calme* it all was, and then fell gently at his friend's feet. The doctor says his heart just gave out, and he would have felt no pain. The same man has been telling Maurice for years that drinking would be the death of him, she says, so at least our friend has had the last laugh.

We ask if René has been told, and Ghislaine says that he has not shown his face since leaving La Puce. He is probably too embarrassed after his last visit to the bar. There is talk that he has gone to work for the farmer at the grand manoir at St Jacques, and has a cottage there as part of their agreement. If that is true, he is a traitor and has yet another reason for not appearing in Néhou. But it seems a shame that he may not know his oldest friend in the village is dead.

We return to La Puce, wrap a bottle of my precious malt whisky in Christmas gift paper, and set out to track the Fox of Cotentin down to his new earth.

Under cover of darkness, we cross the unmarked but scrupulously observed frontier between Néhou and St Jacques-de-Néhou. My wife rides shotgun and keeps watch for hostile natives, but the streets are deserted. The bar in the square is closed and unlit, as is the restaurant next door. Our villagers are apparently exaggerating when they say the residents of St Jacques only go out at night to indulge their unspeakable feeding habits, and spend their days sleeping on beds of local soil in dark cellars.

At last, we see a lone figure, furtively darting between the pools of light cast by the new street lamps of which the Néhou commune is so jealous. I take a chance and pull up, crank the window down and call him. The man looks about wildly for a bolthole like a rabbit caught above ground in a field of hunters, then shuffles over when he sees we are driving an English car. Deliberately speaking in my worst French so that he will not suspect I am actually a member of the community across the crossroads, I ask him if he knows René Ribet and he says everyone knows René Ribet, and many to their cost.

I ask him if he knows where Mr Ribet is staying as I have a business matter to discuss, and he tells us that I should look for a small cottage at the end of the track leading to the grand manoir. I will know it from the new roof tiles and window frames, and the mobile home by the broken gatepost. As we drive away, he shouts after us to be on our guard, and makes off in the direction of the church. Either, my wife says, he realised we are from Néhou and is planning to ring the bells and raise the village, or to pray for our souls because we are going to talk business with René Ribet.

We find the cottage and park beside the recently broken gatepost. A light is flickering beyond the sacking curtain across the new window frames, and I take the bottle of scotch and leave my wife and Victor on guard. As I walk down the path, my wife reminds me to count my fingers after shaking hands if we do effect a reconciliation.

For some reason, I hesitate and adjust an imaginary tie before knocking, and quickly consider how I will approach our first encounter for more than two months. I decide to take the bluff no-nonsense English approach, and rap smartly on the door. From inside, I hear movement, and eventually the door is opened and René peers out into the night. He has put on weight and looks well, and is obviously sober. For a moment, his face is expressionless, then he sees who his visitor is, and steps back from the doorway. I nod and he nods, and we remain motionless till I hold out the bottle. He reaches out, hesitates for a long moment then takes it. He looks at it, then back at me, then steps further away from the door and nods at the table. I nod stiffly back, walk in and sit down as he starts to unwrap the bottle.

～

Two hours later, the bottle is nearly empty and René has spent more time talking than even that night by the big pond in August. He has told me further stories of his childhood and happy years in the countryside, and how he met his wife and had a daughter, then lost them both. His wife is with someone else, and his daughter lives in Cherbourg with her child. We may have seen her with him at the méchoui. He tries to give her money when he can, and wants to impress her and to make her see that he is not just a tramp who has been living in a caravan on someone else's land. He explained how he lost his home when the Parisian owner of the cottage at Néhou threw him out after he heard about the English who would pay crazy prices for worthless country properties. And this after René had worked so hard to restore the place with materials left over from other jobs. He said how he had resented the clever English writer and his wife for being rich enough to buy La Puce and pour money into making it so grand. He said how, in spite of all this, he grew to like me and respect my wife, and thought we were true friends until the bad night in the Bar Ghislaine. As to the arrangements between us, he did not really intend to cheat us, but we seemed to have so much and I seemed so stupid with my money and my ignorance of the land, and my mad spending on putting fairy lights on a farm.

He had always wanted to have the life and status of a farmer, but it is just a dream that he knows can never come true. He is truly sorry for what has happened between us, but I must bear some of the responsibility. I have been a chicken to his fox, and even opened the gate of the coop myself.

Then it was my turn, and I told him that, far from being a wealthy writer, I am so much in debt to the bank in England that we may have to sell up and leave La Puce. That I may have been stupid with my money and ideas for making a home and a future in this part of the Cotentin, but he must know that we are not like others who come to take over, change the local ways and be absent and uncaring owners. I am here to stay and to learn, and have learned a great deal. Especially from him, whom I would still like to be my friend, whatever has happened in the past. As I paused to drain my glass, he said that, whatever happens between us in the future, we have no choice but to be friends; as they say in the countryside, he is my *pote* for life, and there is not much we can do about it.

Another hour passes, then I rise to leave. Before I walk unsteadily back to where my wife is now asleep in the car, he asks me to wait, then returns with something wrapped in an old newspaper. It is his present to us for Christmas, perhaps I will put it in the mill cottage, next to the pictures of John Chevalier and Mr John Major.

As he stands and watches from the doorway, I unwrap the parcel on my lap and see that it is a photograph of a young

René with a middle-aged man who must be his father. I wave and start the car, and as we bump along the potholed track back towards St Jacques, my wife stirs, makes herself comfortable again and sleepily asks if I still have all my fingers.

Epilogue

We are gathered in the Bar Ghislaine to prepare for the Christmas warm-up party.

JayPay is at the counter, having managed to slip away from preparing the spicy couscous which will set the North African theme for our soirée in the village hall. He has one giant arm resting affectionately on his wife's shoulders, while Madame JayPay is smoking more furiously than ever as she considers the odds on a childfree year.

All around me, the Jolly Boys' Club is in full convention, but the seat from where Mr Maurice would have been looking thoughtfully into his suze has been left vacant. As chairman of the wine committee Freddo is consulting with Madame Ghislaine about final amendments to the list of one. He sees that I am watching, smiles knowingly, nods and holds up his two index fingers as if demonstrating the size of one of the hundreds of hapless trout he has caught this morning. I smile back as he nods towards the pissoir outside the grocery-shop window and tap my watch to indicate that we will meet later to play the sausage game. What he does not know is that I have already visited the village hall and adjusted the names written on the relevant paper table-cloths. I shall now be sitting elsewhere, with the older and more diminutive members of the Jolly Boys' Club, while I have ensured that he will be sharing a table with Hubert Audouard. I went swimming in the big pond with Hubert this summer, and know that it is not only his moustache that is bigger than Freddo's.

At my side, Néné Ribet is making plans on the back of a

beer mat for our farm at La Puce. He has been almost rehabilitated into the commune, and next year, we have decided, we are going into partnership to beat the bloody English at their own game. We shall produce the finest lambs in all Normandy, and perhaps all France.

While he happily scribbles details of stock numbers and costs, overheads and potential resale prices, he stresses how important it is that we must be totally honest with each other and share all expenses and whatever profits may be made in our first year as real farmers. As he gets to the part about his specialist knowledge of negotiating for the best prices for buying and selling, and how it is vital that the control of all financial matters be left entirely to him, I merely look knowingly at him, and he falters, smiles wryly and goes back to his plans.

A little later, the Jolly Boys' Club prepares to move on to the village hall and I excuse myself, leave the bar and cross the road to spend a few moments alone with John Chevalier.

~

In the churchyard, the flowers around John's grave are as fresh as ever. I sit down and begin to tell him about the latest news from La Puce and his commune. He will be pleased to know that Néné is back with us, and I am sure that John will not mind if we use his fields by the road for our sheep farm. I know the grass is good and the land well drained, but I shall need his help and guidance to make a success of the venture. There also may be good news from England. I have sent some pages of a book I am writing about our past year at La Puce and Néhou to a big publishing company, and so far they have not sent it back, which is very encouraging. As he will know, it looks like being a long and hard winter, but the new year and seasons will arrive as always, and we will do our best to make the most of what time we have left to enjoy the good days and put up with the bad.

I hear the sounds of laughter as the villagers make their way to the hall, and stand to say goodnight. Before I leave, I tell John that Donella has still not met her badgers, and I have finally given up my plans for finding the miller's gold. Now, though, I am beginning to see that the real treasure at La Puce has been all around us, all the time.

French Letters

There follows a glossary of those French words and expressions I feel may benefit from translation and further explanation. My thanks are due to Jean-Marie Guedeney and Robert Simon for attempting to curb my worst mistakes and excesses. I would only add that the reader should remember that my interpretation of most or all the following may still be totally inaccurate, as they, like the book itself, represent a very unscholarly and individual approach to the subjects covered.

Académie Française Very exclusive club for a collection of venerable old buffers whose avowed and statutory role is to preserve the language, culture and Establishment values of France. A bit like our House of Lords without the hypocrisy.

Acte de vente The final, final completion of a property sale, when vendor and buyer congregate solemnly in the notaire's office to see the transfer through.

Ancien Moulin Old mill (in all agents' detail sheets, 'ancient' can generally be taken as an euphemism for 'ruined').

Apéritif Technically, any drink taken to stimulate the appetite. In our part of the Cotentin, the usual understanding of the word is any drink taken to stimulate the appetite for the next one.

Appellation contrôlée Cunning French system of labelling certain wines to persuade the buyer to pay more for a perfectly ordinary bottle of wine just because the makers say they know where it all comes from.

À Vendre For Sale. Since the English property-buying invasion and French amazement at what we will pay for an old building, now seen in sign form on virtually every uninhabited house or derelict farm building from barn to byre.

Baguette Long and very crusty loaf specifically designed to cause severe gum bleeding in foreigners who over-indulge. Also totally impossible for use in making any sensible sort of English sandwich.

Barrière The fence

Bocage Distinctive Norman countryside feature resulting from the tradition of hedging small fields with sturdy trees to ward off the legendary *vent* (wind). And, of course, to make it very clear where one property stops and the next begins...

Boeuf bourguignon Burgundian Irish stew.

Bottes Boots. In the Cotentin climate, invariably of the Wellington variety, though it is not wise to use his name in a dockside bar on a Friday evening.

Boudin blanc White pudding, as in Cornwall, but different.

Boucherie Butcher's shop or department.

Brio Enthusiasm.

Calva If you need an explanation of this word, you have been reading the book backwards. On second thoughts, if you *have* been reading the book backwards, it is quite probable that you are already familiar with calva, so don't bother.

Chambre Room, though usually referring to one with a bed in it. Not to be confused with *chambrer* or *chambrière*, which mean, respectively, bringing wine to room temperature and a chambermaid. In France, of course, there is a natural affinity between the pursuit of the last two subjects in the confines of the first.

Chambre de Commerce Professional version of our Chambers of Commerce, excepting that their executive officers are voted in and actually do a great deal more for local business than holding cheese and wine parties and going on goodwill trips.

Chambre d'hôte Bed and breakfast establishment, usually rural and often offering a fascinating glimpse of how French people really live.

Charcuterie Cooked cold meats, or the shop that sells them. Usually, every village or town has the undisputed Finest Charcuterie Store in northern France (at least).

Chasseur Hunter, an expression used to describe anyone in possession of cartridges, a gun, blood lust and generally very bad eyesight and aim.

Chasse Interdite The optimistic legend on the 'No Hunting' signs which are the second most popular targets for the above.

Château Literally 'castle', but commonly used by the French to describe any particularly grand and large house. Commonly used by British owners to describe their place if it has more than three bedrooms. The real thing, as foreign owners usually discover to their cost, always has lots and lots of rooms, outbuildings and twiddly bits which cost a fortune to restore and maintain.

Chef Actually 'boss', but inevitably applied in the UK to any cook with pretensions.

Chêne antique Old oak.

Choucroute Alsatian (the region, not the dog) dish of boiled pork on a bed of pickled cabbage. Actually, much nicer than it sounds, and popularised in Normandy by refugees from wartime Alsace.

Cidre Cider. Not to be confused with SIDA, which means AIDS, but is pronounced very similarly, as the author has found to his embarrassment on several occasions.

Cidre bouché Norman equivalent of champagne, without the ridiculous overpricing. Seen on signs at farms that sell traditionally corked and wired bottles of sparkling cider. 'Bouché' can also mean 'kiss of life' which, when you think about some of the high-voltage apple distillations found in Normandy, is particularly apt.

Complet Complete. Full. Ready.

Compromis de vente The first stage of a property contract. When you have signed it and paid the ten per cent deposit, you are then bound to complete on the mutually agreed date or lose the money and the property (unless otherwise agreed).

Couscous A North African speciality dish of semolina flakes and hot stew. Like our Indian curry, popularised as a result of colonial conquests.

Crédit Agricole One of the major banking houses, with branches conveniently located throughout France.

Croque-monsieur 'Mr Bite.' A Welsh rarebit sandwich, with ham inside and cheese outside.

Demi A half. When used in the context of 'une demi pression' (a half of keg beer) in a bar, the French customer is actually ordering a quarter of a litre, which works out at just under a half of an Imperial pint.

It is a little-known fact that the ancient Normans are responsible for this misnomer, which occurs all over France millions of times a day. After colonising our shores in 1066, William & co imposed the traditional Norman liquid measure of 'une pinte'. We, as usual, made it our own, while France evolved to their Euro-litre. Thus the anomaly.

Douve Large river running from Carentan in the south, and picking up La Puce en route through Néhou.

Digestif Supposed to be the opposite of apéritif (see p.268) and taken only after eating, but actually having exactly the same application and usage.

Disque bleu Foul-smelling cigarette, even by French standards.

Douanerie Customs checkpoint, usually manned by bored and anglophobic officials who would (allegedly) happily let tons of smack cocaine go through in favour of catching a bloody rosbif trying to smuggle a new three-piece suite in to the country.

Épicerie Grocery shop. In a village setting, often to be found doubling as the local and only bar, and therefore more than likely to be situated within close proximity of the pissoir (see p.275).

Équipe Team.

Étang Any confined piece of water of a size between a goldfish pond and a proper lake.

Fagot Technically a conveniently sized log for the above, but in practice anything up to a fair-sized dead tree if you are a dealer trying to buy one, or kindling twig if you are a dealer trying to sell one.

Fantôme Ghost, as in of the Opera.

Fils Son.

Fusil Shotgun. Not to be confused with fusée, which is a guided missile capable of great destruction and loss of life if used indiscriminately. Bearing in mind the way many French hunters use their shotguns, the similarity of names is probably more than coincidental.

Frites Like English chips, only different.

Gîte A self-catering property or part of a property equipped for holidaying visitors. Gîtes (like official chambre d'hôtes) have to conform with very strict regulations with regard to general standards and facilities.

Gendarmerie Military police force (or their station) found in the countryside or small towns. Universally and deeply despised by motorists, who will go so far as to risk a big fine by flashing their headlights to warn even approaching Brits that they are entering a speed trap. On that note, always beware of *les flics'* (cops) favourite dirty trick of sitting another one further along the road just as you have safely negotiated the first one and are putting your foot down again...

Grand tournoi Big match.

Haute cuisine Posh nosh.

Huit-à-Huit Eight (AM) to Eight (PM). A grocery store franchise that doesn't live up to its name in our neck of the woods.

Képi Peaked uniform cap, as in French Foreign Legion.

Kir A sickly sweet and highly intoxicating mélange of white wine and cassis, allegedly invented by a bishop of that name. The pretentious version is made with champagne and called *kir royal*. Our local version is *kir normand*, with sparkling cider making a much, much cheaper and therefore much, much more enjoyable substitute for the champagne.

Lave-linge Washing machine.

Louis d'or Gold coin, which every Norman countryman believes to be buried in vast quantities on his land, if only he can discover where.

Livre In this context, a book. In others, a British banknote or weight (pound).

Lude Our river, which is really a stream but gets big billing because it is named on regional maps.

Mairie Mayor's official place of administration, which can be anything from a grand town hall to a room in the local school. Unlike the UK, even the smallest communities have their own elected mayor. A man of enormous fixing power locally, and sometimes in effect a marginally milder version of a mafia godfather.

Maison de mariage (First) marriage home.

Maître Master (as in notaire).

Manoir A grand farmhouse, often appearing to have been designed by a gallic ancestor of Walt Disney. In pre-Revolution times, each great estate would have its own château and manoir. The château went to the eldest son, whilst the second fils (see p.272) inherited the manoir. Thus, it was overblown and embellished to show the status of the owner (and probably to stop him sulking about missing out on the proper family home).

Mélange Mixture or mess, as in 'you look a right mélange this evening, chérie'. Also used for mixed-oil-and-petrol fuel for a mobylette.

Ménage Household, as in ménage à trois.

Merde A multi-purpose slang word or curse, as in 'oh, shit' or 'you little shit'.

Méchoui Barbecue of lamb (the event), popularised during France's North African adventuring.

Métier Special skill, interest or occupation.

Mobylette The favourite French moped, able to tow and carry quite incredible loads. Often seen in the countryside posing as a builder's van or, in extreme cases, heavy-earth-moving equipment. The reason for this vehicle's popularity and adaptation to all sorts of functions is that it requires no driving licence or tax disc, only minimum insurance and can cover more than 150 kilometres for every gallon of petrol – providing, of course, it is not towing a broken tractor.

Monsieur Mister, sir or 'oi, you!' depending on context.

Monsieur le maire 'Mister mayor.' An elective and very important office within any commune. The mayor enforces (or ignores) local and national regulations and statutes, and arbitrates on all and every issue affecting the community. Of particular importance to the British property buyer, as he is the key figure in all matters to do with planning. He can make you go through a bureaucratic nightmare to gain permission to put a road mirror outside your property... or turn a blind eye to a massive new extension if it suits him.

Moulin de la Puce, Le Mill of the Flea.

Non-fumeur Non-smoker/smoking. Still as rare a breed as vegetarians in rural France. NB. A *fumerie* is an opium den, while a *fumier* is a dunghill. This can make for some interesting reactions if you make a slight slip while asking someone if you are allowed to smoke on the premises, or if they are a smoker.

Non-potable Not drinkable, which may apply to any beverage not containing alcohol as far as many Cotentinese are concerned.

Notaire Local legal eagle. In rural France, a combination of solicitor, estate agent and local mafia boss (as in 'mayor').

Pastis The favourite drink for French workers, which is a more sophisticated and less deadly version of the original aniseed-based liqueur, absinthe, traditional choice of all mad French artists, poets and authors.

Pâtisserie Cake and confectionary shop.

Paysan 'Peasant.' Used in France to quite respectfully refer to any person making a living from the land, rather than in the highly insulting British context.

Pépinière Tree nursery.

Pétanque Oversized steel marbles and game, of which the author is supreme local champion (Valdecie Ricard league).

Petite puce 'Little flea.'

Petit pois The ubiquitous 'little pea', which seems one of the few vegetables the French buy en masse. In the average hypermarché, whole shelves will be devoted exclusively to thousands of cans of this infant delicacy.

Peut-être 'Perhaps.' As with '*mañana*' in the Iberian peninsula, the classic Norman procrastination is '*peut-être bien oui, peut-être bien non*' ('*...p'tet bankwee, p'tet bankno*' in patois), which literally means 'perhaps, well, yes, perhaps, well, no'. In fact, and especially when asking your Norman plumber if he will be arriving to complete the job tomorrow, it invariably means 'non'.

Pied-à-terre 'A foot on the earth', usually referring as in Britain to an apartment at some distance from the family home, and traditionally used during the week when the husband is at his city business. Or, even more traditionally, when he wants to continue working with his secretary after office hours...

Pissoir Self-explanatory. The original and official men-only very public urinals in big towns were as ornate and striking as they were unique. Nowadays, virtually all have gone, to be replaced by much cruder but nevertheless fascinating examples of male French inventiveness under pressure.

Poêle A stove for burning wood (preferably someone else's).

Poissons rouges Goldfish. Very popular in some regions, especially cooked à la whitebait in flour.

Pompier Fireman.

Pot au feu Another type of stew.

Pote 'Mate', as in special male friend.

Presse de la Manche, La Regional newspaper.

Quarante-quatre Literally 'forty-four'. In this context, a fiery homemade orange liqueur, but also used in Cotentin to refer to the D-Day landings. The identical usage is coincidental, though both have had significant long-term effects on the Norman psyche and landscape (see the recipe on p.88).

Ragoût Stew when made by pretentious cook (see 'chef').

Repas d'affaires Business lunch.

Ricard The JBC's favourite brand of the above beverage.

Rocher Boulder, large stone or rock, as in Gibraltar.

Saucisse paysanne In this context, 'countryman's sausage'.

Soirée Any evening gathering or do, inevitably involving something to eat and drink.

Sou Ancient French coin of insignificant value (five old centimes), alleged to be secreted in vast hoards by Normans who know they are worthless nowadays, but can't bear to let any form of money out of their custody.

Supermarché Supermarket.

Tête-à-tête Literally 'head-to-head' and used to describe an intimate conversation or position, which may actually involve a little more than talking.

Tout de suite 'At once' or 'very quickly', but meaning exactly the opposite when used by most Cotentinese tradesmen.

Tonto Norman patois for 'see you later' (today).

Tracteur Tractor, unless in the case of a moped in disguise (see 'mobylette').

Vendu Sold. A sign to gladden the heart of both buyer and seller. The British buyer because he has finally captured his little corner of a foreign field; the French seller because he's got rid of that decrepit building at long last...